Media Culture in
Transnational Asia

Global Media and Race

Series Editor: Frederick Luis Aldama, The Ohio State University

Global Media and Race is a series focused on scholarly books that examine race and global media culture. Titles focus on constructions of race in media, including digital platforms, webisodes, multilingual media, mobile media, vlogs, and other social media, film, radio, and television. The series considers how race—and intersectional identities generally—is constructed in front of the camera and behind, attending to issues of representation and consumption as well as the making of racialized and antiracist media phenomena from script to production and policy.

Hyesu Park, ed., *Media Culture in Transnational Asia:*
Convergences and Divergences

Melissa Castillo Planas, *A Mexican State of Mind:*
New York City and the New Borderlands of Culture

Monica Hanna and Rebecca A. Sheehan, eds., *Border Cinema:*
Reimagining Identity through Aesthetics

Media Culture
in Transnational Asia
··
Convergences and Divergences

EDITED BY HYESU PARK

Rutgers University Press

New Brunswick, Camden, and Newark, New Jersey, and London

978-1-9788-0413-5
978-1-9788-0412-8
978-1-9788-0414-2
Cataloging-in-Publication data is available from the Library of Congress.
LCCN 2020022241.

A British Cataloging-in-Publication record for this book is available from the British Library.

♾ The paper used in this publication meets the requirements of the American National
Standard for Information Sciences—Permanence of Paper for Printed Library Materials,
ANSI Z39.48–1992.

www.rutgersuniversitypress.org

Manufactured in the United States of America

Contents

Part II Single-Nation Approach

**Media Culture in
Transnational Asia**

Introduction

■■■■■■■■■■■■■■■■■■■■■■■■■■

HYESU PARK AND MAYA DODD

Media[1] have become an essential part of our everyday life. While it is true globally that media impact our daily experience and are intricately interwoven
into what we do, think, and feel, media are also regional phenomena situated
in specific times and places. These specificities of media, however, transform
and transgress across borders. Indeed, media are built out of shared idiomatic
and audiovisual and verbal aesthetic systems that can be deployed and appropriated in a myriad of ways for different purposes and configurations. Moreover, media, no matter where they originate from and what form they take, have
a common goal of engaging media recipients cognitively and affectively and pro-
voking different forms of human communication and narrative meaning. The
development of the internet and mobile communications in recent years, on
the other hand, has given new meanings and shapes to more traditional media,
accelerating their adaptations and consumptions across geographic borders. It
is, for instance, now common for people in Vietnam to watch popular Indian
soap operas online (Arora and Jotwani, chapter 2 in this volume), while the
remake of Korean television shows in China has become a popular practice.
The intended audience for a specific narrative is far exceeded, and although dissemination is unpredictable, it is not surprising when narratives are adapted
in new contexts and forms. What catches the fancy of which national mood is
anyone's guess. Such global practices of transgression and adaptation of media
and narrative are reconstituting the boundedness of regions, while the transnational flow of media across borders challenges the very stability of categories
of identity. The so-called new media and their open platforms are also breaking

down the barrier between media producer/professional and consumer/amateur, giving way to the new mode of cultural production (Lau, chapter 3, and Wang, chapter 4, in this volume).

This book investigates the production, consumption, and transnational exchange of media in Asia, in which over half of the world's population resides. This book's contributors bear a few things in mind. First, defining Asia and developing models for Asian regional integration involve Asia's many complex and contradictory features. As Wang Hui points out, "Buddhism, Judaism, Christianity, Hinduism, Islam, Sikhism, Zoroastrianism, Daoism, and Confucianism all originated in [Asia]," while the idea of Confucian Asia cannot "fully represent the characteristics of even China alone."[2] Any attempt to summarize Asia as one unitary culture will inevitably face challenges. A high degree of flexibility, consideration for plurality, and willingness to explore and mitigate potential conflicts of interest among nations are hence required. Second, a widespread trend in media studies, especially in the Anglo North, consists of "associating media with specific technologies of communication, such as writing, film, photography, TV, radio, the telephone, and all the uses of digital technology known as 'new media.'"[3] This conception of media as technologies, however, excludes many culturally relevant narrative forms. It also downplays the crucial aspect of media as regional and cultural practices informed by and informing behaviors, thoughts, and feelings of the people consuming and producing them in specific times and places. This book therefore turns to Asian sociopolitical and cultural milieus and actively engages with them to understand and interpret media in Asia. It also questions how these milieus complement and challenge more established methodological and theoretical approaches used actively by the book's contributors in their investigations. These approaches may include examining media semiotically (focusing on image, language, sound) and technologically (focusing on media-defining features), as well as interpreting media narratologically, historically, cross-culturally, linguistically, and so forth.[4] Lastly, old and new media are closely interconnected and cannot be discussed in isolation. Jay Bolter and Richard Grusin's concept of "remediation" highlights this idea of media ecology. Bolter and Grusin define remediation as "the formal logic by which new media refashion prior media forms."[5] As Marie-Laure Ryan notes, then, every medium is "developed as an attempt to remediate the deficiencies of another medium. . . . Media need each other to function as media at all."[6] The wide range of both the old and the new media explored in the book and the various ways in which they converge and transform adequately reflect this concept of media remediation. With these three major points as the core to studying media in Asia, the book ultimately questions how different Asian nations and their unique media cultures engage with both local and global concerns and trends leading the development, adaptation, and appropriation of media within, across, and beyond the region.

Transnationalism and Asian Nationalism: Toward Affective Transactions

Chris Berry and Mary Farquhar explain that the term "transnational" is generally used "to refer to phenomena that exceed the boundaries of any single national territory."[7] Although the more common practice is to treat transnational phenomena "as products of the globalizing process," other scholars, such as Ulf Hannerz and Prasenjit Duara, "oppose the rhetoric of universality and homogenization implied in the term globalization."[8] According to their view, transnational phenomena "need to be specified in terms of the particular places and time in which they operate, the particular people they affect, and the particular ways they are constituted and maintained."[9] In order to understand how Asia collectively creates the media culture that is uniquely Asian and universally global and local simultaneously, we need an approach to media that accounts for the pan-Asian and trans-Asian identities to situate them nationally, regionally, and transnationally. Such an approach is especially pertinent when we consider the cultural, political, and religious plurality of diverse Asia as well as the fraught historical and political relations among Asian nations that render transnational integration in the region an emotionally, historically, and politically challenging task.

In the introduction to *Precarious Belongings: Affect and Nationalism in Asia* (2017), Chih-ming Wang notes how painful memories of colonialism circumscribe nation-building in Asia. Historicizing the affective nature of Asian nationalism, Wang emphasizes the social nature of affect that is particularly resonant in an Asian context. The rise of Japan in the early twentieth century and the traumatic outcomes of World War II, for instance, gave Asian nationalisms a unique twist in character by turning the anticolonial agenda into endless conflicts over ambivalent borders and historical memories. The end of the Cold War and the miraculous rise of China contributed further twists to this development. Thus, since the 1940s, we have witnessed one dispute after another over territories: between India and Pakistan (on Kashmir); between Japan, Taiwan, and China (on the Diaoyutai/Senkaku Islands); between Korea and Japan (on the Dokdo/Takashima Island); and between China and Taiwan (on Taiwan's sovereign status). Such disputes are emotionally charged with painful memories from the past. Wang in his introduction to the book hence adds to the dimension of colonial history "multilateral migration, traumatic territorial disputes and the intersectionality of disgrace, suffering and precarity," which together constitute what he, borrowing John Hutchinson's concept, calls "inter-referencing nationalisms."[10] Moreover, as Wang makes clear, these inter-referencing nationalisms turn nations into "affective communities" of a unique kind that would act according to the affective dispositions of the sense of hurt, fear, dispossession, and intolerance of differences that are "not just personal but rather social in origin and political in character to register the complex interactions between the affective, the social, and the political."[11] These affective communities and their wide range of emotions and feelings turn multiculturalism into a ground for introverted nationalisms in Asia.

The history of the region on borders and conflicts, however, is the motivation for this volume to look for an alternative approach to conceptualize Asia—by, for instance, emphasizing the underrepresented cultural sharing that also defines Asia. Vivian Shaw on antiracism activism in post-3/11 Japan[12] offers an especially illuminating account on how antiracist activists have tried to rebuild the disaster-plagued nation into an inclusive space through what she calls "affective transactions"—sharing food, music, cosplay, and the conviction that people, despite their differences, are "already living together."[13] One may find the possibility for these affective transactions much needed in the face of the introverted nationalisms in Asia in technological innovations. The technologies of the internet and mobile communication interlink people across geographic borders. The consequence, as Eugenia Siapera points out, is that of the diminished relevance of the nation-state, as people are able to be "connected and brought together in a space outside their real or imaginary homeland."[14] Siapera further conceptualizes this space "outside their real or imaginary homeland" using Manuel Castells's notion of "network society." In network society, the advancement of the electronic media leads to fundamental shifts in society, mobilizing and reorganizing its actors and their activities in a space not of places but of flows.[15]

Castells highlights that the rise of the network in new technologically advanced societies has given birth to a new notion of space based "not on physical proximity but on the exchange of flows."[16] Moreover, within this space of flows and exchanges, ethnicity and race, while never ceasing to exist, are no longer bound to specific territories and providing "the basis for a common identity." As Castells further elaborates, in network society, "ethnic roots are twisted, divided, reprocessed, mixed, differentially stigmatized, or rewarded, according to a new logic of informationalization and globalization of cultures and economies that makes symbolic composites out of blurred identities. Race matters, but it hardly constructs meaning any longer."[17] Of course, it is possible to question Castells's theory about the diminished status of race and ethnicity in network society. Consider, for instance, the emergence of pan-Asian or trans-Asian identities, fostered in part by the transnational dialogues that exchanges of media in the region make possible, which in fact become especially prominent in network society. Nevertheless, it is clear that media and their flows contribute to the very "affective transactions" (of images, narratives, ideas, music, and so forth) and the formation of nation and national identities that are less introverted and more open to fluid integrations.

Circulation of Media in Asia: The Asian Turn

In their interdisciplinary 2015 collection, David Roh, Betsy Huang, and Greta Niu build on David Morley and Kevin Robbins's 1995 concept of techno-Orientalism. As a term used to describe a tendency of the West to discursively construct the East, techno-Orientalism indicates "the phenomenon of imagining Asia and Asians in hypo- or hypertechnological terms in cultural productions and political discourse."[18] While much attention has been paid to Western constructions of Asia, much less ink has been spilled on Asian constructions of Asia. The effort to shift the focus to Asia by Asia is timely given the recent development and spread of digital technologies and networked media, of which Asia is a significant part. According to the 2019 statistics from the Internet World Stats, Asia constitutes 50.1 percent of the world's internet population with 2,197 million internet users in total.[19] Not surprisingly, "Chinese, Japanese, Arabic, and Korean are among the top ten most used languages on the web," while Chinese speakers alone "form almost a quarter (23.2 percent) of the world's internet population."[20] Meanwhile, South Korea's Samsung Electronics and SK Hynix are the world's largest and third-largest suppliers of semiconductors that are essential to the production of microelectronics.[21] India, on the other hand, is the world's largest exporter of information technology. The digital revolution in Asia, empowered by the region's rapid economic growth, proactive governmental policies,[22] and relatively younger and more technophilic consumers, is causing fundamental shifts in the existing economic, cultural, and political systems of the region, instigating new ways of life and spreading innovations across and beyond the region. The results, as Sun Lim and Cheryll Ruth R. Soriano point out, are the "boost in domestic innovation in information technology (IT), considerable growth in the quantity and quality of the region's IT clusters, and a thriving start-up ecosystem," which together generate "trend-setting innovations in social media, online games, mobile commerce, and mobile health," among other things.[23]

In spite of the significant position that Asia occupies in the production, consumption, and appropriation of new digital media and other internet-related technologies, analytical frames deployed to understand media predominantly originate from the Global North, with a few mostly Western societies consistently reappearing as the sites for media examination.[24] Indeed, as James Curran and Myung-Jin Park lament in *De-Westernizing Media Studies* (2000), "Whether it be middle-range generalization about, for example, the influence of news sources on reporting, or grand theory about the media's relationship to postmodernity, the same few countries keep recurring as if they are a stand-in for the rest of the world."[25] Yet the world is changing—globalization is no longer a Western cultural force (the spread of *hallyu* [the Korean wave] in Europe and Anglo America, for instance), Asia with its young and educated populace is leading the global economic growth (China, Japan, and India are three of the five world's largest economies), and Asia has become the alternative center for media production (Bollywood of India and K Pop of South Korea, for instance). Asia is also home to "some of the world's oldest, most advanced civilizations, with lasting legacies of artistic, cultural, and scientific innovations of widespread influence."[26] These cultural and philosophical traditions and legacies of Asia are an essential part of the ever-growing media landscape of the region, with overarching impact around the globe.

For this very reason, while acknowledging that media are undeniably global phenomena, whose systems and experiences are shaped by global flows and exchanges, contributors to this book adopt what Kuan-Hsing Chen in 2010 called "Asia as method." Like Goh and Wang's inter-referencing method, Chen's Asia as method describes how "using Asia as an imaginary anchoring point can allow societies in Asia to become one another's reference points so that the understanding of the self can be transformed, and subjectivity rebuilt."[27] This method helps contributors of the book join the effort to de-Westernize and de-parochialize media studies. That is, contributors capitalize on their local knowledge and incorporate the live and direct experience in the specific nationally identified geographical region into their analytical methodology and expertise to bear on the exploration of media that is formal, thematic, and cultural concurrently. Importantly, too, the spirit of Engseng Ho's "local cosmopolitanism" shapes contributors' discussion of Asia and its media in the book. Ho writes that "much recent literature on Asian transnationalism has focused on Asian elites and on textual modes of interaction, notably focusing on the writings of pre-eminent Asian intellectuals and literary figures."[28] In contrast to such privileged sites of readings, contributors in the book engage with both the mainstream and the nonmainstream media of diverse forms, themes, and configurations and consider how these media texts help reconstruct our understanding of Asia. Similarly, it is important to note that thirteen of the book's fifteen contributors are currently researching and teaching in diverse locations in Asia. Their writing styles and scholarly approaches are hence more receptive toward Asian theoretical concepts and academic traditions, appealing well to the audiences outside the Western world. Some Western audiences, on the other hand, may find the manner of writing in some chapters of the book unfamiliar and foreign initially. This unfamiliarity, however, must be celebrated, as one of the many strengths of this book lies in the sheer diversity of the voices and perspectives of the contributors that productively fall outside the Anglophone paradigms. These Asian perspectives will take all audiences in a new direction that pays close attention to how Asia collectively creates the media culture that is uniquely Asian and trans-Asian and universally global simultaneously.

The Book in Outline

As Youna Kim notes, emphasis on global and transnational flows in media studies inevitably raises concerns about cultural homogenization, as "there are also distinctive trends towards fragmentation at multiple levels—regional, national, local—fostering resistance and individual's critical engagement with the media to suit their cultural priorities."[29] Keeping this resistance in mind and recognizing that "certain experiences of media use strongly resonate with locally entrenched and even regionally recognized rituals, histories, or values,"[30] this book takes two distinct and yet interrelated approaches to media in Asia, using a transnational approach on the one hand and a single-nation approach on the other hand. Chapters under the transnational approach propose a trans-Asian model for media studies, examining carefully the cultural, historical, political, demographic, and technological relationships between specific selective locations in Asia, India and Japan (Amit in this volume) or Japan and the rest of East Asia (Yamamoto in this volume), for instance. By doing so, contributors show how these relationships make possible and further foster transnational circulations and exchanges of media and their narratives, affects, and values across national borders. These chapters are also interested in investigating how the trans-Asian model challenges existing paradigms of media studies more generally, as seen in John Gagnon's discussion of Southeast Asian media representations of human trafficking as the alternative to the Western portrayals in this volume. Chapters under the single-nation approach, on the other hand, are more concerned with media phenomena within specific nationally identified geographic locations, as seen in Hyesu Park's studies of YouTube channels in South Korea as well as Asantha U. Attanayake's discussion of British colonialism's legacy in Sri Lankan advertisements today. Nevertheless, these chapters ultimately join the trans-Asian media conversation. The convergences and divergences among the chapters allow readers to notice that there exist shared rituals, histories, and values across the region. These shared commonalities add a certain degree of consistency to the region's media culture and help form meaningful regional structures—even if these structures take widely different forms from nation to nation with a strong sense of heterogeneity. The book's fifteen contributors from ten different national backgrounds discuss fifteen Asian nations as the rich sites for media production, consumption, and exchange. Readers are thus encouraged to treat the book as a palette consisting of a wide range of colors, which intersect to constitute a big, coherent picture that ultimately contributes to a broader media debate.

Although the choices of medium, nation, and analytical and methodological frames differ among chapters, the book's contributors share a common interest in narrative as an integral part of what media do and how media create influence. After all, medium is defined as a channel of communication and expression, and the dominant approach to media studies has been to explore "how institutional, economic, and political factors influence what is and what is not conveyed through media; whether media messages accurately reflect various dimensions of reality; how different audiences interpret the same content differently; and so on."[31] This study of narrative is complemented by the focus on "medium," "the particular characteristics of each individual medium or of each particular type of media," leading to Joshua Meyrowitz's question, "What are the relatively fixed features of each means of communicating and how do these features make the medium physically, psychologically, and socially different from other media and from face-to-face interaction?"[32] Bearing in mind the significance of narrative and medium in the study of media, then, the contributors commonly recognize media as material supports of information that are at once cognitive (enabling human minds to deal with time and space, to express and to communicate), aesthetic (material or technical means of artistic expression), and sociological (contextually situated practices).[33]

The book's regional focus on Asia, on the other hand, allows contributors to further specify their media conversation, as they consider deeply elements of culture, society, and region that situate and shape media dynamics in Asia. Ultimately, contributors together raise some quintessential questions to explore: How do media, depending on the specific form they take, filter different aspects of narrative production and consumption and reflect changes in social interaction and structure? How do media influence media recipients cognitively, emotionally, ethically, and psychically? What do narratives produced by media tell us about ourselves and our social order in rapidly growing Asia? How does the interconnectedness of nations in Asia shed light on media sharing actively occurring across the region?

Rea Amit in chapter 1 commences the transnational discussion of media in Asia by focusing on the cross-border adaptations between Japanese and Indian media, examining films, documentaries, animations, magazines, and letters, among other things. Concentrating on medial representations of Japan in India, and vice versa, as a "cultural Other," Amit posits that Western preconceptions about the non-West gave rise to clichéd images of the East and continue to influence the way the non-West itself depicts other non-Western cultures. Amit cautions that such inter-Asian transposition unfortunately falls into outdated categories of Orientalism and other stereotypical archetypes. Shubhda Arora and Juhi Jotwani in chapter 2 further the discussion of inter-Asian media exchange by looking at the Indian soap opera *Balika Vadhu* (child bride) and its wide popularity in Vietnam. Through their detailed analysis of the show and comprehensive overview of Indian and Vietnamese cultures, Arora and Jotwani show that the extraordinary success of *Balika Vadhu* in Vietnam is attributable to the (Indian) themes explored in the show that resonate well with the material and social reality of people in some parts of Vietnam.

Dorothy Wai Sim Lau in chapter 3 draws our attention to the convergence between the old and new media, examining the transportation of film star personae from cinema to cyberspace through the instance of the Chinese martial arts actor Donnie Yen. With Yen's global presence in mind, Lau analyzes transnational Chinese stardom and the emerging role of amateurs equipped with new digital technology—and also how this technological development fuels active participation of global audiences in the star-making mechanism. Lau asserts that fan-made online videos on Chinese stars by knowledgeable and technophilic fans reconfigure Chinese icons in the global mediascape and alter how the Chinese image is approached, represented, and appropriated. Similarly, W. Michelle Wang in chapter 4 explores the technological impact of media culture in Asia by discussing the adaptation of Chinese online fiction for television and transnational circulation of such television serials. Using the televisual adaptation of the Chinese web novel *When a Snail Falls in Love* (2016) as her case study, Wang outlines how the digital age has shaped the circulation of Chinese culture. At the end, Wang asserts that media culture in transnational Asia must take into account the fact that diasporas are heterogeneous rather than homogeneous groups, whose complex engagements with popular culture are mediated by more than ethnic identification.

John Gagnon in chapter 5 conducts a rhetorical analysis of Southeast Asian media representations of human trafficking in his attempt to provide an alternative perspective to the human trafficking narratives in Western media. These Western representations, Gagnon notes, are almost always rooted in the rhetorics of rescue and liberation. This rhetorical tendency results in reductionistically breaking down the lived experiences of those who have been trafficked and fails to offer a truly complete picture of the issue. Gagnon hence turns to local lenses, that is, Southeast Asian media representations, and argues that to more fully understand the narratives that circulate about human trafficking, we need to look locally to gain a more robust understanding of the global issue. Chapter 6 by Hiroki Yamamoto, on the other hand, takes us to East Asia as he examines the contested legacies of Japanese colonialism in the region through the examples of contemporary Japanese art, including performances, sculptures, and video installations. Yamamoto posits that the remaining legacies of Japanese colonialism can be best identified transnationally throughout the whole of Asia. He therefore promotes visual art as an effective medium for nonverbal communication that allows for thinking and speaking about the sensitive war-related subjects among the people of Asia.

Hyesu Park in chapter 7 turns to the single-nation approach to media in Asia in her study of *mukbang* in South Korea, an online audiovisual broadcast in which a host eats food in front of a camera. Park's investigation of media is narratologically and culturally oriented, as she employs transmedial narrative studies (i.e., narrative studies across media) and South Korean cultural precepts and concepts as her theoretical frameworks to make sense of the mukbang phenomenon. Park argues that the bridging of technology, semiotics, and culture adds depth to our understanding of the production and consumption of mukbang in South Korea. Asantha U. Attanayake in chapter 8 continues this single-nation approach by looking closely into how advertisements in Sri Lanka contribute to the construction, consumption, and representation of white supremacy in Sri Lanka. She argues that the legacies of British colonialism still shape islanders' attitudes toward life, allowing neocolonial powers to embrace the nation easily. Through her close analysis of advertisements that reflect and promote what she calls the speak, eat, dress, and act white tendency, Attanayake shows how these media feed into and insert white supremacy into the mindset of ordinary Sri Lankans.

Sabiha Huq in chapter 9 takes us to Bangladesh as she discusses the role of national cinema in the construction of national identity and culture in Bangladesh. While offering a comprehensive overview of Bangladeshi history and its film industry, Huq in her chapter is critical of the current Bangladeshi film industry dominated by commercial and international films. However, Huq's goal is not to challenge the internationalization of the film industry or to protect the national culture of a museumized kind. Instead, Huq posits that fantasy devoid of imaginative potential, the absence of clear policies on how to evolve a national imaginary, and the lack of a vision of the future constitute a triad of forces that leads to the production of a hotchpotch Bengali culture. Similarly, Darlene Machell de Leon Espena in chapter 10 discusses the role of cinema in nation-building by looking at Indonesia, Philippines, Malaysia, and Singapore during the time of decolonization and their shared colonial history. Unlike Huq, Espena notes positive contributions of national cinema to the construction of national identities in these Southeast Asian nations. She also points out that film producers and directors from these nations shared their narratives, techniques of filmmaking, and political ideas transnationally. Espena hence argues that Southeast Asians employed cinema to conjure the earliest imaginations of their budding nations, and these films reflect the creativity, resilience, and strength of Southeast Asians.

The last two chapters of the book take us to the Middle East. Alireza Dehghan in chapter 11 discusses Afghanistan and its media and culture in transition. Dehghan points out that between 2005 and 2015, the number of internet users in Afghanistan grew from 1 percent to more than 8 percent. Notably, too, Dehghan asserts that Afghanistan's media culture is to some degree in line with that of other Asian nations, as social networks are lessening social and economic deprivations for women and other ethnic and regional minorities in Afghanistan. Overall, Dehghan explores the development of the internet and new media in the nation since the Taliban's collapse in 2001 and questions to what extent the growth and spread of media diminish ethnic, racial, gender, and class problems in Afghan society. Hamid Abdollahyan and Hoornaz Keshavarzian in chapter 12, the last chapter of the book, locate Instagram, the image-based application and social networking site, within one of the world's oldest societies, Iran. They posit that Instagram provides Iranian users opportunities to ostentatiously display a wide range of economic, social, and cultural capitals. This act of display in Iran becomes especially significant given the nation's religious, political, and historical environments that render public displays of many kinds challenging and even dangerous. Their discussion of female Instagram users in Iran is especially notable in this regard. By putting together the sociological and cultural study of Instagram in Iran and considering Instagram's technological specifications, this last chapter of the book makes a meaningful contribution to our understanding of the new media in the Middle East.

By challenging what have been traditionally viewed as sites of Asian interaction, this book probes less visible circuits, furthering an effort to reconstitute Asian and media studies. In the spirit of historians, Tim Harper and Sunil Amrith complicate the idea of site as geographical boundedness: "Pursuing the theme of sites of interaction in an Asian setting allows us to interrogate assumptions about the boundaries of regions and sub-regions. . . . Thinking in terms of particular spaces allows us to refine what we mean by 'inter-Asian connections': by focusing on the agency of particular sites in producing different modes of interaction."[34] By examining technological, artistic, cultural, and social innovations and forces shaping media culture in Asia, we can explore the complex and multifaceted ways in which media are also shaping Asian cultural and political concepts and precepts. An Asian approach to media as regional, transnational, technological, and narrative phenomena enables an understanding of accelerated cultural adaptations across the region. Such understanding leads us to appreciate newly emerging pan-Asian and trans-Asian identities mediated significantly by media flows and exchanges.

Notes

1   Media can be generally thought of as the main means of mass communication as well as the material or form used by the artist, composer, writer, or anyone who wishes to communicate, express, or entertain. While contributors to the book examine widely different aspects of media production and consumption, they commonly emphasize media's narrative potential, that is, what messages they convey and how media recipients interpret and further reconstruct these messages in various ways. Contributors also pay keen attention to the ways in which this

narrative potential is informed by the particular form that media take as well as the specific spatial and temporal setting within which media are situated.

2 Wang Hui, "The Politics of Imagining Asia: A Genealogical Analysis," in *The Inter-Asia Cultural Studies Reader*, ed. Kuan-Hsing Chen and Beng Huat Chua (London: Routledge, 2007), 97.

3 Marie-Laure Ryan, "Story/Worlds/Media: Tuning the Instruments of a Media-Conscious Narratology," in *Storyworlds across Media: Towards a Media-Conscious Narratology*, ed. Marie-Laure Ryan and Jan-Noël Thon (Lincoln: University of Nebraska Press, 2014), 27.

4 Note that contributors to the book engage with sociopolitical and cultural milieus of Asia not simply as the background and setting for media production and consumption used broadly and generally but as what we may call Asian concepts and precepts, that is, concrete theoretical frameworks. This means that contributors examine how these milieus as theories intersect with and further unsettle the more established conceptual framework that originates in the West. See, for instance, Park's use of narratology in her discussion of Korean mukbang shows in chapter 7 as well as Dehghan's challenging Benedict Anderson's theorization of the origin and spread of nationalism in the context of Afghanistan's low literacy rate, insufficient infrastructure, and increasing national insecurity in chapter 11.

5 Jay Bolter and Richard Grusin, *Remediation: Understanding New Media* (Cambridge, MA: MIT Press, 1999), 273.

6 Marie-Laure Ryan, *Narrative across Media* (Lincoln: University of Nebraska Press), 31.

7 Chris Berry and Mary Farquhar, *China on Screen: Cinema and Nation* (Hong Kong: Hong Kong University Press, 2006), 4. For more, please see W. Michelle Wang's chapter in this volume.

8 Hannerz and Duara's view on globalization is quoted in Berry and Farquhar, *China on Screen*.

9 Ibid.

10 Chih-ming Wang, "Introduction: Tracking the Affective Twists in Asian Nationalisms," in *Precarious Belongings: Affect and Nationalism in Asia*, ed. Chih-ming Wang and Daniel Pei Siong Goh (London: Rowman & Littlefield International, 2017), xi.

11 Ibid., ix.

12 March 11, 2011, marks a pivotal moment in Japanese activism and activist consciousness as the country suffered "a devastating triple disaster of a 9.0-magnitude earthquake, a tsunami, and reactor meltdowns at the Fukushima nuclear power plant." These events ignited both the activists and ordinary Japanese people by exposing "the myth of safe nuclear energy and the state's failure to protect its own citizens." For more, please see Vivian Shaw, "'We Are Already Living Together': Race, Collective Struggle, and the Reawakened Nation in Post-3/11 Japan," in *Precarious Belongings: Affect and Nationalism in Asia*, ed. Chih-ming Wang and Daniel Pei Siong Goh (London: Rowman & Littlefield International, 2017), 60–61.

13 Ibid.

14 Eugenia Siapera, *Cultural Diversity and Global Media* (Oxford: Wiley-Blackwell, 2010), 184.

15 Ibid.

16 Ibid., 185. Castells's conceptualization of "network society" is extensively quoted in Siapera.

17 Manuel Castells, *The Rise of the Network Society* (Oxford: Wiley-Blackwell, 2000), 63.
18 David Roh, Betsy Huang, and Greta Niu, "Technologizing Orientalism: An Introduction," in *Techno-Orientalism: Imagining Asia in Speculative Fiction, History, and Media*, ed. David Roh, Betsy Huang, and Greta Niu (New Brunswick, NJ: Rutgers University Press, 2015), 2.
19 "Internet Usage Statistics: The Internet Big Picture," *Internet World Stats*, last modified March 31, 2019, https://www.internetworldstats.com/stats.htm.
20 Sun Sun Lim and Cheryll Ruth R. Soriano, "A (Digital) Giant Awakens— Invigorating Media Studies with Asian Perspectives," in *Asian Perspectives on Digital Culture*, ed. Sun Sun Lim and Cheryll Ruth R. Soriano (New York: Routledge, 2016), 3.
21 "Top-15 Semiconductor Suppliers 2018," Anysilicon, August 20, 2018, https://anysilicon.com/top-15-semiconductor-suppliers-2018/.
22 Consider, for instance, Taiwan's technocracy-centered economic planning.
23 Lim and Soriano, "A (Digital) Giant Awakens," 4.
24 For more criticisms on this Western approach, see James Curran and Myung-Jin Park, "Beyond globalization theory," in *De-Westernizing Media Studies*, ed. James Curran and Myung-Jin Park (New York: Routledge, 2000), 3.
25 Ibid., 3.
26 Lim and Soriano, "A (Digital) Giant Awakens," 4.
27 Kuan-Hsing Chen, *Asia as Method: Toward Deimperialization* (Durham, NC: Duke University Press, 2010), xv.
28 Engseng Ho, *The Graves of Tarim: Genealogy and Mobility across the Indian Ocean* (Berkeley: University of California Press, 2007), 1.
29 Youna Kim, "Media Globalization in Asia," in *Media Consumption and Everyday Life in Asia*, ed. Youna Kim (New York: Routledge, 2008), 13.
30 Lim and Soriano, "A (Digital) Giant Awakens," 7.
31 Ryan, *Narrative*, 50.
32 Joshua Meyrowitz, "Medium Theory," in *Communication Theory Today*, ed. David Crowley and David Mitchell (Stanford, CA: Stanford University Press, 1994), 50.
33 For a more detailed discussion on each aspect of media, including also see Ryan, *Narrative*, 2–5.
34 Tim Harper and Sunil Amrith, *Sites of Asian Interaction* (Cambridge: Cambridge University Press, 2014), 2.

Bibliography

Berry, Chris, and Mary Farquhar. *China on Screen: Cinema and Nation*. Hong Kong: Hong Kong University Press, 2006.

Bolter, Jay, and Richard Grusin. *Remediation: Understanding New Media*. Cambridge, MA: MIT Press, 1999.

Castells, Manuel. *The Rise of the Network Society*. Oxford: Wiley-Blackwell, 2000.

Chen, Kuan-Hsing. *Asia as Method: Toward Deimperialization*. Durham, NC: Duke University Press, 2010.

Curran, James, and Myung-Jin Park. "Beyond Globalization Theory." In *De-Westernizing Media Studies*, edited by James Curran and Myung-Jin Park, 3–18. New York: Routledge, 2000.

Harper, Tim, and Sunil Amrith. *Sites of Asian Interaction*. Cambridge: Cambridge University Press, 2014.

Ho, Engseng. *The Graves of Tarim: Genealogy and Mobility across the Indian Ocean*. Berkeley: University of California Press, 2007.

Hui, Wang. "The Politics of Imagining Asia: A Genealogical Analysis." In *The Inter-Asia Cultural Studies Reader*, edited by Kuan-Hsing Chen and Beng Huat Chua, 1–33. London: Routledge, 2007.

"Internet Usage Statistics: The Internet Big Picture." Internet World Stats. Last modified March 31, 2019. https://www.internetworldstats.com/stats.htm.

Kim, Youna. "Media Globalization in Asia." In *Media Consumption and Everyday Life in Asia*, edited by Youna Kim, 1–24. New York: Routledge, 2008.

Lim, Sun Sun, and Cheryll Ruth R. Soriano. "A (Digital) Giant Awakens— Invigorating Media Studies with Asian Perspectives." In *Asian Perspectives on Digital Culture*, edited by Sun Sun Lim and Cheryll Ruth R. Soriano, 3–14. New York: Routledge, 2016.

Meyrowitz, Joshua. "Medium Theory." In *Communication Theory Today*, edited by David Crowley and David Mitchell, 50–77. Stanford, CA: Stanford University Press, 1994.

Roh, David Roh, Betsy Huang, and Greta Niu. "Technologizing Orientalism: An Introduction." In *Techno-Orientalism: Imagining Asia in Speculative Fiction, History, and Media*, edited by David Roh, Betsy Huang, and Greta Niu, 1–19. New Brunswick, NJ: Rutgers University Press, 2015.

Ryan, Marie-Laure. *Narrative across Media*. Lincoln: University of Nebraska Press.

———. "Story/Worlds/Media: Tuning the Instruments of a Media-Conscious Narratology." In *Storyworlds across Media: Towards a Media-Conscious Narratology*, edited by Marie-Laure Ryan and Jan-Noël Thon, 25–43. Lincoln: University of Nebraska Press, 2014.

Shaw, Vivian. "'We Are Already Living Together': Race, Collective Struggle, and the Reawakened Nation in Post-3/11 Japan." In *Precarious Belongings: Affect and Nationalism in Asia*, edited by Chih-ming Wang and Daniel PS Goh, 59–76. London: Rowman & Littlefield International, 2017.

Siapera, Eugenia. *Cultural Diversity and Global Media*. Oxford: Wiley-Blackwell, 2010.

"Top-15 Semiconductor Suppliers 2018." Anysilicon. August 20, 2018. https://anysilicon.com/top-15-semiconductor-suppliers-2018/.

Wang, Chih-ming. "Introduction: Tracking the Affective Twists in Asian Nationalisms." In *Precarious Belongings: Affect and Nationalism in Asia*, edited by Chih-ming Wang and Daniel Pei Siong Goh, vii–xxi. London: Rowman & Littlefield International, 2017.

Part I

Transnational Approach
■■■■■■■■■■■■■■■■■■■■■■■■■

1

Converging on Love and Indifference
■■■■■■■■■■■■■■■■■■■■■■■■■

Mediated Otherness
in South and East Asia

REA AMIT

The Indian film, *The Japanese Wife* (directed by Aparna Sen, 2010),[1] is emblematic of the compromised transnational flows between East and South Asia, while at the same time also of the anachronistic media convergence by which such flows are contrived. The film depicts an impossible love story between an Indian man and a Japanese woman that develops solely through a letter exchange. It is based on a short story by Kunal Basu, for whom Japan was an imaginary land epitomized by his infatuation with Japanese cinema. Basu's affection for Japanese cinema led him to name his Japanese protagonist Miyagi, after the name of the character in Mizoguchi Kenji's periodic fantasy, *Ugetsu* (1953).[2] This chapter further elaborates on the limited media exchanges between these two Asian regions while highlighting the fundamental self-contradicting motivation that drives them to opposite emotional excesses: affection, identification, or love, on the one hand, as well as disregard, intentional blindness, or indifference on the other. Concentrating on medial representations of East Asia in South Asia, and vice versa, as a cultural Other, I argue that such inter-Asian transposition eventually falls in outdated categories of Orientalism, Japanism, and other stereotypical archetypes.

Scholars have long criticized the West's mystification of the East, many among them influenced by Edward Said's *Orientalism*. Although Said focused mainly on the region known as the Near East, critics used his conceptual analysis to discuss Western depictions of the Far East as well as of South Asia. Surprisingly, perhaps, this chapter identifies similar propensities in various media forms in Asia itself. These do not pertain to new concepts, such as self-Orientalism, by which scholars, particularly in the context of Japanese popular culture, discuss works of fiction or art that lend themselves to Western consumption by exacerbating stereotypes.[3] Rather, the chapter concentrates on how Western preconceptions about the non-West, the ones that gave rise to clichéd images of the East, influence the way the non-West itself depicts other non-Western cultures.

Specifically, the chapter singles out the national characteristics of the production and consumption of mediated imaginaries, both of Japan, as an East Asian nation, and of the South Asian nation, India. Yet, unlike the notion of national character as an outward-projected image of the nation onto the world, I explore the imagining of a cultural Other that India and Japan project inward, catering to a distinct mode of consumption that is unique to a specific community. For both India and Japan, the other country provides an imaginary site that is at the same time near enough to be legitimately toyed with and aesthetically remote enough to serve as a domestic Asian Other. I will elaborate on this by drawing attention to parameters in the consumption and production of images that project communal forms of appropriation, and to the role media plays in circulating such images. While the chapter mainly focuses on film and film culture at large, toward the end I also discuss a Japanese animated work catering to local young audiences that showcases a similar tendency in this medium as well.

I argue that both Japan and India take liberty in depicting their counterpart along lines that are tantamount to Orientalist discourses, a process predicated on the notion that these problematic depictions are wrongly conceived—as if available for their eyes only—much like the compromised and anachronistic media use exemplified in the letter exchange in *The Japanese Wife*. Unlike Sen's film, however, where circumstances prevent the Indo-Japanese couple from meeting, Indo-Japanese media products representing the other country seem to intentionally turn a blind eye to any meaningful transnational exchanges as a form of voluntarily blindness. The chapter concludes by underscoring this point.

Initial Close Encounters of a Special Kind

Unlike the impression created by *The Japanese Wife* and despite the two countries' relative remoteness, there have been real contacts between Japanese and Indian people in the modern era. There is even one early, well-documented account of a real love story between a South Asian woman, born in a part of India that is today Bangladesh, and a Japanese man. The two married, and the woman, Hariprobha Basu Mallik, became Hariprobha Takeda and moved to Japan in 1912. She published her firsthand impression of the country, the people, and her experience as a Japanese wife in 1915. However, having firsthand experience does not always counter stereotypes or cultural biases. Despite her intimate contact with the country and its people, scholar Geeta Keeni indicates that Malik/Takeda highlighted positive Japanese characteristics similar to those identified by Indians who had only briefly visited the country.[4]

Apart from love stories, another early case that demonstrates—despite the good intentions (or indeed, precisely because of favorable inclinations)—how seemingly unmediated[5] impressions conjure up what seems to be a straightforward example of Orientalism, is Indian spiritual leader Swami Vivekananda's comments about the country during his Japanese sojourn. In one of his letters from Japan, he wrote, "The short-statured, fair-skinned, quaintly-dressed Japs, their movements, attitudes, gestures, everything is picturesque. Japan is the land of the picturesque!"[6] Vivekananda's remarks are problematic, but he did not intend to publish his impressions at the time, and writing norms were different in the late nineteenth century. His comments are significant because they are indicative of the fact that seemingly unmediated encounters do not necessarily yield a mindful account of a foreign culture.

Vivekananda also writes that Japanese individuals he met had also expressed unrealistic enthusiasm about India. Indeed, as Fabio Rambelli indicates, India was considered in premodern Japan to be the center of the world, mainly due to its recognition as the birthplace of Buddhism. However, Rambelli also points out that due to the lack of significant direct encounters between the two regions, the image of India (or *Tenjiku*, as it was known in Japan for many centuries), was shaped through an "emphasis on foreignness and exoticism (as signs of Indianness)."[7]

While imaginaries of South Asia in premodern Japan are understandable, in the modern era (much like in Vivekananda's case), Japanese unmediated conceptions of India evince innate tendencies. The most notable example in this regard is those of Kakuzō Okakura (widely known as Tenshin). Famous or infamous for his promotion of the idea of "one Asia," Okakura visited South Asia in late 1901 and early 1902. There, however, Okakura did not see that part of Asia for what it was but rather as a subject with which to promote his own nationalistic ideology. Focusing on India as a concept, Okakura reduced the profusion of South Asian ideas and arts to a single Indian civilization.[8] Although he did acknowledge the multiplicity of "Asiatic races,"[9] his notion of Asia located Japan at its center, in aesthetic terms, as a "museum of [one overarching] Asiatic civilization."[10]

Okakura's host in India, Rabindranath Tagore, who visited Japan several times, criticized the rise of nationalism in Japan and similar nationalistic tendencies in his Japanese acquaintance's theorization of Asia. However, as Rustom Bharucha points out, both men share the erroneous view of an Asian continent that is "more imagined than real, constituting a primordial fellowship and genealogy without which it would have been impossible for them to invent an 'Asia' outside the Orientalist strictures of the West."[11] Thus this is another indication of the fraught outcomes of even unmediated expressions of South Asia by an East Asian and vice versa.

Imagining Asian Identity

Gayatri Chakravorty Spivak traces the use of the name for the continent as it "reflects Europe's eastward trajectory" and convincingly argues that the production of the idea of such a place involves a certain "training of the imagination."[12] While this is undoubtedly true with Westerners, this is also the case with those whose Asian-ness seems unquestioned. For instance, Indian-born writer Salman Rushdie admits that he writes about his home country as an "imaginary homeland." Specifically about the act of writing about India by Indians who no longer reside in India, he states, "Our physical alienation from India almost inevitably means that we will not be capable of reclaiming precisely the thing that was lost; that we will, in short, create fictions, not actual cities or villages, but invisible ones, imaginary homelands, Indians of the minds."[13] It is therefore not surprising that short-time visitors from across Asia will be drawn to somewhat fictitious accounts of the places and people they encounter in other parts of the continent. After all, it is a mere act of human imagination that connects remote geographical locations under the same category.

The intimal contacts in the modern age mentioned earlier between Japan and India shed light on tangible shared imaginary continental relations. While no large region can ever claim even partial homogeneity, whether it is located in the Eastern or Western Hemispheres (a divide that is also fictional), Western nations have long depicted both Japan and India as well as the surrounding areas in South and East Asia as different by nature than what the West is (or is supposed to be). In other words, the West considered both countries as Others to what it conceived itself to be, often reducing them, as Said shows concerning the Near East, to stereotypes and flattened characterizations. It is therefore expected that individuals across Asia would be drawn to favorite depictions of remote cultures within the alleged unified sphere called Asia and that such representations could not avoid at least some degree of fiction, regardless of media.

Given the shared historical background as non-Western, it is less expected, however, that one region would adopt a Western perspective from which to regard another non-Western, Asian country. And yet, there are a growing number of cases that manifest precisely this kind of vision. More surprisingly, unlike textual media that tend to be less realistic, more modern means of representation appear to advance even further the notion of an Asian Other.

Orientalism and Indian Cinema

India is considered by many as the largest global producer of films. It is lesser known, however, that before the famed Indian movie industry became so prolific, Japanese film studios produced the largest number of films in the world. In the first decade after the Second World War, Japan began rebuilding and finding its way out of the desolate situation it faced at the end of the war. Although local studios had released films during and immediately after the war, in the 1950s, Japan experienced a golden age of cinema. That period gave many Japanese their first opportunity to view Indian culture.

Nagamasa Kawakita, the founder and head of the foreign films distributing company, Tōhōtōwa (frequently referred to as Tōwa), bought the screening rights of the Hindi language film *Aan* (Pride, 1952). After shortening its length from 161 to 90 minutes, Kawakita released the film for ten days of consecutive screenings at the Shinjuku Gekiba film theater in Tokyo starting January 1, 1954.[14] Tamaki Matsuoka, the leading scholar of South Asian cinema in Japan, considers the film a moderate box-office success. Beyond its plotline or its South Asian origin, she suggests, the film might have attracted attention because it was India's first Technicolor production.[15]

Although in 1951, Japan had already produced its first color film, *Karumen kokyō ni kaeru* (Carmen comes home), *Aan* was screened at a time of looming debates about media in the country. Although in the mid-1950s cinema became the most dominant medium, eclipsing other media such as the radio, this was also the beginning of public television broadcasts in Japan.[16] One Japanese reviewer of *Aan*, the poet Shinkichi Takahashi, reflects these media transformations. While considering the technological elements that the Hindi film employs, primarily cinemascope, he also contemplates cinema as a medium and compares it to other media, including radio and television.

Takahashi also meditates on the specifically Indian and Asiatic cultural elements the film represents. In contrast to the technological innovations it employs or the emerging new Japanese media ecology within which it is being received, Takahashi discusses aspects in the film that he identifies as non- or even antiscientific (*hikagaku*). In this regard, he emphasizes the role of dance in the film, which he argues is different from Western arts, such as ballet. This is because the latter, he claims, is more technical and even cold, whereas the former is rooted in old tradition. Indian dance is bright, he continues, and the music that accompanies it has a perfect melody (unlike, it seems, Western dance forms).

Like Okakura, Takahashi also adopts an (imaginary) "Asian" perspective from which he states that *Aan* transmits an Indian disdain for Western civilization, and he argues that it showcases an original rhythm of life instead. Ultimately, he concludes, the film is so deeply spiritual that it does not even need to present "our way of life" (*wareware no ikiru michi*).[17] Despite asserting that he, too, is Asian and that he is, therefore, able to understand similar or even shared non-Western sensibilities, he also evokes what Richard King calls "orientalist presumptions about the 'spirituality' of India."[18]

In fact, despite Takahashi's celebration of the film's Indian-ness or Asian-ness, Saad Ullah Khan argues that rather than non-Western qualities, *Aan* might actually have borrowed specific elements from the American Christian religious film, *Ben-Hur: A Tale of the Christ* (1925). He argues that the film demonstrates a "strong influence of Hollywood's style, action as well as direction."[19] As a poet with little or no experience with cinema, Takahashi's insights about the state of the medium among mass media at large are commendable. Yet, even considering his lack of expertise in criticism, it is remarkable that he, likely unconsciously or unintendedly, adopts a view that is based on the premise of a shared Asian or non-Western experience that at the same time reveals the most stereotypical Western presumptions about South Asian Otherness.

Takahashi's culturist generalizations could be dismissed as merely impressionistic remarks by a poet who was drawn to spiritualism.[20] However, his image of India as informed by the film is telling with regard to the process by which the notion of an Asian Other is formed by another Asian. To be sure, Japan was not unique in its reception of Indian films at the time. For example, Dimitris Eleftheriotis writes that *Aan* was also the first Indian film Greece imported, and he points out that there, too, they shortened the film to adjust it to local average theatrical screening time.[21] Ahmet Gurata writes that in Greece's neighboring rival, Turkey, Indian films "arrived" as early as 1947, and he adds that, as in Greece, these films started gaining wider attention and popularity in the mid-1950s.[22] In contrast to the case of Indian films in Japan, however, local critics in both Greece and Turkey considered Indian cinema to be a foreign entity, and similarly expressed their objection to screenings of films from the subcontinent. The early reception of Indian film in Japan represents a singular situation where Indian Otherness expresses a sense of exoticism and remoteness. At the same time, it reveals deep affinity and inherent proximity (as Asian nations), although Greece and Turkey are actually closer to India than Japan and have a much longer history of personal and cultural interactions between them.

Visualizing Affection for Japan in Indian Film Culture

Similar to the reception, albeit limited, of Indian cinema in Japan, early Indian commentators embraced a positive attitude toward Japanese cinema. Although film theaters in India did not commercially screen Japanese films, the Japanese Ministry of Culture[23] organized film screenings to increase the visibility of Japanese culture at Japan's embassies and consulates around the world, including in India. Moreover, in 1947, Chidananda Dasgupta and Satyajit Ray established the Calcutta Film Society, which inspired the establishment of similar societies throughout South Asia.[24] Among other domestic cinematic issues, these societies raised awareness of foreign films and likely helped to convince Indian state officials of the necessity to organize an international film festival in their country.

The Indian film festival opened in 1952. It was broadcast on the radio and toured the country. The festival featured only one East Asian film, the Chinese *Bai mao nu* (The white-haired girl, 1950), but Indian cinephiles, through the network of the film societies, by then had access to other Asian films. Accessing films, however, did not always mean watching them. Film magazines, particularly *Filmfare*, were the most accessible means to films. In the first issue of the magazine, director and critic Khwaja Ahmad Abbas voiced short but powerful praises for the Japanese film *Yukiwarisō* (Hepatica, 1951), specifying its "delicate lyricism." Abbas wrote the essay, not about Japanese cinema but his concerns regarding the local film industry. He mentions *Yukiwarisō* only as an example of a more successful (Asian) national cinematic product.

It is remarkable that Abbas refers to *Yukiwarisō*, because critics in Japan considered the film rather mediocre, and because the film was screened around India along with a more internationally successful Japanese film, *Rashōmon* (1950).[25] Apparently, Abbas was not alone in appreciating that Japanese film, which might have gained more popularity in India than in its producing country.[26] However, unlike India, where distributors publicized the film as an exemplary Japanese film, in Japan the studio that produced the film, Daiei, tried to associate it with European origins by claiming that it was based on the foreign novel *Primula Medesca*.[27]

A clear example of how the film magazine can mediate an image of Japan for potential Indian viewers is the *Filmfare* issue of May 1954, which features an article dedicated to Japanese cinema. It also includes a small box with text celebrating the fact that Japan is an Asian nation that has won two grand prizes at European film festivals.[28] The article itself was not written by a local contributor but rather translated from French. The editors acknowledged that the original article first appeared in the French weekly *Les Lettres Françaises* (The French letters) and was translated into English by a *Filmfare* reader,

FIG. 1.1 Indian star Nargis holding a Japanese fan.

M. K. Panday.[29] The magazine identifies the author of the article as Masayo-shi, a Japanese male first name, but it does not provide any more information about him or the original publication.

The article is, therefore, another indication of the multilayered process of mediation by which South Asia formed an image of Japan. At least, through this magazine, such Japanese imaginary appears sympathetic and remote while at the same time near enough to be considered along the lines of shared geo-politics or cultural identity. A more vivid example of this tendency in the mag-azine is the following large image of Nargis, arguably Indian's most popular actress at the time (and perhaps of all time), with a Japanese fan (fig. 1.1).[30]

Although the peculiar section in the magazine features examples from vari-ous countries where people use fans, including Spain, only Japan gets an entire page and is represented not just by a random actress but by a national icon. As D. A. Windsor points out, Indian critics regard Nargis, in a way, as a Western reincarnation of the Indian girl, one that complicated the East/West divide and problematizes the way India represented itself to the West as well as to the local population.[31] Despite her somewhat compromised status in India due to her Muslim origins, she nonetheless became a symbol of Indian womanhood through her role as the Hindu mother in *Mother India* (1957).[32]

The photograph projects an image of her as a Japanese woman, and it is reminiscent of the Western phenomenon known as Japonism (or *Japonisme*). The term refers to a growing interest in Japanese cultural artifacts, including fans, in Europe and North America in the nineteenth century. It also encompasses an artistic movement led by European artists, including Claude Monet, Vincent van Gogh, and Edgar Degas, who were influenced by Japanese art. Joan Jensen explains that initially "Japonism," along with "Orientalism," simply referred to interest in the East. Artists interested in the East often painted Europeans in Japanese clothes, many of whom held Japanese fans, while other Europeans and North Americans took photographs of themselves wearing a kimono or holding a fan. However, Jensen continues, after Said's publication of Orientalism, Japonism, too, became part of the discourse on postcolonial critique.[33]

Despite its disputes with Pakistan over Kashmir, India is not seen as a colonial power. It thus seems unfitting to consider Nargis's photo holding a Japanese fan in the context of Japonism. Moreover, Nargis did not take the photo to satisfy any individual fascination with a foreign country that has just been discovered as was the case in the West a half century or more earlier. Yet the image is indicative of a tendency to portray Japan in a way that allows individuals in India to see themselves on equal terms with the West by reproducing not just an image but rather a perspective from which Western artists imagined the East.

Seeing Japan as both an exotic Asian Other as well as a source of domestic or even national pride did not start with cinema. Already during Okakura's visit to India, there were Indians who harnessed their affection for Japan in order to promote Indian identity with strong affinity to non-Western, specifically Asian, underpinnings. In this regard, Aida Yuen Wong discusses how Indian artists in the early twentieth century used a technique known as *mōrōtai* (the name of a Japanese painting style) in Japanese woodblock printing (*ukiyo-e*), and highlights one of Abanindranath Tagore's paintings, which became a banner for the Swadeshi Movement, *Bharat Mata* (Mother India, 1905).[34] At the time, Japanese artists considered this technique and paintings outdated, but Indian artists aimed to make a domestic rather than international impact with their works. India's inward-facing cultural production, however, is more pronounced in its largest cultural industry: cinema.

Bollywoodian Japonism

There have been many studies on Orientalism in Western cinema in general[35] as well as specifically in Hollywood.[36] Studies that deal with similar depictions in non-Western film industries are scarce. One exception is Virchand Dharamsey's study that shows how deeply Indian cinema has been engaged with stereotypical depictions of the Middle East.[37] One film among the many that Dharamsey discusses is *Naaz* (1954), which was filmed mostly in Egypt and is probably the earliest example of the now common practice in Bollywood of filming several scenes, particularly song and dance sequences, in exotic locations (often regardless of the plot's main location). Such practices are indicative of the industry's rise in power and the expectation of expansion beyond the subcontinent. For example, in 1956, the president of the Indian Motion Picture Producers' Association, S. K. Patil, announced intentions to expand the Hindi film distribution network to other countries, including, in particular, the East Asian nations of China and Japan.[38]

Distributors did export Indian films outside the subcontinent, but perhaps due to the Sino-Indian War of 1962, Bollywood productions were more successful in the former Soviet Union and the Middle East than in China.[39] In Japan, access to Indian films was largely limited to independent art films, mainly those directed by Satyajit Ray. As studios in India became wealthier in the 1950s, they started filming in more exotic locations, first domestically, in areas such as Kashmir and hard-to-reach scenic areas in northern India, but gradually also outside of India. In the beginning, this was mainly a practice reserved for song and dance sequences and not for the entire production. In contrast to *Naaz*, exotic sites in Indian film are usually in Europe, showcasing lavish green sceneries or snowy mountaintops. Critics widely consider *Sangam* (Confluence, 1964), which was filmed in several countries, including Italy, France, the United Kingdom, and Switzerland, as the film that started this trend.[40]

The 1965 Bollywood production *Love in Tokyo* was unique in that most of it was filmed in Japan, not just several isolated scenes. However, the film fell short of being a transnational phenomenon. In fact, like other films that were filmed in foreign locations, such as *An Evening in Paris*, *Around the World*, and *Night in London* (all three released in 1967), *Love in Tokyo* was more nationalistic than transnational. The film is set at the background of the 1964 Tokyo Olympics, and its narrative revolves around a trip to Japan by a wealthy Indian businessman (played by Joy Mukherjee) on a mission to bring back home to India a boy born to a Japanese mother and an Indian father who have both just passed away. The boy refuses to leave his current home country, Japan, so the man needs to convince him why India is wonderful, even better than Japan, for everyone, but particularly for the boy—and of course, for the Indian viewer.

FIG. 1.2 Indian actress Asha Parekh wearing a kimono and holding a fan in the Indian film *Love in Tokyo* (1965).

Unlike Indian productions that were filmed in Europe, *Love in Tokyo* treats its setting as a peculiar site. First, like other non-Japanese films set in Japan, such as *The Barbarian and the Geisha* (1958), the film ushers in the most stereotypical image of the Japanese people, and mostly Japanese women. This is not to place judgment on this aspect of the film, but rather to acknowledge that it catered to a specific audience, one that had little concern for accuracy, such as the name of the boy's Japanese mother, who is referred to as Nishiyoshi, which is not a Japanese female's name. Second, *Love in Tokyo* offers only minimal meaningful interaction between Indian and local characters, although at least the main Indian female protagonist is said to be fluent in Japanese. The following screenshot from the film brings to mind the aforementioned photograph of Nargis holding a Japanese fan, only now the Indian actress (Asha Parekh) wears full Japanese female garb, which further links the modern Indian image-making of Japan with Japonism (fig. 1.2).

Most of the dialogue in the film takes place indoors, while on-location scenes are in effect just "flourishes"—the term David Bordwell used to describe certain sequences in prewar Japanese cinema.[41] By flourishes, Bordwell points to stylistic elements that are not necessary for the plot but augment it playfully, satisfying a unique mode of appreciation for cinema in prewar Japan. In the same vein, Japan and the Japanese people appearing in *Love in Tokyo* are just an added spice in the masala of the melodramatic extravaganza that became the first in a trilogy of "love-in" films, although none of the sequels even mentions Japan.

In addition to the film's narrative, visually, the film projects images of Japan that are reminiscent of Japanism. The film does celebrate Japan's modernity, showcasing its fashionable department stores, bustling streets, entertainment facilities, and fast-paced urban landscapes. However, to a larger extent, the film shows premodern images of the country, such as Japanese gardens, premodern architecture, and geisha. In one scene, although the characters are supposed to be in Tokyo, they appear at the famous Itsukushima Shrine, which is located far from Tokyo, on an island off the shores of Hiroshima. The film does not mention the atomic bombing of the city, and it flattens the country by presenting Tokyo as a synonym for the entire Japanese archipelago.

The Indian film industry returned to Hiroshima two years later with another production that was set mainly in Japan. The narrative of *Aman* (peace) revolves around an Indian scientist determined to find a cure for radiation victims, who falls in love with a survivor of the Hiroshima bombing. The film's promoters advertised it as "a love story of this atomic age,"[42] but the film's romantic aspects fall short of tying an Indian man with a "Japanese wife." The protagonist (played by Rajendra Kumar) dies after successfully finding a cure for radiation, leaving behind his Japanese love interest. The woman is played by an Indian actress (Saira Banu) who, the film explains, had studied Hindi. Unlike *Love in Tokyo*, Japan and Japanese women in *Aman* appear modern. The film also features a bold and honest (for a Bollywood production, at least) reference to Hiroshima's recent history. Yet, while the film's ominous background is not typical of a popular production, its overall treatment of Japan remains superficial. The film tours Japan for its designated Indian viewers, and while it mostly presents the country as a technologically advanced nation with fast trains, high rises, and flashy nightlife, it highlights a more stereotypical image of premodern Japan with temples, pagodas, and the female protagonist wearing a kimono. Bollywood productions that center on Japan are scarce amid the sum of films the industry releases. Whereas the production of *Youngistaan* (The land of the young, 2014) partially took place in Japan, the 2006 film, *Love in Japan*, was perhaps the last Hindi language production to explore a theme of love between Indian and Japanese people.

From Bollywood to Kollywood

Although some consider Bollywood as synonymous with the Indian film industry, it is, in fact, only one of several regional industries in the subcontinent. For example, the Tamil language film industry in South India is known as Kollywood. While not as international as Bollywood, the South Indian film Industry, too, has made productions that were at least partially filmed in Japan. Starting with the 1985 film *Japanil Kalyanaraman* (Kalyanaraman in Japan), Kollywood increased its output of such productions, including *Theeya Veelai*

FIG. 1.3 Japanese comedian Nanbara at the end of the documentary on *Nattu*.

Seyyanum Kumaru (also released as *You Have Got to Work Like Fire, Kumar!*, 2013) and others.[43] These films demonstrate a wider, national cinematic imagery that is not limited to the Mumbai film industry. The Japanese film industry has displayed only limited affection toward Indian subjects. One exception is Kinoshita Keisuke's 1976 *Love and Separation in Sri Lanka*, which depicts a Japanese woman (played by Takamine Hideko) who is said to have been married to an Indian man who was murdered before the film's events begin.

Japanese media started paying more attention to Indian media following the surprising popularity in the country of the Kollywood production, *Muthu*. As I argue elsewhere, this new interest was not limited to cinema, and it was galvanized by other media, mainly television as well as the internet.[44] One of the highlights in the trend of popular Indian films in Japan was the Japanese production of the 1999 Tamil language short film, *Ucchan Nanchan no Nattu!!* (Up and down, Nattu!), starring TV celebrity Kiyotaka Nanbara. The Nippon Television Network Corporation, which produced the film, also produced a "making-of" documentary, directed by Katō in the same year. After filming the last scene, the documentary shows the film's Japanese star, Nanbara, lifted in the air by two local crew members as he repeatedly declares in English: "I love India!" (fig. 1.3).

The Japanese subtitles imposed on the image not only echo in text Nanbara's words in English but also use a verb that is usually reserved for the utmost expression of affection between partners. Japanese fans of Indian films nowadays have direct access to subtitled Indian films through online websites such as *Ashū kyōdai* (Asian brothers).[45] Fans also discuss forthcoming public screenings of Indian films on social media, and many run blogs dedicated to either their favorite Indian film star or Indian culture at large. On websites such as YouTube, Japanese people share their affection for South Asian culture, posting videos of their trips to the region, such as the one titled *We Love Bangladesh*.[46]

There is no reason to doubt the honesty of such expressions even if those making them are at times supported by commercial or governmental interest groups. However, such online activity ultimately reveals only communication between Japanese people rather than trans-Asian interfusion. In most Japanese accounts, South Asia, whether Sri Lanka, Bangladesh, or the different regions around the Indian subcontinent, is often flattened as one India, and despite their expression of fondness, they nonetheless stress their cultural remoteness. One media event that exposes these undercurrents in Japan is the case of Priyanka Yoshikawa, a product of love between a "Japanese wife" and an Indian man. After becoming Miss World Japan in 2016, numerous bloggers uploaded angry posts refuting her competency in representing Japanese beauty. Even those who supported her raised the question about the need to have a "pure" Japanese (*junsui Nihon jin*) representative for such roles,[47] a question seldom asked when the subject is of Japanese and Western origins.

Conclusion

Writing about possible affinities between India and Japan, film scholar Yomota Inuhiko suggests that blindness might be considered differently in these two countries than in the West. While in the West blindness is often regarded as an extreme form of punishment or tragedy, the epic *Mahābhārata* depicts the case of a woman who chooses to intentionally impair her vision. Similar cases can also be found in Japanese culture, particularly in cinema. Yomota calls this the "voluntary blindness" motif.[48]

Yomota does not mention Japanese or Indian films that depict people who did not choose their disability, such as *Na mo naku mazushiku utsukushii* (Happiness of us alone, 1961), which is arguably the first Japanese film that Bollywood producers remade, *Koshish* (Effort, 1972). However, I would still like to use Yomota's concept to describe the relationship between South and East Asia. Rather than as a narrative principle, the concept can better describe the Indian and Japanese propensity for choosing to see certain aspects while intentionally ignoring others in each other's cultures.

My last example is from a medium that is central to Japan's image in the world: animation. The first direct Indian-Japanese co-production was an

FIG. 1.4 Animated character Karēpanman representing a (stereo)typical Indian in an animated show.

animated adaptation of the South Asian epic, *Ramayana: The Legend of Prince Rama* (1992). The producers released two versions, one for each country. While the legendary depiction of South Asian heroes in both versions is typical and overwhelmingly favorable, other Japanese animated depictions for local consumption are also typical, if not too stereotypical. In a short segment of a video taking place in the Anpanman franchise, these characters represent India (*Anpanman to hajimeyō: Manekko dansu* [Let's begin with Anpanman: Copying dance], directed by Ōga in 2009).

In this section of the video, frequently appearing characters represent several countries, teaching children how to say hello and goodbye in foreign languages. The main characters in this franchise are superheroes associated with different types of bread. Unsurprisingly, representing India on the left side of the image above (fig. 1.4) is Karēpanman, who is a curry-bread hero.[49] The association between India and South Asian food in Japan is a common occurrence; for many years, the most visible South Asians living in Japan were restaurant workers. However, in recent years, most Indians in Japan are probably software engineers, and at any rate, not yoga instructors.[50]

The image of Karēpanman and his female partner representing India, like so many anime characters, is cute. Moreover, it is common for a show catering to children to represent tropes most associated with a foreign culture, rather than presenting real people. However, other characters representing foreign cultures in this segment are stripped from their usual association with bread, replacing it with a new cultural marker not related to food. This is true with regard to France, Hawaii, Russia, and even East Africa. India is seen differently, I argue, not because of a lack of knowledge about it but because Japanese producers turn a blind eye to the notion of a real multilayered South Indian identity.

This is similar in the case of India as it intentionally fails to see Japan in its modern-day complexity. I do not argue that India and Japan must represent one another on equal terms. Nor do I wish to level a critique against media representations of Asian Otherness in these countries. Rather, I see in the production of an Indian and Japanese Other in these two countries an assumption of Westernization, and the role of the media in pushing forward such images, an introversive gaze that both acknowledges its peripherality as well as reinforces its place on the global stage.

Notes

1 Film titles in this chapter appear according to their official U.S. release, when available and in which cases translations are not given. Otherwise, the original title is given with translation.

2 Kunal Basu revealed this in an interview with Reenita Malhotra Hora at the Asia Society in Hong Kong on October 7, 2012.

3 For example, see Shuhei Hosokawa, "Soy Sauce Music: Haruomi Hosono and Japanese Self-Orientalism," in *Widening the Horizon: Exoticism in Post-War Popular Music*, ed. P. Haywood (Sydney: Lohn Libbey and Company, 1999), 114–144. See also Rebecca Suter, "Orientalism, Self-Orientalism, and Occidentalism in the Visual-Verbal Medium of Japanese Girls' Comics," *Literature and Aesthetics* 22, no. 2 (2012): 230–247.

4 Gita Keeni, "Perception of Japan in India—Past and Present: A View from Santiniketan," in *Changing Perceptions of Japan in South Asia in the New Asian Era: The State of Japanese Studies in India and Other SAARC Countries*, ed. Uno Takao (Kyoto: International Research Center for Japanese Studies, 2011), 292–293.

5 By "mediation" here and throughout the chapter, I refer to the means by which a process of identification with and differentiation from media-based representations are made possible, as well to the phenomenological construction of mental images. While it is difficult to conceive of such a process that does not involve at least some degree of cultural abstraction, I still like to posit, somewhat unphilosophically, and unlike thinkers such as Hegel, Heidegger, or even Derrida, that signification of self-identity and otherness diverge from an individuated abstraction and converge when streamlined communally, as a shared process of mediation or interposition. Thus an unmediated recognition of a cultural Other in its own terms would be one that is based on interpersonal experience, rather than one compromised by a communal intermediary agency.

6 Swami Vivekananda, *Letters of Swami Vivekananda* (Kolkata: Vedanta Press, 1960), 62.

7 Fabio Rambelli, "The Idea of India (Tenjiku) in Pre-modern Japan: Issues of Signification and Representation in the Buddhist Translation of Cultures," in *Buddhism across Asia: Networks of Material, Intellectual and Cultural Exchange*, ed. Tansen Sen (Singapore: Institute of Southeast Asian Studies / Manohar Publishers & Distributors, 2014), 269.

8 Inga Shigemi, "Okakura Tenshin to Indo: Ekyō suru kindai koklumin ishiki to han Ajia—idiologī no kisū," *Nihongo Nichibungaku* 24 (2004): 19–20.

9 Kakuzo Okakura, *The Ideals of the East* (San Diego: Stone Bridge Press, 2007), 10. First Published in 1904.

10 Ibid., 12.

11 Rustom Bharucha, *Another Asia* (New York: Oxford University Press, 2006), 74.

12 Gayatri Chakravorty Spivak, *Other Asias* (Malden, MA: Blackwell, 2008), 209.

13 Salman Rushdie, *Imaginary Homelands: Essays and Criticism 1981–1991* (London: Granta Books, 1991), 10.

14 Matsuoka Tamaki, "Nihon ni okuru Indo eiga no kiseki," *Minami Ajia gengo bunka* 4 (2006): 86–87.

15 Ibid., 88.

16 Initial broadcasts began in February 1952.

17 Takahashi Shinkichi, "Indo eiga to shinemasukōpu," *Gunzō* 3 (1954): 177–179.

18 Richard King, *Orientalism and Religion: Post-Colonial Theory, India and "The Mystic East"* (London: Routledge, 1999), 86.

19 Saad Ullah Khan, "A Critical Analysis of Mehboob Khan's Films: Thematic and Technical Treatment," *Pragyaan: Journal of Mass Communication* 8, no. 2 (2010): 36.

20 Takahashi was famous for his work on or his influence by Zen Buddhism.

21 Dimitris Eleftheriotis, "'A Cultural Colony of India': Indian Films in Greece in the 1950s and 1960s," *South Asian Popular Culture* 4 (2006): 103.

22 Ahmet Gurata, "'The Road to Vagrancy': Translation and Reception of Indian Cinema in Turkey," *BioScope: South Asian Screen Studies* 1, no. 1 (2002): 68–69.

23 Known today as the Ministry of Education, Science and Culture.

24 Shampa Banerjee and Anil Srivastava, *One Hundred Indian Feature Films: An Annotated Filmography* (New York: Routledge, 1988), 4.

25 Satō Tadao, *Nihon Eiga shi 2* (Tokyo: Iwanami Shōten, 2006), 239.

26 For example, Christopher Howard notes that the film "had triumphed in India." Christopher Howard, "Beyond Jidai-geki: Daiei Studios and the Study of Transnational Japanese Cinema," *Journal of Japanese and Korean Cinema* 3, no.1 (2014): 9.

27 Information about the novel and its author is obscured. The film credits the author only in the phonetic script kana as Jiāni Furā.

28 Masayoshi, "The Japanese Cinema," *Filmfare* 28 (May 1954): 23.

29 Ibid., 22.

30 *Filmfare* 30 (August 1957): 32. Note that *Filmfare* is a popular Indian film magazine. Whereas some articles in the magazine appear with names of the authors, many others, including those quoted in this chapter, appear without names. This was a common practice when it came to writing in the area of popular culture in the 1950s South Asia.

31 D. A. Windsor, "Nargis, Ray, Rushdie and the Real," *South Asia: Journal of South Asian Studies* 21, no. 1 (1998): 229–230.

32 On the problematic making of her stardom status and the film's iconic image, see Rosie Thomas, "Sanctity and Scandal. The Mythologization of Mother India," *Quarterly Review of Film and Video* 35, no. 3 (2009): 11–30.

33 Joan M. Jensen, "Women on the Pacific Rim: Some Thoughts on Border Cross-ings," *Pacific Historical Review* 76, no. 1 (1998): 9–10.
34 Aida Yuen Wong, "Landscapes of Nandalal Bose (1882–1966): Japanism, Nation-alism and Populism in Modern India," in *Shadows of the Past: Of Okakura Tenshin and Pan-Asianism*, ed. Brij Tankha (Folkestone, UK: Global Oriental, 2009), 95–96.
35 There are many examples for this, but one significant monograph in this regard is Matthew Bernstein and Gaylyn Studlar, *Visions of the East: Orientalism in Film* (New Brunswick, NJ: Rutgers University Press, 1997).
36 For instance, see Brian T. Edwards, "Yankee Pashas and Buried Women: Contain-ing Abundance in 1950s Hollywood Orientalism," *Film & History: An Interdisci-plinary Journal of Film and Television Studies* 31 (2001): 13–24.
37 Virchand Dharamsey, "The Advent of Sound in Indian Cinema: Theatre, Orientalism, Action, Magic," *Journal of the Moving Image* (2010): 22–59.
38 *Filmfare*, 16 (March 1956): 7.
39 Ashish Rajadhyaksha, "The 'Bollywoodisation' of the Indian Cinema: Cultural Nationalism in a Global Arena," *Inter-Asia Cultural Studies* 4, no. 1 (2003): 98.
40 On the film and the "international look" these films created, see Shakuntala Rao, "'I Need an Indian Touch': Glocalization and Bollywood Films," *Journal of International and Intercultural Communication* 3, no. 1 (2010): 1–19.
41 David Bordwell, *Poetics of Cinema* (New York: Routledge, 2008), 375–394.
42 Raminder Kaur, *Atomic Mumbai: Living with the Radiance of a Thousand Suns* (New Delhi: Routledge, 2015), 105.
43 See "Japan Turning into Kollywood's Favourite Location," *The Times of India*, January 15, 2017, https://timesofindia.indiatimes.com/entertainment/tamil/movies/news/Japan-turning-into-Kollywoods-favourite-location/articleshow/22397198.cms.
44 Rea Amit, "Shall We Dance, Rajni? The Japanese Cult of Kollywood," *Participa-tions: International Journal of Audience Research* 14, no. 2 (2017): 636–959.
45 http://asiabros.jp/movie/ind/zztop_mov_ind.html.
46 https://www.youtube.com/watch?v=ws8zp1kXNEw.
47 For example, see https://blog.goo.ne.jp/koube-69/e/485265221cefb372529ad68160140d62.
48 Yomota Inuhiko, "Voluntary Blindness," in *Shadows of the Past: Of Okakura Tenshin and Pan-Asianism*, ed. Brij Tankha (Folkestone, UK: Global Oriental, 2009), 111–118.
49 It is interesting to note that the Indian dish may have become popular in Japan, thanks to an anticolonial Indian man, Rash Behari Bose, and his "Japanese wife." See Takeshi Nakajima, *Bose of Nakamuraya: An Indian Revolutionary in Japan* (New Delhi: Promilla, 2009).
50 On the rise in number of IT Indian workers in Japan, see Bernat Agullo and Midori Egawa, "International Careers of Indian Workers in Tokyo: Examination and Future Directions," *Career Development International* 14, no. 2 (2009), 148–168.

Bibliography

Agullo, Bernat, and Midori Egawa. "International Careers of Indian Workers in Tokyo: Examination and Future Directions." *Career Development International* 14, no. 2 (2009): 148–168.

Amit, Rea. "Shall We Dance, Rajni? The Japanese Cult of Kollywood." *Participations: International Journal of Audience Research* 14, no. 2 (2017): 636–659.

Banerjee, Shampa, and Anil Srivastava. *One Hundred Indian Feature Films: An Annotated Filmography.* New York: Routledge, 1988.

Bernstein, Matthew, and Gaylyn Studlar. *Visions of the East: Orientalism in Film.* New Brunswick, NJ: Rutgers University Press, 1997.

Bharucha, Rustom. *Another Asia.* New York: Oxford University Press, 2006.

Bordwell, David. *Poetics of Cinema.* New York: Routledge, 2008.

Dharamsey, Virchand. "The Advent of Sound in Indian Cinema: Theatre, Orientalism, Action, Magic." *Journal of the Moving Image* 9 (2010): 22–50.

Edwards, T. Brian. "Yankee Pashas and Buried Women: Containing Abundance in 1950s Hollywood Orientalism." *Film & History: An Interdisciplinary Journal of Film and Television Studies* 31, no. 2 (2001): 13–24.

Eleftheriotis, Dimitris. "'A Cultural Colony of India': Indian Films in Greece in the 1950s and 1960s." *South Asian Popular Culture* 4, no. 2 (2006): 101–112.

Gurata, Ahmet. "'The Road to Vagrancy': Translation and Reception of Indian Cinema in Turkey." *BioScope: South Asian Screen Studies* 1, no.1 (2002): 67–90.

Hosokawa, Shuhei. "Soy Sauce Music: Haruomi Hosono and Japanese Self-Orientalism." In *Widening the Horizon: Exoticism in Post-War Popular Music,* edited by Philip Hayward, 114–144. Bloomington: Indiana University Press, 1999.

Howard, Christopher. "Beyond Jidai-geki: Daiei Studios and the Study of Transnational Japanese Cinema." *Journal of Japanese and Korean Cinema* 3, no.1 (2014): 5–12.

Inaga, Shigemi. "Okakura Tenshin to Indo: Ekyō suru kindai koklumin ishiki to han Ajia—idiologī no kisū." *Nihongo Nichibungaku,* no. 24 (2004): 13–30.

Jensen, M. Joan. "Women on the Pacific Rim: Some Thoughts on Border Crossings." *Pacific Historical Review* 76, no. 1 (1998): 3–38.

Kaur, Raminder. *Atomic Mumbai: Living with the Radiance of a Thousand Suns.* New Delhi: Routledge, 2015.

Keeni, Gita. "Perception of Japan in India—Past and Present: A View from Santiniketan." In *Changing Perceptions of Japan in South Asia in the New Asian Era: The State of Japanese Studies in India and Other SAARC Countries,* edited by Takao Uno, 287–299. Kyoto: International Research Center for Japanese Studies, 2011.

Khan, Saad Ullah. "A Critical Analysis of Mehboob Khan's Films: Thematic and Technical Treatment." *Pragyaan: Journal of Mass Communication* 8, no. 2 (2010): 27–39.

King, Richard. *Orientalism and Religion: Post-colonial Theory, India and "The Mystic East."* London: Routledge, 1999.

Matsuoka, Tamaki. "Nihon ni okuru Indo eiga no kiseki." *Minami Ajia gengo bunka* 4 (2006): 85–117.

Nakajima, Takeshi. *Bose of Nakamuraya: An Indian Revolutionary in Japan.* New Delhi: Promilla, 2009.

Okakura, Kakuzo. *The Ideals of the East.* San Diego: Stone Bridge Press, 2007.

Rajadhyaksha, Ashish. "The 'Bollywoodisation' of the Indian Cinema: Cultural Nationalism in a Global Arena." *Inter-Asia Cultural Studies* 4, no.1 (2003): 25–39.

Rambelli, Fabio. "The Idea of India (Tenjiku) in Pre-Modern Japan: Issues of Signification and Representation in the Buddhist Translation of Cultures." In *Buddhism across Asia: Networks of Material, Intellectual and Cultural Exchange,* edited by Tansen Sen, 259–290. Singapore: Institute of Southeast Asian Studies/ Manohar Publishers & Distributors, 2014.

Rao, Shakuntala. "'I Need an Indian Touch': Glocalization and Bollywood Films." *Journal of International and Intercultural Communication* 3, no.1 (2010): 1–19.

Rushdie, Salman. *Imaginary Homelands: Essays and Criticism 1981–1991*. London: Granta Books, 1991.

Spivak, Gayatri Chakravorty. *Other Asias*. Malden, MA: Blackwell, 2008.

Suter, Rebecca. "Orientalism, Self-Orientalism, and Occidentalism in the Visual-Verbal Medium of Japanese Girls' Comics." *Literature & Aesthetics* 22, no. 2 (2012): 230–247.

Tadao, Satō. *Nihon Eiga shi 2*. Tokyo: Iwanami Shōten, 2006.

Takahashi, Shinkichi. "Indo eiga to shinemasukōpu." *Gunzō* 3 (1954): 177–179.

Thomas, Rosie. "Sanctity and Scandal. The Mythologization of Mother India." *Quarterly Review of Film and Video* 35, no. 3 (2009): 11–30.

Vivekananda, Swami. *Letters of Swami Vivekananda*. Kolkata: Vedanta Press, 1960.

Windsor, D. A. "Nargis, Ray, Rushdie and the Real." *South Asia: Journal of South Asian Studies* 21, no.1 (1998): 229–242.

Wong, Aida Yuen. "Landscapes of Nandalal Bose (1882–1966): Japanism, Nationalism and Populism in Modern India." In *Shadows of the Past: Of Okakura Tenshin and Pan-Asianism*, edited by Brij Tankha, 93–110. Folkestone, UK: Global Oriental, 2009.

Yomota, Inuhiko. "Voluntary Blindness." In *Shadows of the Past: Of Okakura Tenshin and Pan-Asianism*, edited by Brij Tankha, 111–118. Folkestone, UK: Global Oriental, 2009.

2

The Child Bride

■■■■■■■■■■■■■■■■■■■■■■■■■■■

Unpacking the Popularity of
the Indian Television Show
Balika Vadhu in Vietnam

SHUBHDA ARORA AND

JUHI JOTWANI

Balika Vadhu (Child bride), a popular soap opera, was broadcast on Colours TV in India for eight years, from 2008 to 2016. The plot follows struggles of a child bride Anandi from childhood to adulthood. Her problems are very gendered and structural, informed by the institutional violence of child marriage and the systemic discrimination of women in a patriarchal society. This Indian soap opera has been dubbed into Vietnamese for the local population in Vietnam and has drawn much attention from and popularity among viewers. The drama was first aired in Vietnam in 2014. By 2015, it was the ninth most searched item on Google in Vietnam.[1] The show's audiences discuss and follow updates on social media, such as Zing Me,[2] Badoo,[3] and Facebook, and watch missed episodes on mobile phones. The brand of *Balika Vadhu* has been extended to other merchandise, including, for instance, chips and snacks, which have also gained popularity in Vietnam due to the show's extensive viewership. The death of Pratyusha Banerjee in 2016, who played the lead role of Anandi, was greatly mourned in Vietnam. There was a public outpouring of grief in Hanoi, Ho Chi Minh City, Hoi An, Danang, and other cities across the country.[4]

Although *Balika Vadhu* has also been broadcast in eastern Europe and parts of Southeast Asia, the show has been particularly successful in Vietnam. This is probably the result of several factors, including the low domestic television production rate in Vietnam. As a consequence of this, Vietnam has seen an influx of cultural commodities sourced from India, China, the Philippines, Thailand, and South Korea. More importantly, however, the shared cultural codes between Vietnam and India, which help Vietnamese audiences relate to the show, significantly contribute to the positive reception of the show in Vietnam.

For example, two important cultural similarities and common motifs that stand out between the two nations are the influence of society and family on the institution of (child) marriage and the viewing culture of watching together, where family members gather to watch television and share their viewing experience communally. Vietnamese audiences are familiar with the concept of child marriage. The UNICEF (United Nations International Children's Emergency Fund) State of the World's Children report (2016) indicates that 11 percent of the nation's female minors are married before the age of eighteen, while the rate is as high as 33 percent among the ethnic minority community, Mong.[5] In addition to this, child brides are trafficked from Vietnam to China and forced into marrying Chinese men who tend to be much older. Apart from the prevalence of child marriage, ideas of family honor and respect for elders are considered important in both India and Vietnam. The necessity of parental consent for choosing a marital partner is another cultural code that both the Indian and Vietnamese audiences understand and embrace readily.

This chapter hence argues that the extraordinary success of *Balika Vadhu* in Vietnam is attributable to the themes explored in the show that resonate well with the material and social reality of people in some parts of Vietnam. Additionally, this chapter pays particular attention to the television viewing culture in Vietnam that turns television viewing into a communal, familial activity. The culture of watching together, which is not uncommon in many other parts of Asia, assumes special significance in the sociopolitical context of postwar communist Vietnam. In Vietnam, particularly around urban centers, the family structure is changing from the joint, patrilocal, and extended system to the nuclear structure. In spite of this ongoing change, *Balika Vadhu* still manages to maintain and reinforce the traditional viewing culture of watching together for reasons discussed later in the chapter. Overall, I discuss cultural, thematic, and transcultural elements of the show *Balika Vadhu* through, among other things, cultural reception theories and global cultural economy[6] to allow for an understanding of its popular audience response in Vietnam.

It has been almost three decades since Arjun Appadurai popularized the idea of "global flows" of cultural economy. These flows, according to Appadurai, are "ephemeral, disjunctive and chaotic." Whereas geography is considered static, the flow of people, ideas, technology, and money is always fluid. The "mediascape," according to him, is part of these global flows—media help the flow of ideologies through the electronic capabilities of the production and dissemination of information.[7] According to Appadurai, the mediascape and the ideoscape are closely interconnected, and travel, trade, and media are the three major ways in which different cultures and ideologies spread and fuse with one another.[8] However, there are global inequalities in the flow of cultural commodities through media, which are highly hegemonic to begin with.[9] So the question regarding which cultural commodity is consumed by what audience in which static geography requires an understanding of audiences as "markets" and an inquiry into audiences as active "meaning makers" in the process of reception.[10] Hence three relevant questions emerge: Why did Vietnam become a potential market for this particular Hindi language soap? Why does the show *Balika Vadhu*, which talks about the trials and tribulations of a child bride from rural Rajasthan, find heavy viewership in urban cities like Hanoi and Ho Chi Minh?[11] How are the Vietnamese audiences making sense of this particular show? The show had high TRPs (television rating points) in India, but its popularity in Vietnam has not been explained.

Researchers have been trying to understand similar questions about why certain mass cultural commodities, which make the most sense within a particular cultural context, find a way to be received positively in foreign contexts. For example, the rise of K pop (Korean pop) in some of the Northeastern states of India,[12] the popular reception of Bollywood films like *Dangal* (name of the traditional wresting of India, 2018) and *3 Idiots* (2009) in China,[13] the extreme popularity of the actor Rajnikanth from the Tamil film industry in Japan,[14] and many other such cases are difficult to explain conclusively. In many such instances, there are cultural flows through mediascapes from fixed geography A to B, but not in the opposite direction from B to A. While economic and global market forces play an important role in regulating these flows, the positive reception of *Balika Vadhu* in Vietnam would require an understanding of the following questions: Are audiences in Vietnam enjoying the show because they relate to the characters and story arc as well as the major themes and plot points of the show? Is it due to their curiosity toward the cultural other? Is it just an attempt at engaging with something other than domestically produced content? While I am unable to answer all these questions within the scope of this chapter, I will focus on understanding the popular reception of the show in Vietnam by making connections with the political, social, and media histories of Vietnam and considering how these histories have perhaps made

Vietnam a fertile market for a show like *Balika Vadhu*. The following section looks at the history of television production in Vietnam and a few significant foreign shows that were imported for the consumption of Vietnamese audiences.

Television Soaps in Vietnam

Although 99 percent of Vietnam's households own a television set,[15] the domestic television production industry hasn't been able to compete with foreign cultural products in terms of production quality, content (themes), and demand (number of shows).[16] According to a Nielsen report in 2015[17] television is still the dominant media platform for Vietnamese viewers. The first television broadcast occurred in 1966, when the United States set up two channels in Saigon. Later in 1970, Vietnam Television (VTV, a government-run channel) was established with the assistance of Cuba, which intermittently broadcast the Vietnam War.[18]

After the end of the Vietnam War in 1975, North and South Vietnam were unified into a communist state, which continues to this day. The Cold War era greatly impacted the kinds of cinema and domestic cultural production in Vietnam. The Vietnamese language cinema was mostly controlled by the government's Ministry of Information and Propaganda, which encouraged production of propagandist films on the war. The shift to a market economy in 1986 caused a serious blow to domestic production in Vietnam. During that time, many American, Mexican, and Brazilian shows became some of the first entrants. From 2010 onward, Vietnam has grown into a good market for foreign cultural commodities, whereas its own film and television industries are not growing fast enough to keep up with the demand. India and Vietnam in particular enjoy good bilateral ties in the economic and cultural spheres, with educational scholarships and religious tourism (mostly Buddhist) from both countries. India's Look East policy, for instance, has fostered economic relations with Vietnam, mostly in oil exploration, agriculture, and manufacturing.[19] In the cultural sphere, Bollywood has been entering Vietnam not only as a visual cultural product but also in the form of collaboration between two cinematic industries.[20]

Apart from Indian shows, many other television serials from other Asian countries, such as South Korea, China, Thailand, and Philippines, as well as some other more remote nations, such as Peru and Mexico, have found an audience in Vietnam. These shows form part of a larger cultural influence. In the 1990s, when communist Vietnam first opened up its entertainment sector, many telenovelas, such as *Simplemente Maria* (Simply Maria, 1992) from Peru and *The Rich Also Cry* (1979) from Mexico, became popular among the Vietnamese. These shows were very different from what Vietnamese were used to watching. Vietnamese audiences in the pre-reform era (between 1970, when

VTV was first launched, and the economic reforms of 1986) were mostly limited to watching propagandist shows with socialist and revolutionary themes. Black-and-white Vietnamese films made during and after the second Indo-China War were repeatedly played on the television. These shows and films talked about heroism, sacrifice, revolution, and war. There was no entertainment in these shows, as entertainment was completely banned from the public discourse.[21] Indeed, "too much romance or amusement was considered the harmful legacy of the bourgeois culture that only led to an erosion of youth's revolutionary and military spirit."[22]

Given this context, when audiences in Vietnam were first introduced to these dramas, they found them as an enjoyable alternative to the scarcity and ideological boredom of the previous cultural products in Vietnam. The cultural deprivation under political oppression had created a void for stories of everyday life and struggle. The larger-than-life revolutionary heroism had been a narrative with which most Vietnamese had been saturated. Shows featuring ordinary concerns of normal living and daily stories of struggle and happiness connected well with Vietnamese audiences.

Simplemente Maria was one such show that gained extreme popularity in Vietnam in 1992. Arvind Singhal, Rafael Obregon, and Everett M. Rogers unpack the story of the show in their paper to understand the popularity of this Peruvian show in Latin America in 1969.[23] This is a show about a country girl who moves to the city to make a life for herself. The show talks about premarital pregnancy, love affairs, and stealing husbands, among other things. In the beginning of the telenovela, Maria works as a maid for a rich family to make a living, but by the end of the telenovela she moves to Paris, where she owns a highly successful clothing boutique. Singhal and others note that "the easy mobility from rural to urban, from poor to rich, made the show very appealing."[24] They further discuss the "edutainment" potential of telenovelas in general. They argue that telenovelas such as *Simplemente Maria* became popular in Latin American countries in the late 1960s because their messages about social changes (promoting adult education, family planning, and women's equality, among others) are packaged in an entertaining format, which had not been common earlier.

Simplemente Maria and *The Rich Also Cry* started a tradition of drama-fueled telenovelas in Vietnam with themes that especially resonated with audiences in terms of some social struggles of Vietnamese society. These shows mostly feature a woman protagonist from a rural/small town who undergoes a journey of hardships and meets antagonistic characters but ultimately emerges successful by challenging the status quo in society. Other popular Filipino shows, such as *Vietnam Rose* (2006), look at the journey of a woman whose family was divided by the Vietnam War. While this show is about the war, it is fundamentally different from the communist-era propagandist films. The narrative looks at the everydayness of a family torn by war rather than patriotic heroism and revolutionary fervor.

South Korean shows have also had a cultural influence on Vietnamese people. Daniele Bélanger from the University of Western Ontario posits that South Korean shows have influenced many Vietnamese women's decision to marry South Korean men.[25] Stephen Epstein,[26] on the other hand, notes that a disproportionate number of Korean dramas with a thematic focus on international marriages have singled out relationships between Korean men and Vietnamese women. These dramas include *Hanoi Shinbu* (The bride from Hanoi; Seoul Broadcasting System, 2005), *Hwanggeumui Sinbu* (Golden bride; SBS, 2007), *Kkocheul Chajeureo Wattdanda* (Flowers for my life; Korean Broadcasting System, 2007), *Sannomeo Namchoneneun* (In the southern village over the mountains; KBS, 2007), and *Barami Bunda* (The wind blows; KBS, 2008).

Therefore, Vietnamese audiences have seen an influx of foreign productions after the reforms and have a history of viewing television soaps or telenovelas with female leads who undertake a difficult journey to emerge successful, stronger, and independent at the end of it. The next section of this chapter explores Indian television soaps and their dominant narratives to make a case for their popularity in Vietnam.

Indian *Saas-Bahu* Soaps

Indian soap operas or Indian serials are soap operas written, produced, and filmed in India, with characters played by Indians and episodes broadcast on Indian television. India's first soap opera was *Hum Log* (We the people), which concluded with 156 episodes.[27] *Hum Log* was heavily inspired by the Mexican telenovela *Simplemente Maria*, the same show that was extremely popular in Vietnam after the reform. The influence of *Simplemente Maria* in Vietnam and India is a crucial point to note. *Hum Log* became one of the most popular and influential pro-social, development soaps after India's independence in 1947. Most Indian soaps use *Hum Log* as a template to create successful television soaps.[28] Over the years, the pro-social element from shows has gradually decreased, while the drama element has increased. An Indian spin on the telenovelas are the *saas-bahu* (mother-in-law, daughter-in-law) soaps. Indian dramas such as *Kahani Ghar Ki* (Story of every household) and *Kyunki Saas Bhi Kabhi Bahu Thi* (Because a mother-in-law was once a daughter-in-law) have been extremely popular and narrate family sagas about strong women (who often don't have careers) and their relationships with their mother-in-law.[29] These saas-bahu soaps are specific to the Indian context but follow formats similar to telenovelas. Telenovelas have a centrality in everyday life in much of Latin America. A typical narrative in these shows incorporates social commentary on current events that directly impact people's lives. Another specific characteristic of telenovelas is the format. Telenovelas last for an average of nine months and are directed toward a happy ending that is immediately followed by the beginning of another telenovela. The audience knows and expects this, which is very different from American soaps.[30] Audience research on telenovelas by Lucas Telles (2004)[31] and Samantha Nogueira Joyce (2013)[32] has indicated that people tend to relate to the central characters in these telenovelas and use the characters and their actions as guidelines for their own personal problems and aspirations.

In India, as Nivedita Menon points outs, a dominant patrilocal system[33] (i.e., the woman moves into the husband's home or community after marriage) ensures constant interactions between the mother-in-law and the daughter-in-law under one household. At the same time, there are not enough opportunities for women to be employed in the formal organized workforce outside the house. Certain social constraints also prevent women from moving out of the household for work opportunities, which creates a situation where both the mother-in-law and daughter-in-law are forced to be together inside the house. As in a patriarchal society, the older mother-in-law exerts her power and authority over the newly wed woman who enters the house.[34] The mother-in-law expects her younger daughter-in-law to accept her authority without questioning it. While in urban areas there has been a shift from patrilocal to nuclear family setups, the majority of rural women still continue to move into their in-law's house after marriage.

This dominant social situation defines the relationship between two women, the saas (mother-in-law) and the bahu (daughter-in-law), has given rise to the popular genre of the saas-bahu soap in the Hindi language shows. The saas-bahu soap is a clichéd formula for characters like the saas, who is typically evil and conniving, and the bahu, who is almost always humble and kind with a loving and congenial personality. The narrative plot points in most of these soaps explore the tussles and fights for power and decision making between the saas and the bahu within the household. The mean and controlling saas conspires to humiliate the bahu, but the kind-hearted bahu never suspects her saas of any misdemeanor. The bahu is shown as a resourceful woman and a pillar of strength who keeps the family from drifting apart. The joint and extended family, for her, is more important than her marital life, and she is fully devoted to taking care of them. The plot points in these saas-bahu serials are familiar and repetitive. Time and again the bahu is tested for her loyalty to the family she is married into. She is expected to exhibit maturity and be demure, yet strong. A usual show twist is when the bahu learns of her mother-in-law's cruel intentions but decides to respect her anyway. Another familiar plot is the forced exit of the bahu from the family, which is orchestrated by the saas. Nevertheless, the evil saas loses in most of her conspiracies while competing with her bahu.

The format of most of these soaps is extremely long, spanning over more than a thousand episodes and carrying on for years. They usually play on prime time, 8 to 10 P.M. slots, and almost five days a week.[35] This time slot is meant for family where children, adults, and elders can all sit together and enjoy these soaps, which is complementary to the viewing culture in Indian middle-class households.[36] As mentioned earlier, the same applies to the transitioning Vietnamese households in the sociopolitical context of postwar communist Vietnam.[37] These shows are marked by dramatic music, cliffhangers, and plot twists. The evil characters line up against the bahu over a period of time. However, in the end, the saas has a change of heart toward the bahu, and their relationship starts to grow and blossom from enemies to best friends. The saas then helps the bahu achieve things outside of the family and domestic sphere. Other common narrative themes include generational leaps that involve significant fast-forwards and face-change operations.

Saas-bahu soaps are popular in India because they reflect the complexity of patrilocal joint families commonly seen in the country. Women, on an everyday basis, need to negotiate and navigate difficult circumstances within the household and have to work hard to establish their position in their family of marriage. Saas-bahu shows reflect this everydayness, and audiences can relate to the characters in the soap. Joanne Cantor suggests that "humans are naturally inclined to emphasize with the emotions of the protagonists."[38] Likewise, Dolf Zillmann and Joanne Cantor in 1977 indicate that regardless of the source of empathy, its existence predicts that viewers may vicariously experience the emotions displayed by the protagonist.[39] These fictional characters help guide viewers through some troubling domestic situations and give creative solutions to their problems. At the same time, like any other telenovela, saas-bahu soaps always have a happy ending, which gives people hope and a positive future to look forward to.

Balika Vadhu is a typical saas-bahu soap (regressive stereotypical representation) mixed with selective pro-social messages on women's empowerment. It tells the story of an eight-year-old Anandi who is married to a 10-year-old Jagdish (or Jagia, as he is lovingly known) and moves into a joint family to assume her role as a daughter-in-law. Anandi faces many challenges, from being asked to cook for everyone in the house to being forbidden from studying, while Jagdish completes his education. *Balika Vadhu* uses many of the narrative arcs described earlier, where characters like Dadisa (grandmother) prevent Anandi from studying and push her into the kitchen to become a devoted, dutiful daughter-in-law. It has dramatic music, generational leaps, and also the cruel saas plot. In fact, after the generational leap, when Anandi returns to her in-laws' house, Jagdish abandons his family and Anandi for a woman he met in college in the city. Anandi is now 18 years old, the differences between Dadisa and Anandi are reconciled, and Anandi is encouraged to teach other women in the village. In spite of these regressive and stereotypical representations of the saas-bahu relationship, however, the show includes themes that allow for productive discussions on social issues, such as widow remarriage, education of girls, and female feticide or preference for a male child. The show entered the *Limca Book of Records*[40] in May 2016 for being India's longest-running show after completing over two thousand episodes.[41] In its second season, the story shifts from Anandi to her daughter Nimbodi, who is also a child bride constantly being harassed by her in-laws.

Having established that *Balika Vadhu* is a saas-bahu serial, very similar in format, style, and themes to the Latin American telenovelas (which have historically been popular in Vietnam), I next explore the changes in Vietnamese society that may offer a plausible decoding of the show's popularity.

Decoding the Popularity

John Fiske in 1987 argued that television is a subject that is worthy of a critical investigation: "The characteristics of its texts and modes of reception enable an active participation in the sense making process which we call 'culture.'"[42] According to Stuart Hall, cultural coding and decoding are processes that are integral to the "readings of a text."[43] Hall emphasizes that there could be three different kinds of "readings of a text," namely (1) hegemonic, (2) negotiational, and (3) oppositional. A hegemonic reading would be the one where the audience meaning-making is as intended by the author or the sender of the media text, whereas an oppositional reading would be an opposite reading of the text. A negotiational reading is an in-between meaning-making by the reader or the audience. For Hall, audiences use their culture to decode meanings from any text. Therefore, the same text may be interpreted differently in different cultural contexts.

Cultural codes embedded in the narrative of *Balika Vadhu* include a societal shift from rural joint families to urban nuclear families, women's empowerment, societal preference for a male child,[44] and the problems of child marriage.[45] There is also empirical evidence to show that the patrilocal residence pattern is in fact quite popular in Vietnam. Within this patrilocal family structure, the burden of domestic labor primarily rests upon women.[46] This pattern also influences parental socialization of children and values placed on sons and daughters, respectively. As in India, families in Vietnam in the twenty-first century are still a source of caregiving for their members. These cultural similarities between India and Vietnam lead to a predominantly hegemonic reading of the cultural codes embedded in the text of *Balika Vadhu*. This implies that audiences in Vietnam interpret *Balika Vadhu* as a show which highlights the evils of child marriage and gender inequality in society. However, the text of *Balika Vadhu* is simultaneously polysemic,[47] as it allows

Vietnamese audiences to insert their own meanings and create their own versions of Anandi and Jagia using their culture-specific context. The social context of the show seems familiar to audiences in Vietnam, thereby creating for them character relatability (as discussed in the previous section). The popularity of telenovelas as a genre in Vietnam, on the other hand, provides added favorability and acceptability of *Balika Vadhu*.

The rural-urban migration is another prominent theme explored in the show. This migration has a significant impact on the social, cultural, and economic lives of people. In India, which is predominantly an agrarian society, the bulk of agricultural activity happens in rural areas, where joint and extended families collectively own and cultivate a piece of land. Rural to urban migration for education or in search of jobs or other forms of livelihood shifts family structures from joint and patrilocal to nuclear. Vietnam has also been experiencing high rates of young adult migration from rural to urban areas in search of new economic and social opportunities.[48] These young people as migrants experience new lifestyles, consumer culture, and a changed way of living. However, most of them have family back in rural areas and maintain a strong rural connection. This may be why television dramas with narratives set in rural contexts still find huge viewership among urban audiences. This gives us a possible explanation for the popularity of *Balika Vadhu* in urban areas across India (Delhi and Mumbai)[49] and Vietnam (Hanoi and Ho Chi Minh) alike. In *Balika Vadhu*, the protagonist Anandi belongs to a poor farming family that owes a huge debt to rich landlords. When her family is unable to repay the debt, they decide to marry their daughter to the son (Jagdish) of the landlord (to whom her family owed money). As the show progresses, Jagdish migrates to the city to attain a better education. Upon his return, however, Jagdish is unable to accept the conservative ways of his family and his child marriage with Anandi. This is shown as a clash between the rural and urban lifestyles, where young Jagia drifts away from his family values and falls in love with a woman from the city.

From a cultural studies perspective, it can be inferred that audiences' awareness of these similarities between India and Vietnam creates a sense of togetherness where viewers watching *Balika Vadhu* adopt a solution-oriented problem-solving approach. Vietnamese audiences watch *Balika Vadhu* to know how Indian characters cope with social problems of child marriages, lack of education, and gender-based violence among others. The need to look for creative solutions to such social problems by interpreting the story of Anandi gives this show meaning in the context of Vietnam. The next section of this chapter explores the dominant viewing culture in India and Vietnam to make an argument for how the narratives and themes of *Balika Vadhu* support this viewing culture.

Television-Viewing Culture

Research conducted at the University of Tampere in 2015 suggests that television brings families together. The researchers, Aku Kallio, Katja Repo, Eero Suoninen, and Anja-Riitta Lahikainen argue that a television screen can be easily shared between family members and therefore encourages collective viewing.[50] This collective viewing initiates dialogues between members that create family bonding. Vietnamese audiences value family and the time spent with together. In Vietnam as well as in India, audiences largely follow a collective family viewing culture, where children, parents, and elderly members of the family can all sit together and watch television. In India, typically, middle-class households have one television set for the entire family. This means that television viewing time is divided among family members, with the male patriarch having priority over other members. A survey conducted by the Broadcast Audience Research Council (BARC) in 2018 reported that 98 percent of homes in India still have a single television set, while 82 percent of television-owning households in the country spend 57 percent of their time watching television together. This impacts younger audiences. Although the viewers aged two to fourteen cannot always watch children's channels, they still contribute to the 23 percent of viewership on Hindi general entertainment channels.[51] The content and narratives of the show hence are important. They need to be inclusive and support and encourage viewers from across different age groups in order to promote family viewing (which as mentioned is considered important by both the Indian and Vietnamese audiences).

The show *Balika Vadhu* is sensitive to diverse age groups. While it brings up difficult social issues, these issues are formatted and narrated in such a way that viewers do not feel uncomfortable confronting them. The central character, Anandi, is a child, which encourages younger audiences to watch the show; however, the issues highlighted in the show are very mature (which encourages older audiences). Anandi moves to Jagia's house after their child marriage (patrilocality), where she is not treated like a child but is forced to enter into a world of adult relationships. *Balika Vadhu* benefits immensely from this narrative of a child in an adult world because it captures the attention of families that typically have individuals from diverse age groups. However, keeping in mind the sensibilities of younger audiences, the show carefully avoids visually uncomfortable themes. For instance, the show depicts the relationship between Anandi and Jagia as a platonic friendship and does not venture into uncomfortable themes of sexual intimacies among children in arranged marriages. This kind of self-censorship makes the show a drama that families can watch together in their living room.

Researchers like Omar Souki Oliveira find that audiences use telenovelas to obtain some vicarious relief from the burden of some very real social conditions that telenovelas do nothing to disrupt.[52] *Balika Vadhu* plays a similar role for families in India and Vietnam, wherein families may collectively watch the show but viewing does not necessarily bring about a social change among audiences. *Balika Vadhu* entertainingly packages social problems through the story of Anandi, which can be easily consumed by audiences in the comfort of their living room. The overly dramatic and overpowering music and costumes, among other things, allow families to comfortably critique societal practices while also being entertained. Therefore, Vietnamese audiences appreciate family shows where values such as respect for elders are emphasized. Bonding among extended family members, family honor, respect for elders, care of children, and the authority of patriarchs are themes that audiences in Vietnam associate with. Such comfort with themes, format, and social issues allows for the popular reception of *Balika Vadhu* in Vietnam.

Conclusion

Transnational media flows in the global cultural industry are difficult to understand, and both political economy and audience reception play an important role in the success of a cultural product in foreign markets. By tracing the media history in post-reform Vietnam, this chapter makes a case for the extreme popularity of the Indian television show *Balika Vadhu* in Vietnam. It argues from a political economy perspective that in communist Vietnam, after the unification, people were tired of watching propagandist and nationalist themes and eager to watch shows that portrayed everyday life of normal people. Telenovelas met that desire and brought stories of ordinary people to the homes of the Vietnamese. These telenovelas were fueled by social and pro-development messages but in a manner that was entertaining and engaging. *Balika Vadhu* is one such show that combines pro-social messages with the entertainment of a Saas-Bahu saga. This chapter establishes the importance of telenovelas in Vietnamese society, the pattern of rural-urban migration, and the centrality of family and collective viewing culture in Vietnam. *Balika Vadhu* is a telenovela that supports family viewing and incorporates rural-urban dynamics. This allows for easy cross-cultural acceptability of *Balika Vadhu* in Vietnam.

Notes

1   Alex Millson, "Google's Top Search Terms of 2015 Reveal Asia's Differing Web Tastes," Bloomberg.com, December 19, 2015, https://www.bloomberg.com/news /articles/2015-12-19/google-s-top-search-terms-of-2015-reveal-asia-s-differing-web -tastes.
2   Zing Me is a social network operated by VNG corporation (Vietnamese Technology Company), which was introduced in August 2009.

3   Badoo is a dating-focused social network founded by Russian entrepreneur
    Andrey Andreev in 2006.

4   Charu Sudan Kasturi, "Outpouring of Grief in Vietnam for 'Balika Vadhu,'"
    The Telegraph (New Delhi), April 3, 2016, https://www.telegraphindia.com/india
    /outpouring-of-grief-in-vietnam-for-balika-vadhu/cid/1488924.

5   "The State of the World's Children 2016: A Fair Chance for Every Child,"
    UNICEF, accessed March 12, 2019, http://www.unicef.org/publucations/files
    /UNICEF_SOWC_2016.pdf.

6   As for the cultural reception theory, Hall argued that audiences are not passive
    recipients of information passed through media. Rather, they are active meaning-
    makers, and they make sense of a text through their own cultural context and
    background. As for the global reception theory, Appadurai has argued that global
    culture flows (ethnoscapes, mediascapes, financescapes, technoscapes, and
    ideoscapes) are disjunctive, chaotic, and overlapping.

7   Arjun Appadurai, "Disjuncture and Difference in the Global Cultural Economy,"
    Theory, Culture & Society 7, no. 2–3 (1990): 305.

8   Ibid.

9   Media hegemony is the process by which certain values that are spread through
    the mass media become dominant in a society. Karl Marx had argued that the
    leading economic system gains its legitimacy from social institutions like
    education, religion, family, and mass media and exerts its impact on the same. For
    example, Stuart Hall had argued in his book *Culture, the Media and the Ideologi-
    cal Effect* (1977) how the television news coverage is an extension of the already
    existing and dominant system of capitalism. For more, see Stuart Hall, *Culture,
    the Media and the Ideological Effect* (London: Arnold, 1977).

10 Stuart Hall, *Encoding and Decoding in the Television Discourse Birmingham
    Centre for Contemporary Cultural Studies* (Birmingham: University of Birming-
    ham, 1973), 9.

11 Info Change India, *Info Change India—Entertainment Education: Why Balika
    Vadhu Worked*, Info Change India, August 2009, http://infochangeindia.org/my
    -media/305-media/related-analysis/7915-entertainment-education-why-balika
    -vadhu-worked.

12 "Here's Why K-Pop Is So Popular in North East India," *India Today* (Mumbai),
    June 13, 2017, https://www.indiatoday.in/lifestyle/music/story/k-pop-korean-pop
    -popular-north-east-india-manipur-nagaland-lifest-982550-2017-06-13.

13 Lata Jha, "Bollywood's Love Story in China," Livemint (New Delhi), May 25,
    2018, https://www.livemint.com/Consumer/hWof35fogMMv9cuMcZQPbK/The
    -Bollywoods-love-story-in-China.html.

14 Ashish Rajadhyaksha, "The 'Bollywoodization' of the Indian Cinema: Cultural
    Nationalism in a Global Arena," *Inter-Asia Cultural Studies* 4, no. 1 (2003): 25–39.

15 Broadcasting Board of Governors, *Annual Language Service Review Briefing Book*
    (Washington, DC: Broadcasting Board of Governors, 2011), 119–120.

16 "Vietnam in View," Executive Summary (Hong Kong: Asia Video Industry
    Association, 2018), 7–10.

17 Do Huong, "Television Dominant Media Platform for Vietnamese Viewers,"
    Vietnam Economic Times, April 1, 2015, http://www.vneconomictimes.com/article
    /vietnam-today/television-dominant-media-platform-for-vietnamese-viewers.

18 Michael Mandelbaum, "Vietnam: The Television War," *Daedalus* 111, no. 4 (1982):
    157–169.

19 Dipanjan Roy Chaudhury, "Welcome India's Efforts in Act East Policy: Tran Dai Quang, Vietnamese President," *Economic Times*, March 1, 2018, https://economictimes.indiatimes.com/news/defence/welcome-indias-efforts-in-act-east-policy-tran-dai-quang-vietnamese-president/articleshow/63119555.cms.

20 "Bollywood Is Coming to Vietnam," Saigoneer, January 4, 2016, https://saigoneer.com/saigon-music-art/6054-bollywood-is-coming-to-vietnam.

21 Giang Nguyen-Thu, *Television in Post-Reform Vietnam: Nation, Media, Market* (Oxon: Routledge, 2019).

22 Philip Taylor, *Fragments of the Present: Searching for Modernity in Vietnam's South* (Hanoi: Alan & Unwin, 2001), 40.

23 Arvind Singhal, Rafael Obregon, and Everett M. Rogers, "Reconstructing the Story of *Simplemente Maria*, the Most Popular Telenovela in Latin America of All Time," *Gazette* 54, no. 1 (1995): 1–15.

24 Ibid., 7–8.

25 Daniele Bélanger, "Marriage with Foreign Women in East Asia: Bride Trafficking or Voluntary Migration?" *Population & Societies* 469 (2010): 1–4.

26 Stephen Epstein, "The Bride(s) from Hanoi: South Korean Popular Culture, Vietnam and 'Asia' in the New Millennium," *Citizenship Studies* 12, no. 1 (2008): 9–25.

27 Arvind Singhal and Everett M. Rogers, "Television Soap Operas for Development in India," *International Communication Gazette* 41, no. 2 (1988): 109–126.

28 Ibid.

29 Lee Artz, "Telenovelas: Television Stories for Our Global Times," *Perspectives on Global Development and Technology* 14, no.1–2 (2015): 193–226. doi:10.1163/15691497-12341341.

30 Cristina Costa, *Eu compro essa mulher. Romance e consumo nas telenovelas brasileiras e mexicanas* [I buy this woman. Romance and consumerism in Brazilian and Mexican telenovelas] (Rio de Janeiro: Jorge Zahar Editor Ltda, 2000).

31 Lucas Telles, "Teledramaturgia ganha caráter científico com tra balho do Núcleo de Telenovelas" [Teledramas gain scientific character with the work of the Telenovelas Group], January 27, 2004, http://www.usp.br/agen/repgs/2004/pags/007.htm.

32 Samantha Nogueira Joyce, "A Kiss Is (Not) Just a Kiss: Heterodeterminism, Homosexuality, and TV Globo Telenovelas," *International Journal of Communication* 7 (2013), 49–53, doi: 1932–8036/20130005, https://ijoc.org/index.php/ijoc/article/viewFile/1832/839.

33 A patrilocal system is a social system in which a married couple resides with or near the husband's parents.

34 Nivedita Menon, *Seeing Like a Feminist* (New Delhi: Zubaan, 2012), 44–45.

35 Kavita Awaasthi, "Television's Prime Time Slot Gets Redefined," *Hindustan Times*, February18, 2013, https://www.hindustantimes.com/tv/television-s-prime-time-slot-gets-redefined/story-2qZmrk5ulgU8JMTFebPtQL.html.

36 Shoma Munshi, *Prime Time Soap Operas on Indian Television* (New Delhi: Routledge, 2010), 5.

37 BestMediaInfo Bureau, "82% of Population Watches TV Together, Impacting Choice of Content: BARC India," BestMediaInfo Bureau, October 11, 2018, https://bestmediainfo.com/2018/10/82-of-population-watches-tv-together-impacting-choice-of-content-barc-india/.

38 Joanne Cantor, "'I'll Never Have a Clown in My House'—Why Movie Horror Lives On," *Poetics Today* 25, no. 2 (2004): 297.

39 Dolf Zillman and Joanne Cantor, "Affective Response to the Emotions of a Protagonist," *Journal of Experimental Social Psychology* 13, no. 2 (1977): 155–165.
40 *Limca Book of Records* is an annual reference book published in India documenting human and natural world records.
41 "*Balika Vadhu* Enters *Limca Book of Records* as the Longest Running Daily Fiction Hindi Soap," *Indian Express*, May 31, 2016, https://indianexpress.com/article/entertainment/television/balika-vadhu-enters-limca-book-of-records-2826060/.
42 John Fiske, *Television Culture* (London: Routledge, 1987), 19.
43 Stuart Hall, *Encoding and Decoding*, 9.
44 Christophe Z. Guilmoto, "Son Preference, Sex Selection, and Kinship in Vietnam," *Population and Development Review* 38, no. 1 (2012): 37.
45 Jonathan Haughton and Dominique Haughton, "Son Preference in Vietnam," *Studies in Family Planning* 26, no. 6 (1995): 325–337.
46 Pham Thi Thu Phuong and Dang Thi Viet Phuong, "Vietnam, Families in," *Encyclopedia of Family Studies* (2016): 1–4, doi:10.1002/9781119085621.wbefs205.
47 Polysemy is the capacity for a text to have multiple meanings. It has to do with how individuals interpret and decode readings in different contexts and cultures.
48 Nhu Ngoc K Pham, Mai Do, Hung Van Bui, and Giang T. Nguyen, "Rural-to-Urban Migration in Vietnam: Conceptualized Youth's Vulnerabilities in the City," *International Journal of Migration, Health and Social Care* 14, no. 1 (2018): 117–130, doi:10.1108/ijmhsc-11-2015-0044.
49 Info Change India, *Info Change India—Entertainment Education*.
50 Anja-Ritta Lahikainen, Tiina Malkia, and Katja Repo, *Media, Family Interaction and the Digitization of Childhood* (Cheltenham: Edward Elgar Publishing, 2017).
51 BestMediaInfo Bureau, "82% of Population."
52 Omar Souki Oliveira, "Brazilian Soaps Outshine Hollywood: Is Cultural Imperialism Fading Out?," in *Beyond National Sovereignty: International Communication in the 1990s*, ed. Kaarle Nordenstreng and Herbert I. Schiller (Norwood: Ablex Publishing Corporation, 1995), 116–131.

Bibliography

Appadurai, Arjun. "Disjuncture and Difference in the Global Cultural Economy." *Theory, Culture & Society* 7, no. 2–3 (1990): 295–310.
Artz, Lee. "Telenovelas: Television Stories for Our Global Times." *Perspectives on Global Development and Technology* 14, no. 1–2 (2015): 193–226. doi:10.1163/15691497-12341341.
Awaasthi, Kavita. "Television's Prime Time Slot Gets Redefined." *Hindustan Times*. February 18, 2013. https://www.hindustantimes.com/tv/television-s-prime-time-slot-gets-redefined/story-2qZmrk5ulgU8JMTFebPtQL.html.
"*Balika Vadhu* Enters *Limca Book of Records* as the Longest Running Daily Fiction Hindi Soap." *Indian Express*, May 31, 2016. https://indianexpress.com/article/entertainment/television/balika-vadhu-enters-limca-book-of-records-2826060/.
Belanger, Daniele. "Marriage with Foreign Women in East Asia: Bride Trafficking or Voluntary Migration?" *Population & Societies* 469 (2010): 1–4.
BestMediaInfo Bureau. "82% of Population Watches TV Together, Impacting Choice of Content: BARC India." BestMediaInfo Bureau. October 11, 2018.

https://bestmediainfo.com/2018/10/82-of-population-watches-tv-together
-impacting-choice-of-content-barc-india/.
Broadcasting Board of Governors. *Annual Language Service Review Briefing Book.*
Washington, DC: Government Accountability Office, 2011.
Cantor, Joanne. "'I'll Never Have a Clown in My House'—Why Movie Horror Lives
On." *Poetics Today* 25, no. 2 (2004): 283–304.
Chaudhury, Dipanjan Roy. "Welcome India's Efforts in Act East Policy: Tran Dai
Quang, Vietnamese President." *Economic Times.* March 1, 2018. https://
economictimes.indiatimes.com/news/defence/welcome-indias-efforts-in-act-east
-policy-tran-dai-quang-vietnamese-president/articleshow/63119555.cms.
Costa, Cristina. *Eu compro essa mulher. Romance e consumo nas telenovelas brasileiras e
mexicanas* [I buy this woman. Romance and consumerism in Brazilian and
Mexican telenovelas]. Rio de Janeiro: Jorge Zahar Editor Ltda, 2000.
Epstein, Stephen. "The Bride(s) from Hanoi: South Korean Popular Culture, Vietnam
and 'Asia' in the New Millennium." *Citizenship Studies* 12, no. 1 (2008): 9–25.
Fiske, John. *Television Culture.* London: Routledge, 1987.
Guilmoto, Christophe Z. "Son Preference, Sex Selection, and Kinship in Vietnam."
Population and Development Review 38, no. 1 (2012): 31–54.
Hall, Stuart. *Culture, the Media and the Ideological Effect.* London: Arnold, 1977.
———. *Encoding and Decoding in the Television Discourse Birmingham Centre for
Contemporary Cultural Studies.* Birmingham: University of Birmingham, 1973.
Haughton, Jonathan, and Dominique Haughton. "Son Preference in Vietnam."
Studies in Family Planning 26, no. 6 (1995): 325–337. doi:10.2307/2138098.
"Here's Why K-Pop Is So Popular in North East India." *India Today.* June 13, 2017.
https://www.indiatoday.in/lifestyle/music/story/k-pop-korean-pop-popular-north
-east-india-manipur-nagaland-lifest-982550-2017-06-13.
Huong, Do. "Television Dominant Media Platform for Vietnamese Viewers." *Vietnam
Economic Times.* April 1, 2015. http://www.vneconomictimes.com/article/vietnam
-today/television-dominant-media-platform-for-vietnamese-viewers.
Info Change India. *Info Change India—Entertainment Education: Why Balika Vadhu
Worked.* Info Change India. August 2009. http://infochangeindia.org/my-media
/305-media/related-analysis/7915-entertainment-education-why-balika-vadhu
-worked.
Jha, Lata. "Bollywood's Love Story in China." Livemint (New Delhi). May 25, 2018.
https://www.livemint.com/Consumer/hWof35fogMMv9cuMcZQPbK/The
-Bollywoods-love-story-in-China.html.
Joyce, Samantha Nogueira. "A Kiss Is (Not) Just a Kiss: Heterodeterminism, Homosexuality, and TV Globo Telenovelas." *International Journal of Communication* 7
(2013): 49–53. doi: 1932–8036/20130005. https://ijoc.org/index.php/ijoc/article
/viewFile/1832/839.
Kasturi, Charu Sudan. "In Vietnam, the Soap Operas Are Diplomats." OZY.
March 18, 2016. https://www.ozy.com/fast-forward/in-vietnam-the-soap-operas
-are-diplomats/66919.
———. "Outpouring of Grief in Vietnam for 'Balika Vadhu.'" *The Telegraph.* April 3,
2016. https://www.telegraphindia.com/india/outpouring-of-grief-in-vietnam-for
-balika-vadhu/cid/1488924.
Lahikainen, Anja-Riitta, Tiina Malkia, and Katja Repo. *Media, Family Interaction
and the Digitization of Childhood.* Cheltenham: Edward Elgar Publishing, 2017.

Mandelbaum, Michael. "Vietnam: The Television War." *Daedalus* 111, no. 4 (1982): 157–169.

Menon, Nivedita. *Seeing Like a Feminist*. New Delhi: Zubaan, 2012.

Millson, Alex. "Google's Top Search Terms of 2015 Reveal Asia's Differing Web Tastes." Bloomberg. December 19, 2015. https://www.bloomberg.com/news/articles/2015-12 -19/google-s-top-search-terms-of-2015-reveal-asia-s-differing-web-tastes.

Munshi, Shoma. *Prime Time Soap Operas on Indian Television*. New Delhi: Routledge, 2010.

Nguyen-Thu, Giang. *Television in Post-Reform Vietnam: Nation, Media, Market*. Oxon: Routledge, 2019.

Oliveira, Omar Souki. "Brazilian Soaps Outshine Hollywood: Is Cultural Imperialism Fading Out?" In *Beyond National Sovereignty: International Communication in the 1990s*, edited by Kaarle Nordenstreng and Herbert I. Schiller, 116–131. Norwood: Ablex Publishing Corporation, 1995.

Pham, Nhu Ngoc K, Mai Do, Hung Van Bui, and Giang T. Nguyen. "Rural-to-Urban Migration in Vietnam: Conceptualized Youth's Vulnerabilities in the City." *International Journal of Migration, Health and Social Care* 14, no. 1 (2018): 117–130. doi:10.1108/ijmhsc-11-2015-0044.

Phuong, Pham Thi Thu, and Dang Thi Viet Phuong. "Vietnam, Families in." *Encyclopedia of Family Studies* (2016): 1–4. doi:10.1002/9781119085621.wbefs205.

Rajadhyaksha, Ashish. "The 'Bollywoodization' of the Indian Cinema: Cultural Nationalism in a Global Arena." *Inter-Asia Cultural Studies* 4, no. 1 (2003): 25–39.

Saigoneer. "Bollywood Is Coming to Vietnam." Saigoneer. January 4, 2016. https:// saigoneer.com/saigon-music-art/6054-bollywood-is-coming-to-vietnam.

Singhal, Arvind, Rafael Obregon, and Everett M. Rogers. "Reconstructing the Story of *Simplemente Maria*, the Most Popular Telenovela in Latin America of All Time." *Gazette* 54, no. 1 (1995): 1–15.

Singhal, Arvind, and Everett M. Rogers. "Television Soap Operas for Development in India." *International Communication Gazette* 41, no. 2 (1988): 109–126.

"The State of the World's Children 2016: A Fair Chance for Every Child." UNICEF. Accessed March 12, 2019. https://www.unicef.org/publications/files/UNICEF _SOWC_2016.pdf.

Taylor, Philip. *Fragments of the Present: Searching for Modernity in Vietnam's South*. Hanoi: Alan & Unwin, 2001.

Telles, Lucas. "Teledramaturgia ganha caráter científico com tra balho do Núcleo de Telenovelas" [Teledramas gain scientific character with the work of the Telenovelas Group]. January 27, 2004. http://www.usp.br/agen/repgs/2004/pags/007.htm.

"Vietnam in View." Executive Summary. Hong Kong: Asia Video Industry Association, 2018.

Zillman, Dolf, and Joanne Cantor. "Affective Response to the Emotions of a Protagonist." *Journal of Experimental Social Psychology* 13, no. 2 (1977): 155–165.

3

Star Construction in the Era of Media Convergence

∎∎∎∎∎∎∎∎∎∎∎∎∎∎∎∎∎∎∎∎∎∎∎∎∎

Pro-Am Online Videos,
Co-creative Culture, and
Transnational Chinese
Icons on YouTube

DOROTHY WAI SIM LAU

Rogue One: A Star Wars Story (2016) has been a recent sensation in the popular and cinematic arenas. Set prior to the events of the 1977 episode, *Rogue One* is the first standalone feature in the *Star Wars* anthology series. The blockbuster has grossed over $5 million and nearly $1 billion domestically and worldwide, becoming the third-highest-grossing *Star Wars* film.[1] Evident to the ongoing ambition of the sci-fi franchise to access the global audienceship, *Rogue One*, moreover, features an international cast including the British-Pakistani Riz Ahmed as Bodhi Rook, the Mexican Diego Luna as Cassian Andor, and the Chinese Wen Jiang as Baze Malbus and Donnie Yen as Chirrut Imwe.[2] Elected by more than thirty thousand votes as the most popular *Rogue One* character in a poll on the official *Star Wars* website in May 2017,[3] Chirrut Imwe appears as a blind yet adroit Jedi fighter, or "'the best fighter' in the galaxy,"[4] as Yen simply puts it. Media limelight also rests on the fact that the martial arts actor triumphs the peer candidates, who have been noticeable in the United States, including Jet Li, Stephen Chow, Tony Leung, Daniel Wu, Chang Chen, and Leehom Wang, to gain this "definitely important" role.[5] Being proud to be the first Chinese face appearing in the *Star Wars* narrative,[6] Yen once expressed that "Asians have proven that they can be as good as anybody else"[7] in an interview by Geek Culture, an online network of amateurs and fans of gaming and sci-fi on specific titles as well known as *Transformers* (2007–2017), *Star Trek* (2009), and *Star Wars* (1977–2016).[8]

Shot by tech260.tv, a Singapore-based online TV channel, the interview was then imparted on YouTube on November 30, 2016, attracting 129,857 views and 165 comment entries, and was supplemented with the website and the Facebook link of Geek Culture. Yen's account like this immediately put the issue of ethnicity in Hollywood at the center of public discourse circulated and celebrated by audiences around the globe. This instance is telling as to Yen's star presence in the transnational media network, bridging the screen persona produced in the studio filmmaking and the public image engendered in amateurish visual productions. With the global presence of Chinese stars in mind, this chapter investigates the emerging role of amateurs in the scene of cultural production at the juncture of the convergence of traditional and new media. New technology enables the ease of searching, poaching, copying, posting, and sharing materials, valorizing a heightened participation of global audiences in the star-making mechanism. The phenomenon, particularly matured on the web as an open platform, gives way to the changing role of fans, who are knowledgeable consumers of the industrialized materials and concomitantly keen on experimenting with various modes of creativity. This chapter, therefore, probes how the fan-made videos, which are the outcome of the synthesis of professionally produced materials and amateur creative efforts, reconfigure the Chinese icons in the global media-scape.

The media convergence not only seamlessly transposes star personae from cinema to cyberspace but also alters the ways in which Chinese image is approached, represented, and understood. Recent decades have seen the growing visibility and mobility of Chinese stars as the global media capital and a noticeable plight of Chinese stars engineer their screen identities stemmed from the martial arts cinema. Hollywood's co-opting of Hong Kong film talents in the 1980s and 1990s vitally constitutes the scene of transnational film culture. Émigrés designated to the various stages of the influx include directors like John Woo, Tsui Hark, Ronny Yu, Stanley Tong, and Kirk Wong; choreographers such as Yuen Woo-ping and Corey Yuen; and performers like Jackie Chan, Jet Li, Michelle Yeoh, and Chow Yun-fat. The stars have established the *wuxia* (action fighter) image not only for local cinephiles but also for an audience beyond Hong Kong as the result of distribution in Southeast Asia and overseas Chinese communities. The proliferation of pan-Chinese filmmaking in the 2000s extended the access of charisma of Chinese stars in the milieu of global capitalism. The highly commercialized mode of production, the frequent use of cutting-edge technology, and the merging or rebuilding of state-owned studios as vast entertainment conglomerates valorize the blockbuster outlook of the transnational Chinese cinema.[9] Titles like *Hero* (2002), *House of Flying Daggers* (2004), *Curse of the Golden Flower* (2006), *The Banquet* (2006), *Red Cliff* (2008), and *Let the Bullet Fly* (2010) employed high-powered casts from Hong Kong (Donnie Yen, Tony Leung Chiu-wai, Chow Yun-fat, Maggie Cheung, Andy Lau, Daniel Wu), the People's Republic of China (PRC) (Jet Li, Gong Li, Zhang Ziyi, Jiang Wen, Zhou Xun, Liu Ye, Ge You), and Taiwan (Takeshi Kaneshiro, Chang Chen, Jay Chou). The star vehicles received satisfactory box-office returns in Asia, North America, and worldwide.[10] These movies also capitalized on the visual spectacle of sets, costume, choreography, and special effects, which were highly stylized and exoticized, as part of the marketized discourse. The Chinese icons, who persistently shuttle between various film industries, formulate a "pan-Chinese" or "pan-Asian" creative-productive network, while embodying "mutating currencies of transnationality."[11]

As the Chinese star phenomenon plays out in the co-creative, digital network, it generates new inquiries that demand serious exploration. Copious studies have already focused on an array of transnational Chinese stars, from the most celebrated ones to the less researched ones, including, for example, Jackie Chan, Jet Li, Michelle Yeoh, Chow Yun-fat, Zhang Ziyi, Maggie Cheung, Gong Li, Tony Chiu-wai Leung, Daniel Wu, and Andy Lau—the list may go on. Many scholars have framed the personalities in sundry contexts like Chinese cinema,[12] East Asian cinema,[13] and transnational cinema[14] and have explored them in terms of star agency, cultural nationalism, masculinity, and femininity as well as issues concerned with production and consumption. This corpus of literature predominantly adopts the approaches of Asian American studies,[15] transnational studies,[16] and cultural studies[17] to examine the racial, ethnic, and gender representations of Chinese stars.[18]

More recent research, on the other hand, provides insight on how the convergence of traditional and new media has given rise to the new breeds of amateur video-makers in the scene of star-making. Pioneering essays written by Julian Stringer and Sabrina Yu inquire into the star construction and audience reception of Jet Li on the internet. Stringer probes how the ambivalence of Asian American devotees has shaped Li's image: while some audiences relish Li's "perfect" Chineseness as embodied in his Hollywood roles, others highlight his own limitations as an ethnic actor.[19] Sabrina Yu examines the construction of Li's star presence through his publicity at the official Jet Li website.[20] By investigating the contradictory onscreen-offscreen personae, Yu extrapolates the equally central roles the star and fans play in the star-making process. Expanding the previous effort, I have analyzed Jackie Chan and Jet Li in the social media platforms of Flickr[21] and Facebook.[22] In both studies, I have argued for the cosmopolitical, rather than ethnic, celebrity-philanthropist presence engineered on the user-oriented sites that have become part of the industrial machinery of persona management. Intellectuals, moreover, have positioned video-sharing sites as the venue of engendering public memories of dead personalities, such as Chinese kung fu megastar Bruce Lee[23] and Taiwanese singer Teresa Tang.[24] They explain how the digitalized clips from private collections become part of the fan-based memorial culture, as far as they are turned into video uploads. In addition to the shared memories of fallen stars, researchers have also dealt with the shared taste of the artist-like figures alive. These attempts demonstrate how the merging of media cultures generates sensitivity and potency that work within and outside the industrial mechanism. Nonetheless, the attempts still remain incipient and scarce in the field. In response to such incipiency and scarcity, this chapter, integrating media studies and star studies, aims at filling the gap by intervening in the current debates about Chinese stardom reconfigured in the backdrop of media convergence.

Pro-Am Online Videos as a Co-creative Star-Making Phenomenon

No longer dominated by professionally produced media texts, film stardom has become an intertextual, versatile venture at the convergence of celluloid and digital means, possibly led by the clash of various modes of creativity. Proliferating, synergistic Web 2.0 platforms like YouTube and Facebook have made possible the "ever-expanding terrain of the amateur,"[25] valorized by the user-generated content and the migratory effort of media audiences. Since the mid-2000s, the maturation of broadband infrastructure and open-source image-making software has further evinced the escalating professionalization of amateur visual productions. Cinephiles easily search, cull, copy, and share movie clips, trailers, making-of footages, and celebrity interviews obtained from television, DVDs, and internet websites. On top of borrowing texts directly, they also produce parodies, mashups, and remixes as if they are professional video makers. Stars of Chinese cinema, as captured in the transnational dialectics, exemplify the changing mode of popular construction in a complex web comprising professionals and amateurs, producers and consumers. Chinese icons, as the source of the entertainment fodder in Asia and the West, are extensively discussed, followed, and tweeted on the web, proving their global fame not only in the Chinese-speaking world but in other language communities as well. Leveled to the popular Hollywood stars like Brad Pitt, Robert Downey, Angelina Jolie, Johnny Depp, and Leonardo DiCaprio, the Chinese personalities' presence in televised interviews, online entertainment tabloid news, viral video advertisements, and downloadable movie trailers further universalizes their crossover image and Orientalist allure.[26] Fans are keen on appropriating the materials from the mainstream media and reposting them on the amateur-inhabited web-based conduits. Thus amateurs threaten the "hegemony" of professional image makers by reconstruing the star texts produced by the institutionalized system through different lenses. The practice collapses the dividing line between the professional and the amateur, although, as Marjorie Garber posits, the two groups allegedly "are always in each other's pocket."[27] The effort validates the trend that popular texts no longer stay in the cultural terrain as they used to, but move across diverse media platforms, driven by both the mainstream industrial initiative and the alternative business initiative.

Among others, YouTube is one of the most amateur-friendly websites that exemplify alternatives to large-scale productions in subcultural fields. It is an open platform that enables users without explicit cultural, institutional, and generic affiliations to create the amateur expressions which many content creators seek to exploit. It invites us to see ourselves as potential bona fide media producers or even celebrities-in-waiting, in Jean Burgess's words.[28] The site's ongoing formalization and legitimation in its operation further suggest a tendency to pursue a relatively profitable and stabilized cultural space[29] inhabited by both trained and untrained practitioners. It is also exemplary of the disruptive influence that novel networks of content production and distribution can cast on current media business models.[30] "Symptomatic to a changing media environment,"[31] YouTube encompasses sundry groups of participants. The three groups of participants on YouTube that Jean Burgess and Joshua Green identify include (1) traditional media companies, (2) Web-TV companies, and (3) "ordinary user" or individual, amateur participants that are not representatives of mainstream media.[32] This chapter concentrates on the cultural activity that happens within the second group, which is considered neither completely corporatized nor completely independent but most actively and reflexively engaged in YouTube's "co-create" culture.[33] Put another way, it dwells in the mediated space that registers a myriad of interrelated occurrences of participation.

More specifically, I hypothesize the transnational Chinese star phenomenon on YouTube as a partly amateur, partly professional co-creative outcome by focusing on Donnie Yen. Ranked as the sixth most influential Chinese celebrity in the Forbes 2011 list,[34] Yen is "one of the most popular and prolific action star choreographers"[35] whose appeal is established and mobilized on celluloid screens and is frequently attended and reworked by cinephiles and media users. Drawing on his solid martial arts training, Yen electrifies viewers of diverse cultural backgrounds with authentic dexterity and kinetic agility. Yen began his film career in the mid-1980s, but it was not until the 2000s that his martial arts status was concretized in the local film industry and in Hollywood. In the early 2000s, he attained newfound success in the Chinese-language cinema with titles such as *Hero* (2002), *SPL: Sha Po Lang* (2005), *Empress and the*

Warriors (2008), and most markedly, *Ip Man* and *Ip Man II: Legend of the Grand Master* (2008 and 2010). His breakthrough role in the *Ip Man* series earned him immense popularity among Chinese-language viewers and Wing Chun (a traditional Southern Chinese kung fu style and a form of self-defense) devotees, propelling him to superstardom. In recent years, he remains active in Hong Kong/Chinese martial arts cinema and Hollywood cinema, and his appearance extends to new screens. Consider as an example *Crouching Tiger, Hidden Dragon: Sword of Destiny* (2016), the sequel of Ang Lee's 2000 sensation that casts Donnie Yen with Michelle Yeoh, which was first released at the phenomenal Netflix as part of the platform's streaming texts. Successfully earning currency in the border-crossing market, Yen manages to engineer a relentless star presence in a multitude of fan-led communication networks, including fan clubs, fanzines, fansites, and blogs. Photographs and videos featuring his screen fighting, gym workouts, and behind-the-scene rehearsals are broadly circulated in both the official and unofficial media outlets. Yen has gained an enormous presence in the digital media world, and the audiovisual texts of him, in particular those pertinent to his hyperkinetic personae, have been widely relayed and reproduced on video-sharing sites like YouTube.

Some questions arise regarding the YouTube-based star texts of Donnie Yen: How is Donnie Yen's personality in *Rogue One* represented and interpreted by YouTube users? To what extent is Yen's persona on YouTube parallel to, different from, or overlaid with the earlier roles, produced by the institutionalized filmmaking system? What is the feasible connotation of the amateur-orchestrated image of Yen? To address these questions, I conducted a survey on YouTube by keyword-searching "Donnie Yen, Star Wars" on June 25, 2017. I identified two videos, among the list of entries that topped the search results, which were distinct from the merely copy-and-paste entries of movie clips and trailers and demonstrated a certain degree of originality. The two entries include (1) Donnie Yen in Rogue One | Generation Tech and (2) Star Wars Stop motion—Donnie Yen VS Storm Troopers. By examining the content and running commentaries of the clips, I plan to analyze how pro-am video makers[36] appropriate and rework images from the corporatized media, emulating and complicating Yen's well-known martial arts personality. I posit that pro-am videos trouble the image of Yen as a martial arts hero by either mixing the action body with other generic components like sci-fi or virtualizing the warrior figure found in other media contexts, such as video game and virtual reality. In doing so, my analysis insinuates how, in a volatile media environment, amateur videos produced outside the institutionalized structure of filmmaking spawn alternative ways of engaging with stars. It also informs the possibilities of Chinese star-(re)making through the collaborative grassroots-corporate effort.

Martial Arts Heroes' Lightsaber Battle

Amateur-produced videos free Donnie Yen from rigid generic and cultural boundaries and present him as an immensely flexible and diverse persona. The first video, entitled "Donnie Yen in *Rogue One* | Generation Tech," explores Yen's expanded image on YouTube as new visual hybrids of disparate symbolic components.[37] The posting date of this video is December 29, 2015, the time before the launch of *Rogue One* and yet after the advertising image of Yen had been publicized. Part of the caption hence insinuates, "We're not sure exactly what his role will be but he appears on a promotional photo as what appears to be a blind monk." The clip combines symbols of the sci-fi hit *Rogue One: A Star Wars Story* and the Chinese martial arts epic *Hero* (2000)—Yen is a member of the main cast in both films. *Hero* is the first global blockbuster produced in mainland China, and it riveted audiences both in and outside of China, setting a model for the transnational mode of production.[38] It also casts a cluster of the most marketable performers in Chinese-language cinema, such as Jet Li, Tony Leung, Maggie Cheung, Zhang Ziyi, and Donnie Yen. Based on Yen's performance in *Hero*, the video maker imagines and speculates on Yen's kinetically robust image as it will appear in *Rogue One*. The opening of the video shows a standout fight scene in *Hero* between Nameless (Jet Li) and Long Sky (Donnie Yen), two accomplished spearmen-assassins. Cinephiles of martial arts cinema do not miss the fact that both Li and Yen are genuine martial artists who are acclaimed for superb dexterity. Certain audiences regard the fight between the two megastars as "the most grounded."[39] Instead of merely copying images, the video maker re-creates the scene by cutting the iconic lightsabers from *Star Wars* and inserting them in the duel (fig. 3.1). In this fashion, the producer turns the Chinese heroes into semi-Jedi knights, hybridizing and re-creating the martial arts image. The new audiovisual text decontextualizes the Chinese body from a clearly defined signifying system that informs martial arts imaginary. It is, too, a showcase of the agency and creativity of amateurs, interrupting the structure of the hegemonic image-making in the martial arts film-making mechanism.

Yen's martial arts image is further debunked as his Churrit role is associated with a virtual personality from the digital game world. Yen's blind Jedi knight persona reminds us of the cinematic icon of Zatoichi, a blind swordsman featured in a long-running series of film and television in Japan. The hypothetical tie between two personalities can be traced back to the cross-cultural popular exchange in the 1960s and 1970s. During that period, Hong Kong cinema drew references from Japanese samurai films, and Zatoichi became a progenitor text of the martial arts films (*wu xia pian*). *Zatoichi Meets the One-Armed Swordsman* (1971), a swordplay movie produced by Shaw Brothers studio, exemplifies such a connection between Hong Kong and Japan.[40] Yet the YouTube

FIG. 3.1 The re-creation of dual heroes in *Hero* (2002), Donnie Yen and Jet Li, with the iconic lightsabers from *Star Wars*.

user's neglect, conscious or not, of the Zatoichi's role in the video narrative downplays the orientation of Yen's persona in the martial arts cinematic tradition. Instead, it shows a proclivity toward a digital visual logic, as Yen's persona is in parallel to the Miraluka, the fictional character in the multiplayer online game *Star Wars: The Old Republic*. With its human-like appearance, Miraluka is a sentient species existing in the galaxy around the time of Clone Wars. The members of the species have tanned brown skin and gray or white hair, and yet their racial or ethnic origin remains unclear. One of the distinct features of Miraluka is a lack of eyes, which leads them to perceive their surroundings with force-inflicted sensitivity rather than regular vision. In addition, they adopt the traditions and teachings of the Jedi Order and can fight skillfully with lightsabers due to their trust in the Force.[41] As Yen's Churrit persona appears alongside the Miraluka, it looks closer to a kind of "mobile identity," which Mary Flanagan designates as the new category of "digital stars,"[42] not the "'real' . . . action actor."[43] In addition, the video displays a portrait of a Miraluka female that likely makes Yen's screen masculinity woolly and fluid. Underlining the separation of the image and the body,[44] the video narrative shapes the disembodiment of the hero, making a stark contrast with his well-known presence grounded in his physical prowess and martial authenticity.

Nonetheless, the obscurity of Yen's martial arts appeal can still motivate fan engagement. The clip attracts an inventory of comments from individual users, encompassing evaluations of Yen's former personalities and expectations for his new role in *Rogue One*. The video title "Donnie Yen in *Rogue One* | Generation Tech" includes the name of the uploader, Generation Tech, which means, as indicated in the Facebook Page hyperlinked with the YouTube entry, "the place to be for video content covering the latest and greatest technologies."[45] Alongside the 67,471 views, the entry has attracted 88 comments, and one of the most recurring themes points to the "mashup" part, as expressed by phrases such as "looked . . . cool," "great work," and "great video." Equally notable, the other category of comments refers to the anticipation of Yen's *Rogue One* personification. For example, in January 2017, a user named "Joy Comilang" writes, "I hope he is a Jedi . . . a vanished one." At a similar time, user "Thomas Muller 7-1" writes, "imagine donnie yen wielding a lightsaber." Some users' feedback, furthermore, recognizes Yen's status derived from his martial artistry and his acting skill. For instance, some of the users' comments posted in January 2016, right after the posting of the video, demonstrate interactions by the knowledgeable fans. Part of the exchange appears as follows:

MIMA KAKE (JANUARY 2016) It would be a waste if they did not use Donnie
 Yen's martial arts skills. Or it is a challenge for him to do some different
 acting. We will see in about a year.;)
GENERATION TECH (JANUARY 2016) Yea can't wait, it's about time Donnie Yen
 becomes more mainstream outside of the Asian market.
PTIGRIS7 (JANUARY 2017) +Mima Kake If you have seen bodyguards and
 Assassins, Ip Man 3 or . . . perhaps All Well Ends well 2012, you will
 see that Donnie's acting is really superb, outside of his martial arts
 skill.
MIMA KAKE (JANUARY 2017) Cool, I shall check them out. Thanks.
KAPTIONIST (JANUARY 2017) +Mima Kake I did hear that Ip Man 3 was his last
 movie that displays any sort of kung fu . . .
MIMA KAKE (JANUARY 2017) Well, I definitely will check some more movies
 with him before I see Rogue one.;)

The interplay among users, elicited over a year, echoes the affective responses invoked by the desire of film moments in the era prior to the popularization of digital media. It arouses the cinephilic pleasure that Paul Willemen has conceptualized in terms of "the moment of revelation," or "a moment of excess."[46] The moment either operates out of a rigid framework or allows viewers to realize the "illusion" that "what is being seen is in excess of what is being shown."[47] The producer "selects a fragment,"[48] reworking it in resourceful ways like "an aspect of cinema that is not strictly programmable in terms of aesthetic strategies."[49] Akin to the discourse of cinephiles, this amateur video encapsulates the momentary encounter between web users and Yen's films. It is capable of recalling personal and collective memories about a range of Yen's previous personalities in martial arts films, such as *Ip Man 3* (2015) and *Bodyguards and Assassins* (2009), as well as in comedies like *All Well Ends and Well 2012* (2012). It also acknowledges users as productive viewing subjects, facilitating copious social encounters, exchanges, and identifications. It is worth noting here that the video maker, moreover, participates in the commentary conversation. As the uploader and the commenter, Generation Tech assumes the double roles in generating the intertextual star image, complicating the relationship between producers and consumers, between uploaders and viewers, in the digital co-creative culture.

Furthermore, the video narrative given by a host functions as an "extended brand narrative,"[50] a characteristic in the phenomenon of media amateurization, shaping viewers' understanding of Donnie Yen. As Kathy Bowrey points out, the proliferating amateur media allow a "greater personal identification with brands."[51] This clip reveals a predilection for self-branding and amateur agency through the presence of a host named Allen Xie, who engineers his online presence in a number of amateur-based platforms, such as YouTube and Facebook. Positioning himself as more an aficionado than an industrial practitioner, Xie unfolds his fondness of traveling and video shooting, as he self-introduces on his Facebook page. As the approximately three-minute clip indicates, the *Hero* battle scene is followed by Xie's articulate, elucidatory speech of the screen persona of Yen as he provides an exposition of *Rogue One*'s cast in a manner similar to a video essay. Framed in a medium shot in this video, the presenter demonstrates his digital-cultural capital by speaking in fluent English, implying possibly that the video addresses the Anglophone online community. He assumes the introductory and expounding positions as he eloquently guides the audience to consider and observe the Chinese *Star Wars* warrior. Although the author of the video is not clearly identified as to whether it is the host Xie or the uploader Generation Tech, both of them reside in a parallel position, embodying a mode of authority marked by the privilege of enunciation and commentary. In this fashion, the video maker/uploader (invisible) and the presenter (visible) show mastery over and judgment of Yen's personalities traversed in *Hero* and *Rogue One*, providing a star narrative that operates adjacent to, if not out of, the industrial cinematic undertaking.

Virtualizing the Star Persona

The second video, "Star Wars Stop Motion—Donnie Yen VS Storm Troopers," demonstrates the intertextual potentiality between Yen's cinematic role and a sort of virtualized personification.[52] In the approximately two-minute entry, the video maker, named "counter656," who presumably works outside the commercial filmmaking circle, produces an animated text based on one of the frequently quoted scenes of *Rogue One*—the fight between Donnie Yen and the Stormtroopers. This clip was uploaded on December 16, 2016, a day after *Rogue One*'s theatrical release in many regions, drawing on the sensation of the new sci-fi hit. The clip is a joint effort of Hot Toys and Lucas Film, as indicated in the caption of the entry. The other part of the caption reads "This time he wants to fight ten Storm Troopers." The phrase "this time" implies a reference to Yen's earlier character in *Ip Man* (2008), directed by Hong Kong filmmaker Wilson Yip. It alludes to the most-recalled fight scene in the 2008 martial arts epic between Yen, who plays the role of the Wing Chun master called Ip Man, and a throng of Japanese karatekas.[53] The plot of the film depicts that Ip Man seeks revenge for the death of a fellow master from Foshan, a city in the Guangdong Province in southern China, by engaging the ten karate black belts in a bout. Underscoring the dynamism of the hero's body, the director in the film adopts quick editing and moving frames to suggest the ferocity of the Wing Chun acrobatics and maximize the action's vividness. The amateur vide maker here bridges two personalities, preserving the martial vigor from the Wing Chun hero in the image of the Jedi knight. As a cognizant fan-producer, the video maker hence re-creates Yen's *Rogue One*, role not as an independent, isolated presence but as a continuation of the actor's previous cinematic image.

The clip has restaged Yen's Wing Chun body but makes it ambivalent as it is decontextualized from the Chinese martial arts tradition and situated in the *Star Wars* narrative. As a popular form of martial arts with a century-old history, Wing Chun is a highly codified entity conjuring a specific identification of Chinese culture. *Ip Man* portrays Yen as a man of honor who celebrates family ties, friendship, modesty, and ethnic comradeship through his Wing Chun presence. Similar to the personality of Wong Fei-hung, a Chines folk hero inspired by a real-life martial artist and widely depicted on martial arts screens,[54] Yen's Ip Man character appears as a good-natured family man who, as Yen puts it, is "essentially a nerd who fights well."[55] As the plot of the film unfolds, the Wing Chun master always holds back in the face of combatants' challenges and defeats them without hurting them. One illustrative scene is the duel between Master Liu and Ip Man. The scene depicts that Master Liu comes and demands a duel from Ip Man, who refuses to fight until the family dinner is finished. The fight is also held behind closed doors, as Ip Man does not wish to embarrass his opponent or harm the latter's public reputation. The other parts of the plot depict that during the Japanese occupation of China, Ip Man is brave enough to stand against the oppressors by teaching Wing Chun to the locals and encouraging them to unite and help each other. Yen's impersonation of Ip Man signifies an "ideal" set of Confucian virtues with which most Chinese people are eager to associate.

This second amateur video problematizes Donnie Yen's martial arts image by repositioning his persona in a digitally visual setting. Throughout the second video, Yen's Jedi knight personality is merely presented as the form of a collectible figure, by virtue of the star existence bound to codes that operate in the logic of digital production (fig. 3.2). We do not even have a glimpse of the real face of the actor. Yen appears closer to the category of digital stars, like Lara Croft in the computer game series *Tomb Raider*, than to that of real actors. Neither static in time and space nor fixed in the diegetic context, Yen shares the qualities of the computer-generated personalities, such as the ones in video games, and becomes a specific mode of (dis)embodiment. In the past, one could

FIG. 3.2 The digital figure of Donnie Yen's Jedi knight battles with a group of *Star Wars* troopers, alluding to the "Ip Man" personality confronting ten karatekas.

hardly imagine Yen as associated with such a degree of artificiality, especially in regard to seeing him fight. Now the video maker replaces the performer's authentic presence with a virtual presence, transiting to the virtual star system, which is a relatively new star system as compared to the film history's star discourse.[56] The video's reconfiguration of Yen has further unsettled the potency of the martial arts body. Put another way, the lack of human presence of the digitally coded persona in the amateur video becomes an additional or alternative dimension of how one can approach and configure Yen.

Conclusion: Converging Media, Diverging Personae

Through the instance of Donnie Yen, this chapter has analyzed transnational Chinese stardom in the transnational, digital context as a co-creative upshot of professional and amateur initiatives. As I have argued, while Yen's star appeal principally anchors on his Chinese image that stresses his martial prowess and acrobatic dexterity, amateur video makers unsettle such image in innovative manners. Amateurs can fuse elements from various generic systems, such as sci-fi and martial arts, that lead to a new representation of Yen's personality. The first video is one such example. Users can also alter the coded persona of Yen by refashioning him as a digitalized figure rather than a human figure, the outcome of which is a total synthesis like that seen in computer games. The second video provides an illustration of this idea. The manifestation is a mutating, diverging imaginary that cannot be encapsulated within well-delineated cultural and industrial boundaries. In this manner, this chapter reveals how untrained or partly trained video makers open up novel aspects of star-making through co-creative effort inhabiting a culture of media convergence. It also articulates the ever capricious and fluid relations between different players in the capricious media environment.

Notes

Portions of this chapter appeared in "Donnie Yen's Star Persona in Amateur-produced Videos on YouTube." *Transformative Works and Cultures* no. 28, September 15, 2018. DOI: https://doi.org/10.3983/twc.2018.1329.

1   Nancy Tartaglione, "'Rogue One' Blasts Past $1B At Global Box Office; 'Moana' Sails To $500M+," Deadline | Hollywood, last modified January 24, 2017, https://deadline.com/2017/01/rogue-one-star-wars- crosses-1-billion-disney-moan a-500-million-worldwide-box-office-1201891739/.
2   Edmond Lee, "Hong Kong Action Star Donnie Yen on How He Changed *Rogue One: A Star Wars Story*," *South China Morning Post*, last modified December 13, 2016, http:www.scmp.com/culture/film-tv/article/2054237/hong-kong-action-star -donnie-yen-playing-blind-warrior-rogue-one.
3   Star Wars, "Poll: Who Is Your Favorite Rogue One Character," StarWars.com, last modified May 18, 2017, https://www.starwars.com/news/who-is-your-favorite -character-in-rogue-oneem.
4   Lee, "Hong Kong Action Star."
5   Brian Truitt, "Donnie Yen Is the 'Man' in Hong Kong Action Scene," *USA Today*, last modified January 28, 2016, http:www.usatoday.com/story/life/movies/2016 /01/18/donnie-yen-ip-man-crouching-tiger-star-wars/78860818/.
6   Joseph Baxter, "Star Wars: Episode 8 Wants to Cast Hong Kong Action Star as a Jedi," CinemaBlend, last modified April 2015, https://www.cinemablend.com /news/593789/Star-Wars-Episode-8-Wants-Cast-Hong-Kong-Action-Star-Jedi.
7   Lee, "Hong Kong Action Star."
8   "Geek Culture," last modified January 31, 2019, https://geekculture.co/.
9   Zhang Yingjin, "Transnationalism and Translocality of Chinese Cinema," *Cinema Journal* 49, no. 3 (2010): 136.
10 Zhang Yimou's three films, *Hero* (2004), *House of Flying Daggers*, and *Curse of the Golden Flowers*, respectively garnered $177,394,432, $92,863,945, and $78,568,977 worldwide (Box Office Mojo). The global box office revenue of Feng Xiaogang's *The Banquet* was $22,598,772 (imdb.com). John Woo's *Red Cliff* globally grossed $2,545,912 worldwide (Box Office Mojo), while Jiang Wen's *Let the Bullet Fly* grossed $104,336,887 (Box Office Mojo).
11 Vivian Lee, "Introduction: Mapping East Asia's Cinemascape,' in *East Asian Cinemas: Regional Flows and Global Transformation*, ed. Vivian Lee (New York: Palgrave Macmillan, 2011), 1.
12 Mary Farquhar and Yinjing Zhang, eds. *Chinese Film Stars* (New York: Rout- ledge, 2010).
13 Wing-Fai Leung and Andy Willis, eds. *East Asian Film Stars* (New York: Palgrave Macmillan, 2014).
14 Russell Meeuf and Raphael Raphael, eds. *Transnational Stardom: International Celebrity in Film and Popular Culture* (New York: Palgrave Macmillan, 2013).

15 Julian Stringer, "Talking about Li: Transnational Chinese Movie Stardom and Asian American Internet Reception," in *Political Communications in Greater China: The Construction and Reflection of Identity*, ed. Gary Rawnsley and Ming-Yeh Rawnsley (London: Routledge Curzon, 2003), 275–290.

16 Sabrina Yu, *Jet Li: Chinese Masculinity and Transnational Film Stardom* (Edinburgh: Edinburgh University Press, 2012).

17 Dorothy Lau, "The Flickering of Jackie Chan: Transnational Chinese Film Stardom, Web 2.0, and the Signification of Performance," *International Journal of the Humanities* 8, no. 2 (2010): 11–22.

18 Dorothy Lau, "'Friending' Jet Li on Facebook: The Chinese Celebrity Persona in Online Social Network," *Journal of Asian Cinema* 26, no. 2 (2016): 169–192.

19 Stringer, "Talking about Li," 275–290.

20 Yu, *Jet Li*, 167–184.

21 Dorothy Lau, "Actor or Ambassador? The Star Persona of Jackie Chan in Social Media," *Continuum: Journal of Media & Cultural Studies* 30, no. 2 (2014): 1–17.

22 Dorothy Lau, "'Friending' Jet Li on Facebook."

23 Dorothy Lau, "Rearticulating Bruce Lee and His 'Hip-Hop Fury' in Fan Made Videos," in *Lasting Screen Stars: Personas That Endure and Images That Fade*, ed. Lucy Bolton and Julie Lobalzo Wright (London: Palgrave Macmillan, 2016), 291–303.

24 Kai Khiun Liew, "Rewind and Recollect: Activating Dormant Memories and Politics in Teresa Teng's Music Videos Uploaded on YouTube," *International Journal of Cultural Studies* 17, no. 5 (2014): 505.

25 Patricia Zimmermann, "An Amateurized Media Universe." Review of *Amateur Media: Social, Cultural, and Legal Perspectives*, ed. Dan Hunter, Ramon Lobato, Megan Richardson, and Julian Thomas, *Jump Cut*, no. 55 (Fall 2013). https://www.ejumpcut.org/archive/jc55.2013/zimmermanAmateur/text.html.

26 The most recent screen reprisal of the persona of Bruce Lee, impersonated by Mike Moh, is found in Quentin Tarantino's latest film, *Once Upon a Time in Hollywood* (2019). Tarantino uses real celebrities to propel the storyline about two fictional characters played by Brad Pitt and Leonardo DiCaprio. The cinematic "mashup" provokes an array of controversies across sundry media outlets. Discontent of many Bruce Lee fans, including Lee's daughter, points to the racially stereotypical portrayal of Moh's Lee, ranging from his instrumental role as a comedy punchline to his incompetence of conquering Pitt's Cliff Booth in a street fight.

27 Marjorie Garber, *Academic Instincts* (Princeton, NJ: Princeton University Press, 2001).

28 Jean Burgess, "YouTube and the Formalization of Amateur Media," in *Amateur Media: Social, Cultural and Legal Perspectives*, ed. Dan Hunter, Ramon Lobato, Megan Richardson, and Julian Thomas (New York: Routledge, 2013), 53–58.

29 Ibid., 54.

30 Jean Burgess and Joshua Green, "The Entrepreneurial Vlogger: Participatory Culture beyond the Professional-Amateur Divide," in *The YouTube Reader*, ed. Pelle Snickars and Patrick Vonderau (Stockholm: National Library of Sweden, 2009), 89–107.

31 Ibid., 90.

32 Ibid., 92–93.

33 Ibid., 91.

34 Lin Xu. "Top 100 Chinese Celebrities, 2011," China.org.cn, last modified June 23, 2011, http://www.china.org.cn/top10/2011-06/23/content_22845446_5.htm.

35 Lisa Funnell, "Hong Kong's It/Ip Man: The Chinese Contexts of Donnie Yen's Transnational Stardom," in *Transnational Stardom: International Celebrity in Film and Popular Culture,* ed. Russell Meeuf and Raphael Raphael (New York: Palgrave Macmillan, 2013), 119.

36 "Pro-am" is a contraction of professional–amateur that refers to an activity in which professionals and amateurs collaborate. Synonymous terms, chiefly used in the socioeconomic arena, are "amateur professionalism" or "semiprofessional." I borrow the trope "pro-am" in positioning the media, with a fundamental reliance on user-generated creativity, that are operated by the users who reside outside the industries but adopt the professionally produced materials in their creative endeavors. Jean Burgess. "YouTube and the Formalization of Amateur Media," 53.

37 Generation Tech, "Donnie Yen in *Rogue One* | Generation Tech," YouTube, December 29, 2015, https://www.youtube.com/watch?v=5WeLL5Ob_Mo.

38 Gary D. Rawnsley and Ming-Yeh T. Rawnsley, "Introduction," in *Global Chinese Cinema: The Culture and Politics of "Hero,"* ed. Gary D. Rawnsley and Ming-Yeh T. Rawnsley (London: Routledge Curzon, 2010), 4.

39 "Hero with Jet Li # Donnie Yen," Martial Arts + Action Movies, accessed April 1, 2019, https://martialartsactionmovies.com/hero-with-jet-li-donnie-yen/.

40 Gina Marchetti, "Does the Karate Kid Have a Kung Fu Dream? Hong Kong Martial Arts between Hollywood and Beijing." *JOMEC Journal* 5 (2014): 2.

41 "Miraluka," Star Wars: The Old Republic Wiki, accessed March 31, 2019, http://swtor.wikia.com/wiki/Miraluka.

42 Mary Flanagan, "Mobile Identities, Digital Stars and Post-cinematic Selves," *Wide Angle* 21, no. 1 (1999): 77.

43 Funnell, "Hong Kong's It/Ip Man," 119.

44 Flanagan, "Mobile Identities," 82.

45 Generation Tech (@generationtechofficial), "About," Facebook, accessed December 15, 2018, https://www.facebook.com/pg/generationtechofficial/about/?ref=page_internal.

46 Paul Willemen, *Looks and Frictions: Essays in Cultural Studies and Film Theory* (Bloomington: Indiana University Press, 1994), 236–237.

47 Ibid., 237.

48 Ibid., 237.

49 Ibid., 237.

50 Kathy Bowrey, "The Manufacture of Authentic Buzz," in *Amateur Media: Social, Cultural and Legal Perspectives,* ed. Dan Hunter, Ramon Lobato, Megan Richardson, and Julian Thomas (New York: Routledge, 2013), 88.

51 Ibid., 89.

52 counter656, "Star Wars Stop motion—Donnie Yen VS Storm Troopers," YouTube, December 16, 2016, https://www.youtube.com/watch?v=u4oy1o15f4Q.

53 Wing Chun is a form of Chinese martial arts that spawned in the nineteenth century and was popularized in southern China. As a form of self-defense, Wing Chun requires quick arm movements and strong legs to defeat opponents. Ip Man, a real-life figure who was also an iconic practitioner of Wing Chun, was the first one to teach this form of martial arts in Hong Kong. Originated in Japan, karate is a fighting system developed since the early twentieth century. It relies on the use of punching, kicking, knee strikes, elbow strikes, and open-hand techniques. Both

Wing Chun and karate earned mass popularity as "Oriental" martial arts in the Anglo-American world partly due to the import of martial arts movies to the West in the 1970s. Gary Krug, "The Feet of the Master: Three Stages in the Appropriation of Okinawa Karate into Anglo-American Culture," *Critical Studies: Critical Methodologies* 1, no. 4 (2001): 401–403.

54 The historical figure of Wong Fei-hung has been portrayed in over a hundred films and television dramas since 1949, mostly produced in Hong Kong. Hong Kong actor, Kwan Tak-hing, was the actor most frequently cast for the role in over seventy films from the 1940s to the 1980s, while contemporary Chinese performers, including Jet Li and Vincent Zhao, have had their own versions of the figure's personification in recent years.

55 Kit Yan Seto, "Fighting Fit," The Star Online, April 23, 2010, http:ecentral.my/news/story.asp?file=/2010/4/23/movies/6112482&sec=movies.

56 Flanagan, "Mobile Identities," 78.

Bibliography

"About Wing Chun Kung Fu." Wing Chun Concepts. Accessed March 20, 2019. http://www.wingchunconcepts.com/about.php.

Baxter, Joseph. "Star Wars: Episode 8 Wants to Cast Hong Kong Action Star as a Jedi." CinemaBlend. Last modified April 2015. https://www.cinemablend.com/news/593789/Star-Wars-Episode-8-Wants-Cast-Hong-Kong-Action-Star-Jedi.

Bowrey, Kathy. "The Manufacture of Authentic Buzz." In *Amateur Media: Social, Cultural and Legal Perspectives*, edited by Dan Hunter, Ramon Lobato, Megan Richardson, and Julian Thomas, 73–93. New York: Routledge, 2013.

Burgess, Jean. "YouTube and the Formalization of Amateur Media." In *Amateur Media: Social, Cultural and Legal Perspectives*, edited by Dan Hunter, Ramon Lobato, Megan Richardson, and Julian Thomas, 53–58. New York: Routledge, 2013.

Burgess, Jean, and Joshua Green. "The Entrepreneurial Vlogger: Participatory Culture beyond the Professional-Amateur Divide." In *The YouTube Reader*, edited by Pelle Snickars and Patrick Vonderau, 89–107. Stockholm: National Library of Sweden, 2009.

counter656, "Star Wars Stop Motion—Donnie Yen VS Storm Troopers." YouTube, December 16, 2016. https://www.youtube.com/watch?v=u4oyi015f4Q.

Farquhar, Mary, and Yinjing Zhang, eds. *Chinese Film Stars*. New York: Routledge, 2010.

Flanagan, Mary. "Mobile Identities, Digital Stars and Post-cinematic Selves." *Wide Angle* 21, no. 1 (1999): 76–93.

Funnell, Lisa. "Hong Kong's It/Ip Man: The Chinese Contexts of Donnie Yen's Transnational Stardom." In *Transnational Stardom: International Celebrity in Film and Popular Culture*, edited by Russell Meeuf and Raphael Raphael, 117–138. New York: Palgrave Macmillan, 2013.

Garber, Marjorie. *Academic Instincts*. Princeton, NJ: Princeton University Press, 2001.

"Geek Culture." Last modified January 31, 2019. https://geekculture.co/.

Generation Tech (@generationtechofficial). Facebook. Accessed March 2, 2019. https://www.facebook.com/pg/generationtechofficial/about/?ref=page_internal.

————. "Donnie Yen in *Rogue One* | Generation Tech." YouTube. December 29, 2015. Video, 2:59. https://www.youtube.com/watch?v=5WeLL5Ob_M0.

"Hero with Jet Li # Donnie Yen." Martial Arts + Action Movies. Accessed April 1, 2019. https://martialartsactionmovies.com/hero-with-jet-li-donnie-yen/.

Khoo, Olivia. "Fifteen Minutes of Fame: Transient/Transnational Female Stardom in *Hero*." In *Global Chinese Cinema: The Culture and Politics of "Hero,"* edited by G. Rawnsley and M. T. Rawnsley, 121–131. New York: Routledge, 2010.

Krug, Gary. "The Feet of the Master: Three Stages in the Appropriation of Okinawa Karate into Anglo-American Culture." *Critical Studies: Critical Methodologies* 1, no. 4 (2001): 395–410.

Lau, Dorothy. "Actor or Ambassador? The Star Persona of Jackie Chan in Social Media." *Continuum: Journal of Media & Cultural Studies* 30, no. 2 (2014): 1–17.

————. "The Flickering of Jackie Chan: Transnational Chinese Film Stardom, Web 2.0, and the Signification of Performance." *International Journal of the Humanities* 8, no. 2 (2010): 11–22.

————. "'Friending' Jet Li on Facebook: The Chinese Celebrity Persona in Online Social Network." *Journal of Asian Cinema* 26, no. 2 (2016): 169–192.

————. "Rearticulating Bruce Lee and His 'Hip-Hop Fury' in Fan Made Videos." In *Lasting Screen Stars: Personas That Endure and Images That Fade*, edited by Lucy Bolton and Julie Lobalzo Wright, 291–303. London: Palgrave Macmillan, 2016.

Lee, Edmond. "Hong Kong Action Star Donnie Yen on How He Changed *Rogue One: A Star Wars Story*." *South China Morning Post*. Last modified December 13, 2016. http:www.scmp.com/culture/film-tv/article/2054237/hong-kong-action-star -donnie-yen-playing-blind-warrior-rogue-one.

Lee, Vivian. "Introduction: Mapping East Asia's Cinemascape." In *East Asian Cinemas: Regional Flows and Global Transformation*, edited by Vivian Lee, 1–12. New York: Palgrave Macmillan, 2011.

Leung, Wing-Fai, and Andy Willis, eds. *East Asian Film Stars*. New York: Palgrave Macmillan, 2014.

Liew, Kai Khiun. "Rewind and Recollect: Activating Dormant Memories and Politics in Teresa Teng's Music Videos Uploaded on YouTube." *International Journal of Cultural Studies* 17, no. 5 (2014): 503–515.

Marchetti, Gina. "Does the Karate Kid Have a Kung Fu Dream? Hong Kong Martial Arts between Hollywood and Beijing." *JOMEC Journal* 5 (2014): 1–20.

Meeuf, Russell, and Raphael Raphael, eds. *Transnational Stardom: International Celebrity in Film and Popular Culture*. New York: Palgrave Macmillan, 2013.

"Miraluka." Star Wars: The Old Republic Wiki. Accessed March 31, 2019. http://swtor .wikia.com/wiki/Miraluka.

"Poll: Who Is Your Favorite *Rogue One* Character." StarWars.com. Last modified May 18, 2017. https://www.starwars.com/news/who-is-your-favorite-character-in -rogue-oneem.

Rawnsley, Gary D., and Ming-Yeh T. Rawnsley. "Introduction." In *Global Chinese Cinema: The Culture and Politics of "Hero,"* edited by Gary D. Rawnsley and Ming-Yeh T. Rawnsley, 1–18. London: Routledge Curzon, 2010.

Richardson, Megan, and Jake Goldenfein. "Competing Myths of Informal Economies." In *Amateur Media: Social, Cultural and Legal Perspectives*, edited by Dan Hunter, Ramon Lobato, Megan Richardson, and Julian Thomas, 18–26. New York: Routledge, 2013.

Seto, Kit Yan. "Fighting Fit." The Star Online. Last modified April 23, 2010. http:ecentral.my/news/story.asp?file=/2010/4/23/movies/6112482&sec=movies.

Stormtrooperlarry. "Exclusive: The Latest on *Rogue One.* Actor Donnie Yen." Stormtrooper Larry. Last modified June 20, 2016. https:stormtrooperlarry.com /2016/06/20/exclusive-the-latest-on-rogue-one-actor-donnie-yen/.

Stringer, Julian. "Talking about Li: Transnational Chinese Movie Stardom and Asian American Internet Reception." In *Political Communications in Greater China: The Construction and Reflection of Identity*, edited by Gary Rawnsley and Ming-Yeh Rawnsley, 275–290. London: Routledge Curzon, 2003.

Tartaglione, Nancy. "'Rogue One' Blasts Past $1B at Global Box Office; 'Moana' Sails To $500M+." Deadline | Hollywood. Last modified January 24, 2017. https:// deadline.com/2017/01/rogue-one-star-wars-crosses-1-billion-disney-moana-500-mi llion-worldwide-box-office-1201891739/.

Truitt, Brian. "Donnie Yen Is the 'Man' in Hong Kong Action Scene." *USA Today.* Last modified January 28, 2016. http:www.usatoday.com/story/life/movies/2016 /01/18/donnie-yen-ip-man-crouching-tiger-star-wars/78860818/.

Willemen, Paul. *Looks and Frictions: Essays in Cultural Studies and Film Theory.* Bloomington: Indiana University Press, 1994.

Xu, Lin. "Top 100 Chinese Celebrities, 2011." China.org.cn. Last modified June 23, 2011. http://www.china.org.cn/top10/2011-06/23/content_22845446_5.htm.

Yu, Sabrina. *Jet Li: Chinese Masculinity and Transnational Film Stardom.* Edinburgh: Edinburgh University Press, 2012.

Zhang, Yingjin. "Transnationalism and Translocality of Chinese Cinema." *Cinema Journal* 49, no. 3 (2010): 135–139.

Zimmermann, Patricia. "An Amateurized Media Universe." Review of *Amateur Media: Social, Cultural, and Legal Perspectives*, edited by Dan Hunter, Ramon Lobato, Megan Richardson, and Julian Thomas. *Jump Cut*, no. 55 (Fall 2013), https://www.ejumpcut.org/archive/jc55.2013/zimmermanAmateur/text.html.

4

Screen to Screen

■■■■■■■■■■■■■■■■■■■■■■■■■■

Adaptation and Transnational
Circulation of Chinese (Web)
Novels for Television

W. MICHELLE WANG

This chapter examines the technological impact of media culture in Asia by discussing the dominant practice of adapting online fiction for Chinese television and the transnational circulation of such television serials. I begin by explaining how contemporary Chinese narratives "travel"[1] across mediums, languages, and geographical borders, attending to issues of circulation, exportability, and distribution. Using the televisual adaptation of Chinese web novelist Dingmo's *When a Snail Falls in Love* (2016) as my case study, I examine dimensions of intermediality, interactivity, and intertextuality to address adaptation strategies that relate to meaning-making, rendering subjectivity, narrative pertinence, and storyworld extendability.[2] In doing so, I outline how the digital age has shaped the circulation of Chinese culture, even as it mediates the formation and fostering of Chinese diasporic identities. My essay offers an alternate paradigm for thinking about media culture in transnational Asia—one that takes into account the fact that diasporas are heterogeneous rather than homogeneous groups, whose complex engagements with popular culture are mediated by more than ethnic identification.

Situating China's Media Industry amid East Asian Pop Culture Flows

Chris Berry and Mary Farquhar note that the term "transnational" is loosely used "to refer to phenomena that exceed the boundaries of any single national territory."[3] While some theorists treat transnational phenomena "as products of the globalizing process," others, such as Ulf Hannerz and Prasenjit Duara, "oppose the rhetoric of universality and homogenization implied in the term globalization," suggesting that transnational phenomena "need to be specified in terms of the particular places and time in which they operate, the particular people they affect, and the particular ways they are constituted and maintained."[4] One productive way scholars have approached the study of transnationalism in Asia is to examine how "popular cultural products have criss-crossed the national borders of East Asian countries"[5] since the 1920s,[6] between major urban centers, such as Hong Kong, Shanghai, Singapore, Seoul, Taipei, and Tokyo.

As compared to film and music, television dramas are "the most regionally-distributed and circulated product"[7] in East and Southeast Asia, which "'de-center' the relatively unified cultural authority once enjoyed by national television systems."[8] In fact, Sylvia Van Ziegert argues that "it is precisely the commodification of Chinese culture which helps it to circulate throughout diasporic spaces,"[9] since China's television exports are generally "targeted at the overseas Chinese communities, especially in Asian regions."[10] The "imaginary coherence" of these diasporic Chinese communities—now connected by digital and satellite media—is embedded within what Beng Huat Chua terms the larger, "rather long standing project" of constructing a "relatively imaginable" (though by no means culturally homogeneous) "East Asian identity."[11]

Beijing Normal University professor Xing Zhou notes that the 1990s were considered a "golden age of Chinese TV dramas in Southeast Asia,"[12] but by the turn of the millennium, statistics from Mainland China's State Administration of Radio, Film and Television indicate a "lackluster export market": in contrast to more than 70,000 hours of imported television programs in 2005, "China exported only an egregiously disproportionate 6,680 hours of programs" that same year.[13] Several interrelated issues contribute to such feeble transnational circulation: "deeply inscribed and haunted by the history of communist revolution and by authoritarianism,"[14] Michael Keane notes that ideological restrictions "on the thematic content of TV drama" in Mainland China "have led to a glut of dramas" featuring flat or stereotypical characters "molded from the clay of socialist realism."[15] Chua observes that these "ideology/pedagogy-heavy dramas became tiresome over time and eventually did not even attract China's domestic audience, let alone transnational ones."[16]

In comparison, Carstens found that "the strikingly apolitical nature of Chinese popular culture that emerged in Hong Kong's flourishing media industry from the 1970s to the 1990s" likely accounts "for the transnational appeal of Hong Kong productions"—particularly among Chinese diasporas (like Malaysian Chinese) who live in countries with national policies that foster "the separation of cultural and national identities," such that "the apolitical hybrid cultural imaginaries of Hong Kong Chinese productions speak more clearly to local Chinese experience."[17] Though Hong Kong and Taiwanese productions dominated the Chinese-language markets well into the twenty-first century,[18] I argue that Mainland China's television production has eclipsed these earlier centers of Chinese-language pop culture production, with drama serials now being picked up by international streaming services (including Netflix).

Exports of Chinese television dramas amounted to US$80 million (approximately 560 million yuan)[19] in 2016, as compared to US$6.5 million just twelve years earlier[20]—a rapid acceleration propelled not only by China's growing economic influence around the world but also by their sustained investment in television programming. A recent study by IHS (Information Handling Services) Markit notes that China overtook the United Kingdom "to become the second-largest TV programming market in the world after the US" in 2017, reporting US$10.9 billion in television programming expenditure.[21] This "content creation spree" has led analysts to project that by the year 2022, China will invest an estimated 224 billion yuan (US$33 billion) in television programming.[22] I contend that this increased investment in content creation corresponds to an increasing sophistication in China's television productions, which has in recent years been crucially tied to the rising popularity and adaptations of Chinese web novels.

Though online fiction is a relatively recent form of media that emerged only in the late 1990s, its roots date back to the late nineteenth century[23] in the familiar form of serialized fiction—whereby installments of a longer narrative are published in regular intervals via a medium that can be economically and extensively circulated. In China, this medium is now the World Wide Web; with an online literature market that has grown by more than 20 percent annually since 2013, Adam Minter notes that both hobbyists and professional writers circulate their work on platforms such as qidian.com and jjwxc.net.[24] By 2016, 333 million people (more than 40 percent of China's internet user base[25] or one in four Chinese nationals[26]) were reading online fiction, and the industry generated US$1.3 billion in revenue—a figure that almost doubled to US$2.5 billion in 2017.[27] However, a May 2018 article in the *South China Morning Post* points out that though "[o]nline publishing platforms were once hailed for their innovative business models," websites are now "flooded with lowbrow fare and potboilers," given web novels' "pay-by-word model."[28]

The model can be a double-edged sword in that while online Chinese fiction offers attractive flexibility in allowing readers to pay only for material that engages their interest and to enjoy a wide range of offerings at very little cost, authors correspondingly tend "to develop long-winded narratives"[29] in order for web writing to become a viable source of income; the web novel's narrative qualities are thus partly shaped by the medium's economic model. Online Chinese writers typically make substantial earnings only from "a successful novel's adaptation rights,"[30] giving rise to what is popularly termed the "IP" (intellectual property) phenomenon in China—which refers to "original copyrighted material" produced by web novelists "that can be bought and adapted for other formats."[31] The term "IP" thus serves as a shorthand reference for the work's intermediality: specifically, its potential for adaptation into varying mediums and other franchising possibilities. *China Finance Online* reported that in 2016, 15 of 20 most watched Chinese television serials, 14 of 20 most viewed web serials, 13 of 20 highest grossing Chinese films, 15 of 20 most downloaded games, and 16 of 20 most watched Chinese animations were all IP adaptations of Chinese web novels.[32] This IP trend carries through to 2017, where half (including the top four) of ten most highly viewed Chinese television serials online were IP adaptations,[33] while the 2018 adaptation based on Ane's award-winning web novel *Like a Flowing River* clinched multiple honors, including China's prestigious Magnolia Award for best television series.[34]

IP adaptations also export well: for example, the fifty-four-episode Chinese period drama based on Haiyan's *Nirvana in Fire* (2015) has aired in Singapore, Malaysia, Japan, South Korea, Australia, Canada, and the United States, while the forty-two-episode contemporary series based on Ane's *Ode to Joy* (2016) received more than 200 million views on YouTube[35] and has been broadcast in countries including Sri Lanka, Cambodia, Vietnam, and Russia. Producer Hongliang Hou notes that while it used to be necessary for Chinese producers to travel abroad in order to negotiate television deals, foreign companies are now proactively "contacting us to buy series like *Nirvana in Fire* and *The Disguiser*," suggesting that "Chinese titles are gaining influence in overseas markets."[36] Though Chinese television dramas are also distributed in traditional offline formats, such as DVDs, viewers are increasingly accessing such content through online video streaming.

Licensed online platforms (including YouTube) are typically locked in continual technological tugs-of-war with users, given streaming sites' adoption of geoblocking technology—restricting content access based on a user's geographical location—which some viewers then circumvent using a virtual private network. Apart from technological access, viewers may prefer some platforms to others based on reasons relating to immediacy and linguistic access: for instance, the first episode of *When a Snail Falls in Love* was broadcast on

Shanghai Dragon Television at 10 P.M. on October 24, 2016, and made available (with only Chinese subtitles) two hours later on YouTube[37] and China's Tencent Video. *Snail* was released on Netflix in select countries with English subtitles almost ten months later in August 2017, but was available in select regions (due to geoblocking) on the video-streaming website Viki shortly after its initial broadcast in China. It is now fully subtitled in twelve languages, including Croatian, Greek, Portuguese, Romanian, and Spanish.

I contend that issues of technological and linguistic access not only influence distribution but also shape audiences' potential degrees of interactivity with IP works in important ways. Adapting Linda Hutcheon's distinction between "knowing and unknowing audiences"[38] on a continuum, I suggest that where IP drama viewers fall on this spectrum is mediated by language, medium, and technological proficiencies. "Unknowing audiences" include those who are unaware of, unwilling to, or unable to experience the work's "palimpsestic doubleness"[39] due to lack of linguistic access or knowledge of the web novel, or indifference to the television serial's adaptational status. Further along the continuum are those who read Chinese web novels in translation: a *Metro Beijing* article notes that "China's online literature has seen major growth in overseas popularity"[40] as a result of the increasing number of online forums devoted to translating Chinese web novels into English—many of which in turn learn of these novels through their televisual adaptations. Beijing Foreign Studies University professor Mingxing He observes, "What is unique about the internationalization of China's online literature is that armies of online volunteer translators and crowdfunding sponsors propel it."[41] For instance, wuxiaworld.com—which logged "nearly 3 million [daily] page views" in 2016, with more than 200,000 users in "over 150 countries"—has translators who are Chinese citizens, Chinese diasporas living in the United States, Canada, and Singapore (among other countries), as well as individuals who have studied the language for years.[42]

The spectrum of *Snail*'s knowing audience thus includes viewers who have read the novel in translation, in print, and online—many of whom are likely Dingmo fans who are familiar with the author's oeuvre. While knowing audiences are able to appreciate "adaptations *as adaptations*,"[43] it is crucial to note that knowingness is not necessarily privileged (or even desired), given its potential for interfering with viewers' experience of the work. Hutcheon notes that "knowing audiences have expectations—and demands"; in fact, the "more popular and beloved the novel, the more likely the discontent" and "negative fan reaction,"[44] since we tend to cognitively simulate such novels in powerfully vivid (and sometimes highly idiosyncratic) ways. Production teams often have "greater freedom [and] control" in shaping the adaptation for unknowing audiences, who tend to be less "burdened with affection or nostalgia for the adapted text."[45] Hutcheon argues that for "an adaptation to be successful in its own right, it must be so for both knowing and unknowing audiences."[46]

In the case of Chinese IP dramas, "knowingness" encompasses not only knowledge of and linguistic/technological access to the web novel, to paratextual material such as interviews and behind-the-scenes footage, to "intertextual knowledge"[47] of other works by the same novelist/actors/director/production team, but also to a tacit awareness of how China's censorship guidelines shape viewers' expectations of "narrative permissibility" (non-/sanctioned types of stories and ways of telling them),[48] and understanding of genre conventions and "expectation shifts"[49] facilitated by medium changes. Hutcheon notes that viewers can learn to become "knowing audiences in terms of medium"[50] when we become aware of how medium markers (such as cinematic conventions of using long panning shots or televisual conventions of featuring moments of high narrativity) shape our understanding of the adaptation, and to correspondingly consider how and for what purposes productions defy such conventions—an issue to which I now turn.

Intermediality and Narrative Progression

My use of the term "intermediality" (which encompasses adaptation) takes its cue from Lars Elleström, broadly referring to approaches that highlight media similarities and differences in relation to "their constitutive role for meaning-making within communication."[51] Drawing on James Phelan's rhetorical model of narrative progression, I explain how *When a Snail Falls in Love*'s adaptational revisions better motivate narrative cohesion, even as they shift emphasis from the web novel's elements of romance to refocus on the stakes and social dynamics of police work. By attending to the adaptation's reconfigured "instabilities" ("unstable situations within, between, or among the characters") and "tensions" ("unstable relations among authors, narrators, audiences"),[52] I explicate how viewers' sense of *Snail*'s thematic pertinence is shaped by the revised narrative progression. I further address adaptational shifts in conveying subjectivity, pushing back against popularly held assumptions that the screen is more limited than prose for rendering consciousness—which in turn relates to "the larger and much-debated issue of the ability of different media to present inner and outer worlds, subjectivity and materiality."[53]

A central challenge IP productions face in maintaining audience engagement (particularly for the police procedural, as is the case with *Snail*) relates to knowing audiences' familiarity with plot trajectory—with many others who can and do join this segment of the audience as the serial is on air, given the ease of accessibility to the novels on the internet. Production teams partly address this challenge by adjusting textual dynamics to maneuver elements of surprise, even as they maintain varying degrees of fidelity to the web novel. While adaptations' reconfiguration of instabilities can ameliorate uneven knowledge gaps between different segments of the audience, they also risk readerly ire in their challenges to textual fidelity. Another way of balancing audience engagement with adaptational fidelity is to partly shift the narrative load from the *what* to the *how*, in the serial's management of "narrative progression"—which Phelan defines as a synthesis of both textual and readerly/viewerly dynamics, and the way such dynamics shape audiences' interpretive, ethical, and aesthetic judgments about events, characters, and their telling.[54] For IP adaptations, such "aesthetic judgments about the artistic quality of the narrative and of its parts"[55] also include knowing audiences' sense of how effectively the narrative has traveled across mediums. I address both segments of the audience in my discussion, using the term "knowing audience" to specify adaptational dimensions that only *Snail*'s readers are likely to discern, and the more general term "viewer" to denote effects of the narrative progression that both knowing and unknowing audiences are able to appreciate.

Snail's move from web novel to television incorporates new instabilities and tensions that address thematic issues, such as the inadequacy of witness protection,[56] dealing with survivors who are re-victimized into the cycle of crime,[57] police officers who struggle with survivor's guilt and posttraumatic stress disorder,[58] officers sacrificed in the line of duty and their loved ones' struggle with loss.[59] The television adaptation thus renews focus on the stakes and difficulties of police work, even as it challenges the lone figure of the super sleuth popularized in media culture by intensifying the initial instability between *Snail*'s protagonists, where police inspector Ji Bai (Wang Kai)[60] reluctantly takes a gifted new trainee Xu Xu (Wang Ziwen) under his wing. Though Xu Xu is compared to Sherlock Holmes[61] given her exceptional gifts in observational analysis, her intuitive approach to police work comes into constant conflict with her mentor, Ji Bai: for instance, when she urgently insists that an apprehended kidnapper Yang Yu (Zhang Xiaoqian) intends to harm his kidnap victim after he has been taken into police custody, Ji Bai calmly but relentlessly asks for the basis of her reasoning, pointing out that the work of criminal investigation proceeds on the basis of evidence.[62]

While the events that characterize their first meeting follow a fairly similar trajectory across both mediums—in which the inexperienced Xu Xu is taken hostage and rescued by Ji Bai after she goes off alone in pursuit of Yang Yu[63]— the stakes of the narrative progression are substantially altered to foreground the social dynamics involved in police work. Though Xu Xu's solo pursuit of Yang Yu (as her more experienced colleagues are busy apprehending his accomplice) demonstrates her professional acumen—thus appearing to justify her independent course of action—it is later revealed that Ji Bai, who is directing the operation, has already tracked Yang and the victim down in collective efforts with other members of the police force; in other words, the operation's sole target was Yang's accomplice. The necessity of Xu Xu's solitary act is thus subverted in the adaptation, given that it magnifies the police operation by aggravating a situation otherwise under control, causing herself to be taken hostage in the process. Crucially, none of this is explicitly articulated but is a realization that both knowing and unknowing audiences are eventually led to as a result of the revised narrative progression: because the resolution of the crisis is delayed, audiences are aligned with Xu Xu's initial position of believing that her insight has allowed her to perceive what her colleagues have neglected—and they subsequently realize, along with her, the consequences of that misjudgment. The adaptation's handling of the progression in this manner, to paraphrase Phelan, confidently relies on the viewers' ability to recognize and revise their judgments of Ji Bai's initial overbearing insistence that Xu Xu produce evidence for her reasoning not as a close-minded hierarchical act but an instance of turning her mistake into a teachable moment.

While Xu Xu's poor physical fitness (another source of instability in her relationship with Ji Bai) remains a factor in her being taken hostage, the adaptation remotivates the point by partly shifting emphasis onto her acting independently of the team. The television serial pushes back against the lone figure of the sleuthing genius by featuring several new dialogues between Ji Bai and Xu Xu, and Ji Bai and Zhao Han (Yu Heng), where Ji bluntly observes that Xu's failure to pass her physical fitness test signals her belief that being a genius exempts her from baseline rules that ordinary police officers are expected to adhere to.[64] Ji Bai's grueling training of Xu Xu becomes an opportunity for their romance to flourish in the web novel, but the adaptation pares back this dimension, remotivating the strenuous training as a necessary part of Xu Xu's evolving professionalism. The final episode's instability is reconfigured such that her training pays off when she eventually comes to Ji Bai's rescue (rather than vice versa, as is the case in the novel), inviting knowing audiences' positive aesthetic judgments in the strengthened cohesion of the narrative's parts in service of the whole.

Snail's elements of romance are significantly reconfigured in the television adaptation, where intimacy is evoked by rendering characters transparent to select individuals; I use the word "transparent" in Lisa Zunshine's sense of the term, to refer to "moments in fictional narratives when characters' body language involuntarily betrays their feelings."[65] For example, Xu Xu is one of the few characters before whom the typically impassive Ji Bai becomes briefly transparent, particularly when Ye Zixi (Zhao Yuanyuan)—Ji Bai's childhood playmate, whom he regards as a younger sister—is brutally murdered. While Zixi's murder remains a main source of instability across both mediums, as opposed to being a stranger-turned-friend whom Xu Xu encounters during her first case in the web novel, the realignment of Zixi's character is an adaptational shift that foregrounds Ji Bai's ethicality as his personal and professional ethics are put to the test when interrogating the murder suspects. (Ji Bai's involvement in the investigation is a point I return to in the next section.) Ji Bai listens impassively as Zixi's lover blandly remarks that she was merely one of his many mistresses,[66] while her cousin abusively labels her a slut and prostitute.[67] In particular, Hu Zhishan (Tan Xihe) taunts Ji Bai with Zixi's dying moments,[68] while Ye Qiao (Wu Xiaoyu) describes pinning her "to the ground with knives like an entomological specimen," in cruel relish of Zixi's final "bloodied struggle."[69]

While some scholars suggest that prose fiction's advantage in portraying "'res cogitans,' the space of the mind,"[70] proves particularly resistant to adaptation, others, like Hutcheon and Robert Stam, point out that multitrack mediums "can both direct and expand the possibilities of perception"[71] in their "calibration of access to characters' knowledge and consciousness"[72] via actor performance, camera angles, and so on. Snail's successful televisual adaptation is due in no small part to the production team's masterful renditions of character subjectivity, particularly in Ji Bai's purposeful inscrutability given the nature of his profession and his personal relation to the murder victim. His calm, incisive manner during the interrogations betray little more than cold aloofness in the frequent close-up shots where his face occupies one-third to half the frame—paradoxically subverting the conventionally held notion that the tight shot offers a greater sense of access to a character's mind. Instead, viewers share in Ji Bai's subjectivity when Xu Xu's directness renders him transparent during their conversations between the interrogation sessions, where Xu's unexpected offer to light his cigarettes as a way of tracking his emotional (rather than physical) health momentarily pierces his veneer of restraint.[73]

Head-on frontal shots of Ji Bai's guarded impassivity in the interrogation room are in stark contrast with the long shots and close-ups in profile during their conversations, where he averts his eyes and looks out into the distance after wordlessly inviting Xu Xu to sit beside him. To paraphrase Zunshine, such moments of access to character consciousness—in which Ji Bai's emotions are strategically obscured in the "attempt to conceal or restrain" his feelings— paradoxically render him "more interestingly transparent" than "freely emoting" characters.[74] Ji Bai's lack of transparency in fact becomes a subject of their conversation, as Xu Xu frankly admits that even given her professional training as a behavioral analyst, she is unable to discern the extent to which Zixi's death has affected him or if Ji Bai simply has "alarming willpower."

JI BAI What does instinct tell you?

XU XU Professionals do not trade in instinct.

JI (after a pause) Xu Xu's instinct.

XU You're in grief. Even pain.

JI Why?

XU Instinct doesn't require qualifications.[75]

Their quiet intimacy in this exchange builds on earlier narrative progressions, in which Ji Bai explicitly instructs Xu Xu not to base police operations on instinct; here, however, his willingness to defer to "Xu Xu's instinct" allows her to render him transparent in his unspoken grief. The adaptation reworks elements of romance in their sharing of vulnerabilities, as Xu Xu goes on to disclose how she developed her expertise as a result of being alienated by her peers as a child—once again foregrounding the adaptation's emphasis on the significance of social dynamics.

A key adaptational revision includes creating an entire backstory for Zhao Han—Ji Bai's best friend and the team's second-in-command—which is in turn linked to *Snail*'s global instability of transnational drug and human trafficking. This backstory is conveyed in a poignant conversation between Ji Bai and Xu Xu, as they await the outcome of Zhao Han's gunshot wound surgery.[76] Neither is particularly demonstrative nor do they discuss their emotional responses to Zhao's shooting, as the unarticulated hangs heavy between them—where viewers have to infer Ji Bai's state of mind, submerged within his quiet narrative of how Zhao Han came to join the police force. Ji Bai relates his attempt to stop Zhao Han from enrolling in the police academy years ago, after Zhao's father (a police officer and Ji's teacher) went missing during a rescue mission; it was Zhao Han's mother who eventually convinced Ji Bai to let him go. Ji Bai's voice cracks slightly as he recounts her remarks, of how his being alone on the force kept her in perpetual anxiety and that if Zhao Han goes along, at least they can look out for one another. Seated alongside him, Xu Xu silently clasps the back of Ji Bai's hand, as the camera's close-up reveals the quiet anguish and the glint of tear in Ji's eyes, before he tightens his grasp around the tips of her fingers, leaning forward to bury his forehead against the back of her hand.

To borrow Phelan's language, the adaptation's handling of the progression demonstrates a high regard for viewers' "cognitive, emotive, and ethical capacities,"[77] as they are engaged in a rapid series of complex narrative judgments in their inference of Ji Bai's subjectivity. On the one hand, viewers' interpretive judgments are emotionally and cognitively shaped by their simulation of Mrs. Zhao—a character briefly referred to but whom viewers never meet—in their admiration of her strength and courage for respecting her son's decision to join the force despite the loss of her husband. Viewers are further emotionally aligned with Mrs. Zhao in her affection for Ji Bai, a character whom we too have come to care for over the course of the series. Ji Bai's early attempts at dissuading his best friend from applying for a job that he himself is committed to, lead viewers to the interpretive judgment of his tender affection for the Zhaos: his desire to keep his teacher's only child out of harm's way given the high-risk nature of police work, and for fear that Mrs. Zhao may lose both her husband and her son in the line of duty—misgivings that are now realized as

Ji Bai waits with Xu Xu for the outcome of Zhao Han's surgery. On the other hand, our inference of Ji Bai's muted sense of professional and personal failure—his sense of responsibility and implicit self-blame as Zhao Han's boss, and of having failed to "look out for one another" as Mrs. Zhao had hoped—reinforces our positive ethical judgments of all three characters.

The heartrending moment further earns viewers' positive aesthetic judgments, as the nuanced moment of heightened intimacy between Ji Bai and Xu Xu is gripping in the actors' chemistry, particularly in Wang Kai's powerfully restrained performance as Ji Bai. Actor Wang Kai observes in an interview that though the adaptation attenuates the novel's elements of romance, the subtlety or restraint that governs how intimacy is conveyed in the television serial elevates the form of expression.[78] By this point in the narrative (about two-thirds of the way into the series), knowing audiences who have read the web novel and are engaged with paratextual material—for instance, interviews posted on the serial's social media platforms such as Weibo—further judge the addition of this moment as a masterful stroke in adaptational revision, given our recognition of the artistic intention in trimming back romance in favor of accentuating thematic elements about the stakes of police work. Such intertextual and interactive engagements are issues to which I now turn.

Interactivity, Intertextuality, and Storyworld Extendability

New modes of interactivity enabled by digital technologies have given rise to what Lawrence Lessig terms a "Read/Write" (as opposed to traditional print technology's "Read/Only") literacy.[79] Within this revised paradigm, readers and viewers "inhabit the intervals between texts and act as the agent of their transformations and adaptations,"[80] whereby media artifacts are not merely treated as "texts or institutions but also social practices" that are "embedded within specific historical conditions of production and reception."[81] For instance, internet fan communities that upload translations/subtitles to drama serials and web novels are one such form of "participatory culture"[82] that has arguably had the greatest impact on the transnational circulation of East Asian pop culture artifacts.

This renewed emphasis on the audience is particularly crucial in refashioning critical inquiry in the study of Chinese popular culture, which Shuyu Kong rightly observes "has overwhelmingly focused on the political discourse and ideological messages of the end products" at the expense of neglecting viewer agency.[83] Such neglect inadvertently results in the tendency of regarding "popular culture exclusively as a site for ideological domination" and treating viewers as passive "cultural dopes" when, in fact, Kong argues it is precisely because Chinese audiences are immersed in heavily censored cultural environments that they are "accustomed to reading between the lines and discerning hidden meanings" in cultural artifacts' "underlying subtexts," reinterpreting and reappropriating these texts within their own realms of experience.[84]

Chinese online literature and social media platforms have emerged in recent years as new sites of writerly audience participation that warrant consideration as to how such participatory cultures intervene in traditional modes of media production and reception. I propose that such interventions can be effectively examined by attending to issues of interactivity, intertextuality, and storyworld extendability in IP adaptations. I first examine Dingmo's authorial comments that bookend each chapter/installment of *Snail* (sometimes in response to messages readers leave on earlier installments of the web novel), explaining how these and other types of intertextual knowledge bear on knowing audiences' reception of its televisual adaptation, before turning my attention to storyworld extendability by tracing character migrations across Dingmo's fictional universe to suggest both the potential and the challenges of such transmedial gestures in IP adaptations' move from web browsing to video screens.

Though some Chinese web novelists actively foster interactivity, others choose not to include comments or decide to pen them separately, clearly delineating the novel from its paratexts: for instance, while Ane occasionally features posts such as "On the rare occasion of writing a foreword,"[85] installments of her web novel *Ode to Joy* do not include authorial comments. Writers who choose to include such paratextual comments do so in order to engage in various types of author–reader communications: for example, Dingmo has used authorial endnotes in *Snail* to point to textual revisions made in response to reader comments (chapter 21); to initiate conversations about defending web novelists' intellectual property rights (chapter 22); to gloss her references to historical criminal cases, such as the serial murders in China's Gansu province (chapter 63);[86] and to shape readerly expectations about textual dynamics in the unfolding of *Snail*'s narrative discourse.

Such interactivity intensified in *Snail*'s transition from text to television, where lively debates were sparked online about the adaptation's attention to minutiae, such as members of the task force handing over their cellphones before a major operation (a detail that turns out to be a point of peripeteia); if stunts such as special forces leaping down a three-story building are realistic; and whether it is appropriate for Ji Bai to be involved in Zixi's murder investigation given his friendship with the victim—questions that a subdivision of China's Dezhou Public Security Bureau proactively engaged with and responded to on its official Weibo account.[87] Chinese IP productions also maintain their online presence by interacting with the author and audience on social media (typically via Weibo),[88] frequently gesturing toward intertextual knowledge that knowing audiences are likely privy to.

In addition to the web novel, Hutcheon points out that other aspects of knowingness should "be considered in theorizing about the product and process of adaptation. If the audience knows that a certain director or actor has made other films of a particular kind, that intertextual knowledge too might well impinge on their interpretation of the adaptation they are watching," which can "make for amusing in-jokes and ironies."[89] Given that *Snail*'s production team has made several other highly successful IP adaptations—including *Ode to Joy* (2016), *Nirvana in Fire* (2015), and *The Disguiser* (2015)—significant overlaps in cast members and viewership facilitate playful intertextual gestures made by the production team and actors on social media platforms. For instance, *Snail*'s Weibo account features a post juxtaposing animated GIF images of explosions in *Nirvana in Fire*, *The Disguiser*, and *Snail*, where actor Wang Kai is featured in three different roles with the wry observation that things get explosive when he is on the scene.[90] Other posts remark on the changed nature of character relations, such as the adversarial relationship between Ji Bai and Hu Zhishan, played by Wang Kai and Tan Xihe, whose characters were on friendly terms in *Nirvana in Fire*,[91] while actors Wang Ziwen and Zhang Xiaoqian banter about how quickly their relationship has changed, from her character's romantic rejection of his in *Ode to Joy*, to his taking hers hostage in *Snail*.[92]

The most striking intertextual resonances, however, are visual rather than paratextual ones, where "*Snail*'s exquisite use of cinematic language"[93] led some viewers "to a sense of déjà vu"[94]: the eventual pursuit of a drug and human trafficking ring to Myanmar in *Snail* drew comparisons to *Operation Mekong* (2016)—a Chinese film that had premiered just weeks earlier, based on the historical 2011 Mekong River massacre led by a Burmese drug lord. The medium's visual immediacy—in *Snail*'s long panning shots of the Mekong, and of Myanmar's lush forests and iconic temples—inadvertently brought the film to mind, instantiating Jason Mittell's observation that once a text enters cultural circulation "in our media-saturated age," "it becomes part of a complex intertextual web"[95] that makes it difficult (if not impossible) to view in isolation, a form of knowingness that has the potential to distract or disrupt our experience of the work.

Snail's casting choices created further visual resonances given Wang Kai and Wang Ziwen's collaboration in *Ode to Joy*, which aired earlier that year, in which they also play a couple with very different personalities from Ji Bai and Xu Xu. Knowing audiences appreciated the actors' skillful handling of their markedly different characterizations,[96] which speaks to the continual "palimpsestic doubleness"[97] with which viewers experience the (tele)visual medium—a quality that can work for or against the production depending on casting chemistry and performers' abilities to navigate their roles. Wang Kai had also earlier been cast in the role of police officer Li Xunran from *Love Me If You Dare* (2015)—another Dingmo web novel of the same genre adapted for television a year earlier by the same production team—whereby the author expressed hopes of casting the actor in *Snail* after seeing him in *Love*, coinciding with the production team's intended choice.[98]

Fictional crossovers also occur, as several Dingmo characters make cameo appearances in her other web novels: for instance, Ji Bai and Xu Xu have been written into special web novel episodes of *Love Me If You Dare* (chapter 71),[99] *Our Glamorous Time* (chapters 41, 67, 72, and 82),[100] and *Memory Lost* (chapter 13)[101]—though the author embeds these extensions of the narrative discourse within her authorial comments rather than building them into the main body of her novels. Storyworlds continue to proliferate in mini-episodes within Dingmo's authorial endnotes not only across texts but even within the same novel: in chapter 38 of *Snail*'s web novel, for example, Dingmo embeds a 600-word extension in her endnote, which rides on the chapter's events to offer a brief proleptic glimpse into Ji Bai and Xu Xu's future together,[102] shaping readerly expectations about the subsequent narrative progression. The extension caused some alarm when readers later learned of Xu Xu's pregnancy in chapter 56 (posted more than two weeks later),[103] as they wondered if the temporal gap meant she opted for an abortion or suffered a miscarriage—concerns that Dingmo responded to in chapter 58's endnote, apologizing for her oversight in the story's temporal logic.[104]

Though readers clearly treat such extensions as integral components of the narrative, it is worth noting that storyworld extendability has not quite taken off in IP adaptations. While all four Dingmo novels were adapted for television relatively recently between 2015 and 2018, none featured the character migrations that connect (thereby extending) the storyworlds—not even *Love* and *Snail*, which were produced and directed by the same team within a year of each other. It is unclear why this is the case, though one possible reason may relate to narrative cohesion: given their independent feature as special/mini-episodes, such storyworld extensions may not be as compellingly interwoven with the rest of the narrative, leading production teams to decide against their inclusion. Another likely reason relates to franchising rights and differences in production quality: for instance, *Snail* and *Memory* were produced by different companies but premiered on the same day, putting them in direct competition for viewership, ratings, and media coverage—with *Snail* being more favorably reviewed on the bases of overall production quality and character actualization[105]—which tends to discourage the collaborations necessary to effect such intertextual gestures.

Conclusion

In addressing these intertextual, interactive, and intermedial dimensions of Chinese web novels' adaptations into television serials, I hope to have demonstrated the stakes and the complexities of "knowingness" entailed in audiences' receptions of IP dramas, which are in turn mediated by language, medium, and technological proficiencies. The transnational appeal of Chinese television dramas bridges reader/viewer/fan communities by fostering Chinese diasporic identifications not in nationalistic terms but by means of a shared linguistic heritage in a digitally connected world—via Chinese diasporas' engagements with reading and translating Chinese web novels, and/or watching and subtitling Chinese television dramas. Putting media and adaptation studies in productive conversation with diaspora studies allows scholars to widen the focus from how diasporas negotiate their plural identities in terms of ethnicity and nationality, to perceive how such engagements are also crucially entangled with issues of linguistic and digital access.

Thomas Leitch observes that the current "scope of adaptation studies remains largely Anglo-American rather than international"[106]—an imbalance I begin to address by attending to the rich complexities that underlie the Chinese IP drama phenomenon, which is but one of many crucial developments in Asia's contemporary media landscape. My essay offers an alternate paradigm for examining media culture in transnational Asia by forgoing a country-based/region-bounded approach in favor of thinking about audiences in terms of narrative engagement, language proficiency, and digital access, which I argue are strong mediating factors in our cross-cultural engagements with and response to popular culture artifacts.

Notes

I gratefully acknowledge the support of Nanyang Technological University for making the research and writing of this chapter possible (NTU Start-Up Grant No. M40823). A shorter version of this chapter was presented at the annual conference of the International Society for the Study of Narrative (2019).

1 Linda Hutcheon, *A Theory of Adaptation* (New York: Routledge, 2013), xviii. I borrow Hutcheon's metaphor in exploring adaptation as a process of "what can happen when stories 'travel'—when an adapted text migrates from its context of creation to the adaptation's context of reception" (xviii).
2 I use "storyworld" in David Herman's sense of the term, to refer to audiences' cognitive and imaginative responses to and projections of fictional worlds, in our fashioning of "mental models of who did what to whom and with whom, when, where, why, and in what fashion." See *Routledge Encyclopedia of Narrative Theory*, ed. David Herman, Manfred Jahn, and Marie-Laure Ryan (London: Routledge, 2005), 570.
3 Chris Berry and Mary Farquhar, *China On Screen: Cinema and Nation* (Hong Kong: Hong Kong University Press, 2006), 4.
4 Ibid.
5 Beng Huat Chua, "Conceptualizing an East Asian Popular Culture," in *The Inter-Asia Cultural Studies Reader*, ed. Kuan-Hsing Chen and Beng Huat Chua (London: Routledge, 2007), 117.

6   Beng Huat Chua, *Structure, Audience and Soft Power in East Asian Pop Culture* (Hong Kong: Hong Kong University Press, 2012), 3.

7   Ibid., 30.

8   John Sinclair, "The De-Centring of Cultural Flows, Audiences and Their Access to Television," *Critical Studies in Television* 4, no. 1 (2009): 26.

9   Sylvia Van Ziegert, *Global Spaces of Chinese Culture: Diasporic Chinese Communities in the United States and Germany* (New York: Routledge, 2006), 10.

10 James F. Scotton and William A. Hachten, *New Media for a New China* (West Sussex: Wiley-Blackwell, 2010), 97.

11 Chua, "Conceptualizing," 115.

12 Tingting Huang, "Can Chinese TV Shows Recapture Their Former Glory in SE Asia?" *Global Times*, August 22, 2016, http://www.globaltimes.cn/content/1002005.shtml.

13 Scotton and Hachten, *New Media*, 97.

14 Chua, *Structure*, 24.

15 Michael Keane, "From National Preoccupation to Overseas Aspiration," in *TV Drama in China*, ed. Ying Zhu, Michael Keane, and Ruoyun Bai (Hong Kong: Hong Kong University Press, 2008), 147.

16 Chua, *Structure*, 26.

17 Sharon A. Carstens, "Constructing Transnational Identities? Mass Media and the Malaysian Chinese Audience," *Ethnic and Racial Studies* 26, no. 2 (2003): 340–341.

18 Chua, *Structure*, 4.

19 Oxford Economics, "The Economic Contribution of Film and Television in China in 2016," Motion Picture Association of America, last modified December 2017, https://www.mpaa.org/wp-content/uploads/2017/12/MPAA_China_2016_WEB-2.pdf.

20 Scotton and Hachten, *New Media*, 97.

21 Kia Ling Teoh, "Programming Spend by Online Companies in China to Surpass That of TV Broadcasters in 2018," IHS Markit, August 13, 2018, https://technology.ihs.com/605505/programming-spend-by-online-companies-in-china-to-surpass-that-of-tv-broadcasters-in-2018.

22 Ibid.

23 Patrick Hanan, *Chinese Fiction of the Nineteenth and Early Twentieth Centuries* (New York: Columbia University Press, 2004), 104.

24 Adam Minter, "China Reinvents Literature (Profitably)," Bloomberg, November 7, 2017, https://www.bloomberg.com/view/articles/2017-11-06/china-reinvents-literature-profitably; Huanying Song, Yu Pan, and Lu Liu, "Changes in Chinese People's Cultural Life in New Media Environment," in *New Media and China's Social Development*, ed. Yungeng Xie (Singapore: Springer, 2017), 147.

25 Amy Qin, "Craving a Hot TV Show in China? Start Scouring the Web," *New York Times,* October 28, 2016, https://www.nytimes.com/2016/10/29/arts/television/craving-a-hot-tv-show-in-china-start-scouring-the-web.html.

26 Koh Ping Chong, "Lucrative New Chapter for Chinese Online Novels," *Straits Times*, November 13, 2017, https://www.straitstimes.com/asia/east-asia/lucrative-new-chapter-for-chinese-online-novels.

27 Rachel Cheung, "China's Online Publishing Industry—Where Fortune Favours the Few, and Sometimes the Undeserving," *South China Morning Post*, May 6, 2018, http://www.scmp.com/magazines/post-magazine/long-reads/article/2144610/chinas-online-publishing-industry-where-fortune.

28 Ibid. Cheung explains how this "pay-by-word model" functions: budding authors "post the first 100 or so chapters" (of about two to three thousand words each) at no charge, and only when the work acquires "a sizeable following will the writer be offered a contract"; readers then pay about 0.02 yuan per thousand words, which is "shared between the platform and author," with the option of offering further monetary rewards to the authors of works they admire.

29 Ibid.

30 Ibid.

31 Qin, "Craving."

32 Tianyu Cao and Bo Qin, "China Literature Ltd. (0772.HK): Web Literature Pioneer, Double Winner in Content and Platform Delivery" (my trans.), China Finance Online, December 22, 2017, http://hk.jrj.com.cn/2017/12/22103123836774.shtml.

33 Zhiyan Wang, ed., "Multi-billion-Dollar Web Literature Industry Needs to Treat Its Readers Better" (my trans.), China Youth Daily (rpt. *Xinhua News*), February 9, 2018, http://www.xinhuanet.com/book/2018-02/09/c_129808506.htm.

34 Yan Wu, Junfang Deng, and Qiang Zhao, "Magnolia Awards: TV Series *Like a Flowing River* Wins Big," CGTN, June 14, 2019, https://news.cgtn.com/news/2019-06-14/Who-are-the-winners-of-Magnolia-Awards—Hwww6zoZDG/index.html.

35 Fan Xu, "Dramas Spread Wings," *China Daily*, May 24, 2018, http://usa.chinadaily.com.cn/a/201805/24/WS5b0614baa3103f6866eea4cc.html.

36 Ibid.

37 An English-subtitled version was available on the YouTube channel, Yoyo Television Series Exclusive, in March 2018.

38 Hutcheon, *A Theory*, 127.

39 Ibid.

40 Lu Yin, "Novel Reads," Metro Beijing (rpt. *Global Times*), March 14, 2016, http://www.globaltimes.cn/content/973691.shtml. Sites that translate Chinese web novels include webnovel.com, shiroyukitranslations.com, and dorayakiz.wordpress.com/translations, amongst others.

41 Jia Mei, "Web Novels Take Readers into a Whole New World," *China Daily*, April 24, 2017, https://www.pressreader.com/china/china-daily/20170424/281479276299271.

42 Yin, "Novel reads."

43 Hutcheon, *A Theory*, 121.

44 Ibid., 122; 127.

45 Ibid., 121.

46 Ibid., 121.

47 Ibid., 126.

48 Christopher González, *Permissible Narratives: The Promise of Latino/a Literature* (Columbus: Ohio State University Press, 2017), 9–10.

49 Hutcheon, *A Theory*, 123.

50 Ibid., 125.

51 Lars Elleström, "Adaptation and Intermediality," in *The Oxford Handbook of Adaptation Studies*, ed. Thomas Leitch (Oxford: Oxford University Press, 2017), 509–510.

52 James Phelan, *Experiencing Fiction: Judgments, Progressions, and the Rhetorical Theory of Narrative* (Columbus: Ohio State University Press, 2007), 7.

53 Hutcheon, *A Theory*, 56.

54 Phelan, *Experiencing Fiction*, 3; 9.

55 Ibid., 9.

56 *When a Snail Falls in Love* (《如果蜗牛有爱情》), episode 17, November 28, 2016, Shanghai Dragon Television.

57 Ibid., episode 7, November 7, 2016; episode 12, November 14, 2016.

58 Ibid., episode 15, November 21, 2016.

59 Ibid., episode 4, October 31, 2016; episodes 13–14, November 21, 2016.

60 Since performance is a relevant aspect of my analysis, I place actors' names in parentheses alongside first mention of character names. Given that English subtitles adhere to the Chinese convention of putting last names before first names, I retain this order for all references to character and actor names in the main body of the essay to minimize confusion.

61 *Snail*, episode 2, October 24, 2016.

62 Ibid., episode 3, October 24, 2016.

63 Ibid., episode 3; Dingmo, *When a Snail Falls in Love*, chapter 9, April 7, 2013.

64 *Snail*, episode 4; see also episodes 1, October 24, 2016; episode 3; and episode 6, October 31, 2016.

65 Lisa Zunshine, *Getting Inside Your Head: What Cognitive Science Can Tell Us about Popular Culture* (Baltimore: Johns Hopkins University Press, 2012), 23.

66 *Snail*, episode 8, November 7, 2016.

67 Ibid., episode 11, November 14, 2016.

68 Ibid., episode 20, December 12, 2016.

69 Ibid., episode 9, November 7, 2016.

70 Hutcheon, *A Theory*, 14.

71 Ibid., 42–43; 55.

72 Robert Stam, "Introduction: The Theory and Practice of Adaptation," in *Literature and Film: A Guide to the Theory and Practice of Film Adaptation*, ed. Robert Stam and Alessandra Raengo (Malden, MA: Blackwell, 2005), 35.

73 *Snail*, episode 9. This distinctly contrasts the web novel's treatment of their conversation about Ji Bai's smoking habit as a point of flirtatious romantic tension (chapters 22–23).

74 Zunshine, *Getting Inside*, 79–80.

75 *Snail*, episode 9. All Chinese translations from primary and secondary sources are mine unless otherwise stated.

76 Ibid., episode 14, November 21, 2016.

77 Phelan, *Experiencing Fiction*, 190.

78 Kai Wang, "Interview," Tencent video, 17:14, October 24, 2016, http://v.qq.com/x /cover/avuik2dix9zqv8p/m0022rqgpqw.html.

79 Thomas Leitch, ed., *The Oxford Handbook of Adaptation Studies* (Oxford: Oxford University Press, 2017), 5.

80 Timothy Corrigan, "Defining Adaptation," in *The Oxford Handbook of Adaptation Studies*, ed. Thomas Leitch (Oxford: Oxford University Press, 2017), 32.

81 Shuyu Kong, *Popular Media, Social Emotion and Public Discourse in Contemporary China* (London: Routledge, 2014), 12.

82 Henry Jenkins, *Convergence Culture: Where Old and New Media Collide* (New York: New York University Press, 2006), 3.

83 Kong, *Popular Media*, 11–12.

84 Ibid., 12, 44.

85 Ane, "On the Rare Occasion of Writing a Foreword" (my trans.), *Sina Blog*, February 26, 2009, http://blog.sina.com.cn/s/blog_48dbc5c40100c4e2.html.

86 The murders began in the 1980s and remain unsolved at the time of Dingmo's writing of *Snail* in 2013; the murderer was eventually apprehended in 2016 and executed in 2019.

87 Dezhou Public Security Bureau, Canal Economic Development Zone Sub-Bureau (德州运河公安分局), Weibo post, October 29, 2016 (3:55 P.M.), http://www.weibo.com/2403912521/Ef55BDy2w; Weibo post, November 16, 2016 (10:50 P.M.), http://www.weibo.com/ttarticle/p/show?id=2309404042391089726559.

88 Production teams actively foster interactivity in some cases by inviting netizens to pen lyrics to IP dramas' theme songs—an issue I examine at length in my article, "Hearing the Unsaid: Musical Narration in *The Journey of Flower* and *Nirvana in Fire*," *Narrative* 26, no. 1 (January 2018): 81–103.

89 Hutcheon, *A Theory*, 126.

90 *When a Snail Falls in Love*, Weibo post, December 2, 2016 (4:30 P.M.), http://www.weibo.com/5796654162/EkfQG9t1G.

91 *When a Snail Falls in Love*, Weibo post, November 10, 2016 (8:46 P.M.), http://www.weibo.com/5796654162/EgW7J4gj2; December 8, 2016 (3:00 P.M.), http://www.weibo.com/5796654162/El9P83sAW; December 10, 2016 (5:00 P.M.), http://www.weibo.com/5796654162/EltsPiu4J.

92 Ziwen Wang, Weibo post, October 25, 2016 (1:22 P.M.), http://www.weibo.com/1378010100/EesnCd7Yh.

93 Haiqing Han, "Understanding Web Serials' Evolving Sophistication: The Case of *When a Snail Falls in Love*" (my trans.), Today's Mass Media (rpt. *People's Daily*), March 1, 2017, http://media.people.com.cn/n1/2017/0301/c411112-29116266.html.

94 Jing Wen, "What Type of IP Adaptation Does the Audience Need? Like Makeup, It Should Accentuate without Obscuring Authenticity" (my trans.), Chuan Mei Nei Can, October 27, 2016, https://mp.weixin.qq.com/s?__biz=MjM5ODczNDAzNA==&mid=2691619695&idx=1&sn=2e9016781d45acc431801f3ecdb16a9e.

95 Jason Mittell, "Strategies of Storytelling on Transmedia Television," in *Storyworlds across Media: Toward a Media-Conscious Narratology*, ed. Marie-Laure Ryan and Jan-Noël Thon (Lincoln: University of Nebraska Press, 2014), 254.

96 Jun Zeng, "*When a Snail Falls in Love* wins acclaim; Wang Kai and Wang Ziwen Offer a New CP Model" (my trans.), Guangzhou Daily (rpt. *People's Daily*), October 26, 2016, http://media.people.com.cn/n1/2016/1026/c40606-28807629.html.

97 Hutcheon, *A Theory*, 127.

98 Kai Wang, "Interview," Tencent Video, 17:14, October 24, 2016, http://v.qq.com/x/cover/avuik2dix9zqv8p/m0022rqgpqw.html; "The Making of *When a Snail Falls in Love* (Part 2)," Tencent Video, 10:14, November 4, 2016, http://v.qq.com/x/cover/r3bfp2iz9hf9whu/j00223ndyhu.html.

99 Dingmo, *Love Me If You Dare*, chapter 71, August 24, 2013, http://www.jjwxc.net/onebook.php?novelid=1857985&chapterid=71.

100 Dingmo, *Our Glamorous Time*, Jinjiang Literature (January–March 2014), http://www.jjwxc.net/onebook.php?novelid=1982518.

101 Dingmo, *Memory Lost*, chapter 13, August 12, 2014, https://read.qidian.com/chapter/CwaqnrLFUW81/tkcyBxSum5oexoRJOkJclQ2.

102 Dingmo, *When a Snail Falls in Love*, chapter 38, May 5, 2013.

103 Ibid., chapter 56, May 23, 2013.

104 Ibid., chapter 58, May 25, 2013, http://www.jjwxc.net/onebook.php?novelid
    =1766288&chapterid=58.
105 Zeng, *"When a Snail Falls in Love* Wins Acclaim."
106 Leitch, *The Oxford Handbook,* 6.

Bibliography

Berry, Chris, and Mary Farquhar. *China On Screen: Cinema and Nation.* Hong Kong: Hong Kong University Press, 2006.
Cao, Tianyu, and Bo Qin. "China Literature Ltd. (0772.HK): Web Literature Pioneer, Double Winner in Content and Platform Delivery." China Finance Online. December 22, 2017. http://hk.jrj.com.cn/2017/12/22103123836774.shtml.
Carstens, Sharon A. "Constructing Transnational Identities? Mass Media and the Malaysian Chinese Audience." *Ethnic and Racial Studies* 26, no. 2 (2003): 321–344.
Cheung, Rachel. "China's Online Publishing Industry—Where Fortune Favours the Few, and Sometimes the Undeserving." *South China Morning Post.* May 6, 2018. http://www.scmp.com/magazines/post-magazine/long-reads/article/2144610/chinas-online-publishing-industry-where-fortune.
Chong, Koh Ping. "Lucrative New Chapter for Chinese Online Novels." *Straits Times.* November 13, 2017. https://www.straitstimes.com/asia/east-asia/lucrative-new-chapter-for-chinese-online-novels.
Chua, Beng Huat. "Conceptualizing an East Asian Popular Culture." In *The Inter-Asia Cultural Studies Reader,* edited by Kuan-Hsing Chen and Beng Huat Chua, 115–139. London: Routledge, 2007.
———. *Structure, Audience and Soft Power in East Asian Pop Culture.* Hong Kong: Hong Kong University Press, 2012.
Corrigan, Timothy. "Defining Adaptation." In *The Oxford Handbook of Adaptation Studies,* edited by Thomas Leitch, 23–35. Oxford: Oxford University Press, 2017.
Dingmo. *When a Snail Falls in Love.* Jinjiang Literature. April 1–July 20, 2013. http://www.jjwxc.net/onebook.php?novelid=1766288.
Elleström, Lars. "Adaptation and Intermediality." *The Oxford Handbook of Adaptation Studies,* edited by Thomas Leitch, 509–526. Oxford: Oxford University Press, 2017.
González, Christopher. *Permissible Narratives: The Promise of Latino/a Literature.* Columbus: Ohio State University Press, 2017.
Han, Haiqing. "Understanding Web Serials' Evolving Sophistication: The Case of *When a Snail Falls in Love.*" *People's Daily.* March 1, 2017. http://media.people.com.cn/n1/2017/0301/c411112-29116266.html.
Hanan, Patrick. *Chinese Fiction of the Nineteenth and Early Twentieth Centuries.* New York: Columbia University Press, 2004.
Herman, David. "Storyworld." In *Routledge Encyclopedia of Narrative Theory,* edited by David Herman, Manfred Jahn, and Marie-Laure Ryan, 569–570. London: Routledge, 2005.
Huang, Tingting. "Can Chinese TV Shows Recapture Their Former Glory in SE Asia?" *Global Times.* August 22, 2016. http://www.globaltimes.cn/content/1002005.shtml.
Hutcheon, Linda. *A Theory of Adaptation.* 2nd ed. New York: Routledge, 2013.
Jenkins, Henry. *Convergence Culture: Where Old and New Media Collide.* New York: New York University Press, 2006.

Keane, Michael. "From National Preoccupation to Overseas Aspiration." In *TV Drama in China*, edited by Ying Zhu, Michael Keane, and Ruoyun Bai, 145–156. Hong Kong: Hong Kong University Press, 2008.

Kong, Shuyu. *Popular Media, Social Emotion and Public Discourse in Contemporary China*. London: Routledge, 2014.

Leitch, Thomas, ed. *The Oxford Handbook of Adaptation Studies*. Oxford: Oxford University Press, 2017.

"The Making of *When a Snail Falls in Love* (Part 2)." Tencent Video. November 4, 2016. http://v.qq.com/x/cover/r3bfp2iz9hf9whu/j00223ndyhu.html.

Mei, Jia. "Web Novels Take Readers into a Whole New World." *China Daily*. April 24, 2017. https://www.pressreader.com/china/china-daily/20170424/281479276299271.

Minter, Adam. "China Reinvents Literature (Profitably)." Bloomberg. November 7, 2017. https://www.bloomberg.com/view/articles/2017-11-06/china-reinvents-literature-profitably.

Mittell, Jason. "Strategies of Storytelling on Transmedia Television." In *Storyworlds across Media: Toward a Media-Conscious Narratology*, edited by Marie-Laure Ryan and Jan-Noël Thon, 253–277. Lincoln: University of Nebraska Press, 2014.

Oxford Economics. "The Economic Contribution of Film and Television in China in 2016." Motion Picture Association of America. Last modified December 2017. https://www.mpaa.org/wp-content/uploads/2017/12/MPAA_China_2016_WEB-2.pdf.

Phelan, James. *Experiencing Fiction: Judgments, Progressions, and the Rhetorical Theory of Narrative*. Columbus: Ohio State University Press, 2007.

Qin, Amy. "Craving a Hot TV Show in China? Start Scouring the Web." *New York Times,* October 28, 2016. https://www.nytimes.com/2016/10/29/arts/television/craving-a-hot-tv-show-in-china-start-scouring-the-web.html.

Scotton, James F., and William A. Hachten, eds. *New Media for a New China*. West Sussex: Wiley-Blackwell, 2010.

Sinclair, John. "The De-Centring of Cultural Flows, Audiences and Their Access to Television." *Critical Studies in Television* 4, no. 1 (2009): 26–38.

Song, Huanying, Yu Pan, and Lu Liu. "Changes in Chinese People's Cultural Life in New Media Environment." In *New Media and China's Social Development*, edited by Yungeng Xie, 145–164. Singapore: Springer, 2017.

Stam, Robert. "Introduction: The Theory and Practice of Adaptation." In *Literature and Film: A Guide to the Theory and Practice of Film Adaptation*, edited by Robert Stam and Alessandra Raengo, 1–52. Malden, MA: Blackwell, 2005.

Teoh, Kia Ling. "Programming Spend by Online Companies in China to Surpass That of TV Broadcasters in 2018." IHS Markit. Last modified August 13, 2018. https://technology.ihs.com/605505/programming-spend-by-online-companies-in-china-to-surpass-that-of-tv-broadcasters-in-2018.

Van Ziegert, Sylvia. *Global Spaces of Chinese Culture: Diasporic Chinese Communities in the United States and Germany*. New York: Routledge, 2006.

Wang, Kai. Interview. Tencent Video. October 24, 2016. http://v.qq.com/x/cover/avuik2dix9zqv8p/m0022rqgpqw.html.

Wang, W. Michelle. "Hearing the Unsaid: Musical Narration in *The Journey of Flower* and *Nirvana in Fire*." *Narrative* 26, no. 1 (January 2018): 81–103.

Wang, Zhiyan, ed. "Multi-billion-Dollar Web Literature Industry Needs to Treat Its Readers Better" (my trans.). *China Youth Daily* (rpt. Xinhua News). February 9, 2018. http://www.xinhuanet.com/book/2018-02/09/c_129808506.htm.

Wen, Jing. "What Type of IP Adaptation Does the Audience Need? Like Makeup, It Should Accentuate without Obscuring Authenticity" (my trans.). Chuan Mei Nei Can. October 27, 2016. https://mp.weixin.qq.com/s?__biz=MjM5ODczNDAzNA==&mid=2691619695&idx=1&sn=2e901678ıd45acc431801f3ecdb16a9e.

When a Snail Falls in Love. Performed by Kai Wang and Ziwen Wang. 21 episodes. October 24–December 5, 2016, on Shanghai Dragon Television, Tencent Video, and YouTube.

Wu, Yan, Junfang Deng, and Qiang Zhao. "Magnolia Awards: TV Series *Like a Flowing River* Wins Big." CGTN News. June 14, 2019. https://news.cgtn.com/news/2019-06-14/Who-are-the-winners-of-Magnolia-Awards—Hwww6z0ZDG/index.html.

Xu, Fan. "Dramas Spread Wings." *China Daily.* May 24, 2018. http://usa.chinadaily.com.cn/a/201805/24/WS5b0614baa3103f6866eea4cc.html.

Yin, Lu. "Novel Reads." Metro Beijing (rpt. *Global Times*). March 14, 2016. http://www.globaltimes.cn/content/973691.shtml.

Zeng, Jun. "*When a Snail Falls in Love* Wins Acclaim: Wang Kai and Wang Ziwen Offer a New CP Model." Guangzhou Daily (rpt. *People's Daily*). October 26, 2016. http://media.people.com.cn/n1/2016/1026/c40606-28807629.html.

Zunshine, Lisa. *Getting Inside Your Head: What Cognitive Science Can Tell Us about Popular Culture.* Baltimore: Johns Hopkins University Press, 2012.

5

Rhetorical Liminality in Southeast Asian Media Representations of Human Trafficking

■■■■■■■■■■■■■■■■■■■■■■■■■■

JOHN GAGNON

Over the past twenty years, the topic of human trafficking has garnered increasing public attention in the West, having been sensationalized in mass print media and becoming a popular topic in the film-making industry. Nicholas Kristoff, in 2012, famously launched his own anti-trafficking crusade from the pages of the *New York Times* opinion section. Nonprofit organizations, such as Hope for Justice and The Polaris Project, have actively made their own public awareness materials both in print and in film. Movies like *Taken* (2009), *The Whistleblower* (2010), *Reclaim* (2014), *The 11th Hour* (2014), and others have elicited significant box office returns while enhancing public attention to what many now describe as a global human rights crisis.

We must recognize that human trafficking, definitionally, is not limited to a single type of exploitation.[1] Even so, it should be acknowledged that in media-saturated Western countries, portrayals of human trafficking operate through a particular narrative frame that has been defined by sociopolitical forces. Conceptions of human trafficking in the United States, for example, may be understood as growing out of pervasive racial, class, and gender-based fears and the codification of those anxieties via subsequent legislation. Given the global nature of the topic, the investment of governments in expanding awareness and controlling narratives, and the potential for sensationalism, the ways in which media portrayals of human trafficking shape—and reflect—discourse represent an important area of inquiry and engagement. While Western representations have been studied in depth, this chapter examines the rhetoricity of Southeast Asian media portrayals of human trafficking—an area that remains understudied.

The dominant narrative of human trafficking represents a distinctly Western perspective to a global problem. As I've written elsewhere, the dominant narrative is identified by these attributes: "(1) a reduction of complex individuals into simple actors, often within binaries: moral/immoral, criminal/noncriminal, victim/agent; (2) an emphasis on the work of institutional actors in the act of rescuing; (3) a use of the language of victimization and vulnerability; and (4) a de-emphasis on the voice of the individuals subjected to trafficking."[2] The human trafficking narratives we encounter in Western media almost always follow the same format, generally "plotted in terms of the captivity narrative that played such an extensive role in negotiating Native American/settler relations and the enslavement narrative of African Americans."[3] Such narratives are rooted in the rhetorics of rescue and liberation, reductionistically breaking down the lived experiences of those who have been trafficked: they have no voice, no agency, and are saved from criminal actors by culturally sanctioned institutions. As Tryon Woods observes, "The discourse on anti-trafficking repackages the time-worn theme of colonialism's so-called civilizing mission."[4] Indeed, the dominant diagnostic, prognostic, and motivational frames[5] of human trafficking in Western media—particularly American media—reflect human trafficking as the problem of the Other who needs to be saved.

I think it important to acknowledge that the Western framework—the one that dominates and that most scholarship relies on as legitimate—arose out of the social purity agenda of the early twentieth century, associated fears about so-called white slavery, and the continued influence of predominantly white communities and conservative religious groups on issues of female sexual autonomy, gender roles, and interracial sex.[6] Researchers have demonstrated that the dominant narrative constructs limited and limiting discourses. For example, media accounts commonly portray highly sexualized and young female victims, ignoring the trafficking stories of those in the LGBTQ community, and rendering virtually nonexistent exploitation related to nonsexual work (i.e., labor trafficking).[7] Rachel Austin observes that these portrayals create the expectation of the ideal victim: "The rescue narrative that dominates media representation . . . is dangerous because human trafficking victims have more complex experiences that do not fit with the ideal victim seeking rescue from the police or other officials. As the literature and critics reveal, these perceptions are not based on reality, but rather are supported by concepts that the general public has historically accepted.... This becomes problematic when government actors such as police and political figures use these distorted images as their reference to make decisions."[8] This has resulted in significant harms: the criminal prosecution of those exploited for sex, the detention and forced migration of those exploited for labor, the sensationalization and perpetuation of myths about human trafficking in the media, the commodification of trafficking as a revenue generator for private organizations, the emphasis on sex trafficking over labor and other types of exploitation, and many more.

There is little debate about the global nature of the human trafficking problem. But because scholarship on media portrayals of trafficking[9] has mostly focused on Western perspectives, we don't possess a truly complete picture. We need local lenses, a multiplicity of perspectives to reflect a multiplicity of possible experiences. This chapter, then, makes a simple argument: to more fully understand the narratives that circulate about human trafficking, we need to look locally to gain a more robust understanding of a global issue. I don't think this is a simple topic that can be properly considered by looking only at the local; global systems are in play and must be considered. Yet there is a clear need to enable communication between communities of interest, to account for differing cultural discourses, and to incorporate the ideas and needs of those with different perspectives. Emphasis on localized meaning-making and storytelling practices can teach us something about the ways in which we might reconsider academic conversations around human rights. Media play an unquestionable role in generating awareness about human trafficking while also influencing discourse around the issue.[10] Media are an effective way to inform the public of the human trafficking problem—in particular because of their broad reach and capacity to circulate narratives; the discourse generated in Western contexts allows for information about the issue to be more accessible by establishing certain situations as familiar.[11] But this familiarity is dangerous because the realities of trafficking take on different hues in different places.

I have grown increasingly wary of the ways in which media campaigns persistently move specific issues, like human trafficking, "into the discursive realm of global human rights."[12] Jacqueline Jones Royster and Molly Cochran argue that "the rights of human-ness are innate" and, as such "a global enterprise for all humanity,"[13] a position with which I agree—however, I am no longer confident that framing these issues with such broad brush strokes is most effective for actually addressing them. I see such moves as inherently dangerous because of the tendency to paint human rights issues in the abstract, with over-broad generalizations and neat, tidy categories. This abstraction does a great disservice to the individual lived experiences of those who have suffered, fails to account for cultural differentiation across/between West and East, and as such doesn't actually do much for enhancing the project of human rights. Shelley

Wright observes that "much of the abuse which human beings actually suffer cannot be adequately addressed within 'mainstream' human rights discourse."[14] Media projects involving the issue of human trafficking, which apply the mainstream discourse, have rendered us less capable of seeing and less willing to hear the individual and communal voices that exist at the local level. To a very large extent, I see this as a need and responsibility for engaging in the feminist work of "re-mapping boundaries and renegotiating connections."[15] As Inés Hernandez-Avila writes, "This mapping and renegotiating is a necessary process within communities as well as between communities."[16] One of the specific ways that boundaries need to be remapped, or transformed, in the study of media portrayals of human trafficking, is in situating what it means to prioritize the study of local media efforts to make sense of an issue that is certainly not owned by the West. Just because there may be commonalities of circumstance to any given trafficking scenario, whether in the United States or, say, Thailand, it doesn't mean that they are represented, understood, or even experienced in the same way.

Because media functions over time in both constructing and affirming cultural discourses about gender, sexuality, race, and migration, in the context of human trafficking it is important to think about how the dominant Western narrative of human trafficking circulates and moves via media across global contexts. While scholars have engaged in substantive critiques of the dominant narrative, there has been virtually no work done that examines how local discursive spaces in Southeast Asia interact with the dominantly circulated narrative. Indeed, as Erin Kamler—who works at the intersection of feminist social justice and the arts—argues, we need to better account for the complexities of this work by listening to unheard stories, particularly those that fail to align with the dominant narrative.[17] Michel Foucault's notion of discursive formations[18] is useful for understanding the differences in human trafficking discourses that exist in competing spaces. If a discourse is a group of statements belonging to a single system of formation, then we must understand each competing discourse—for example, the broader cultural discourse situated around human trafficking in the West and the everyday discourses addressing human trafficking found in Southeast Asia—that are necessarily different in how they operate linguistically, enunciatively, and logically. My claim that researchers have not seriously considered the more local discursive spaces around human trafficking media portrayals then connects both with Foucault's notion of discursive formations and with the question of how/why some discursive concepts enter into broader discourse and how/why some do not.

As in the West, media portrayals of human trafficking in Southeast Asia have expanded considerably over the past couple decades. In many ways, this is unquestionably linked to the passage of the Trafficking Victims Protection Act of 2000, which resulted in U.S.-led international pressure on countries to more substantively address human trafficking. This pressure is most notably visibilized in the annual Trafficking in Persons Report, issued by the U.S. Department of State, and which ranks governments based on their efforts to acknowledge and combat trafficking. With increased pressure, international funding, and intergovernmental coordination, government awareness campaigns have increased across the region, and with them, portrayals in print, news, and film media have risen as well. While Southeast Asia is not as media saturated as the United States, and the media landscape remains woefully understudied by way of comparison, the proliferation of human trafficking portrayals in media has been noted by scholars such as Tien Hoang Le and Meghan Sobel, who have done important work in opening up this area of study in recent years.

Notably, the research conducted by Tien Hoang Le[19] and Meghan Sobel,[20] respectively, centers on government-sponsored media campaigns and formal news media. Their publications, while important, do not address the more organic forms of media production at the local level, via locally based organizations' development of media projects. In limiting their research to government-sanctioned media, their findings demonstrate that much of the dominant narrative that has been constructed and circulated in the West remains intact and circulated throughout Southeast Asia. The framing we see in the Western narrative is the same framing most visibly used in Southeast Asian media portrayals of human trafficking: it is represented primarily as a criminal problem, sex trafficking is emphasized over other forms of trafficking, and the language used is largely reflective of the three-P's paradigm (prosecution, prevention, protection) articulated in the U.S. Trafficking Victims Protection Act.

For example, in 2018, the government of Thailand partnered with A21, an anti-trafficking organization based in Costa Mesa, California, to develop a media campaign called "Can You See Me?" The campaign launch video, which features a series of government officials and A21 representatives speaking, claims that the campaign "shows us the real story" and that the videos produced as part of the campaign "best represent the problem [of human trafficking] in Thailand and the Mekong region."[21] The primary messages of the launch video are (1) the campaign will lead to "more victims rescued and more criminals brought to justice"; (2) to remind individual citizens "If you see something, report it. If you suspect something, report it"; and (3) to give ordinary people information so that "they now have the power to rescue others and stop trafficking in Thailand."[22] Notably, the video fails to define human trafficking, identifies it as a criminal issue (as highlighted by the video's focus on the deputy commissioner general of the Royal Thai Police), and falls into the same narrative framework that we see at work in Western media portrayals of trafficking. Indeed, the phrasing "if you see something, report it" is strikingly similar to the U.S. Department of Homeland Security's "if you see something, say something" campaign. The three primary messages of the launch video, as already detailed, map clearly onto the United States' three-P's paradigm: bringing criminals to justice aligns with prosecution, encouraging reporting aligns with prevention, and the idea of stopping trafficking aligns with protection. While the A21 representatives in the video give lip service to the Thai-specific nature of the campaign, the reality is that the framing of the campaign is undifferentiable from similar campaigns developed and circulated in the West.

The media productions of the joint Thai-A21 campaign further demonstrate the distinctly Western narrative frame. In one of the campaign videos—which exhibit high production value and professional actors—a sex trafficking scenario is presented where minors are lured through the promise of false jobs.[23] The A21 campaign describes the video in these terms:

> Nok and her sister Aom were approached by a broker at home in the village and told about a job opportunity in the city. Together with their parents, the girls decided to travel with the broker to help provide a better life for their families. When the girls arrived at their destination it became clear that they had been deceived. Unsure of what to do, the girls decided to get out of the truck. However, Aom was held back while Nok was taken inside. She had her papers taken from her, was beaten, and afraid. Nok had no choice but to do what she was told. Girls like Nok and her sister are tricked into working in the sex industry frequently. Girls are looking for a better life to support their families or to provide for themselves and are taken advantage of.[24]

The video features two young-looking and highly sexualized female actors who never speak, are voyeuristically subjected to physical (and implied sexual) violence on-screen, and who helplessly and tearfully look at passersby in an implied plea for rescue. The video concludes with the campaign's catchphrase "Can You See Me?" in English superimposed over a female face frozen in a painful grimace. The video reinforces the notion of the Westernized "ideal victim" and the imagery, rhetorical moves, and narrative tropes are nearly identical to those used in U.S.-based antitrafficking campaigns.[25] The irony of this is that the most visible narrative we see circulating in and throughout Thailand is the same narrative that is circulated in Western countries, like the United States. In this we can see the Western influence of media production and consumption on this issue in the region.

The narrative we see emerge from this campaign on human trafficking is oriented by the colonial mindset, and its agenda set in the West: it operates in a top-down categorizing manner, talks about trafficking scenarios rather than with the local communities impacted by trafficking, and fails to fully consider the informative value of survivors' lived experiences in the development and dissemination of narrative. As Julie Cruikshank has observed, the colonial mindset "move[s] forward by devising and reinforcing categories."[26] In devising and reinforcing these categories, those with power and privilege monopolize and control the human trafficking narrative while marginalizing and silencing—that is, writing out—the voices of the Asian Other. In other words, the dominant narrative operates as a particular language that belongs to the historical process of colonization by silencing the individuals and communities that would, or could, create their own locally based narratives about human trafficking.[27] In this sense, the human interest stories we see in government-approved Southeast Asian media are little different than those in the West, albeit perhaps more damaging because they render the trafficking subject as a colonized Other who is used discursively for the purposes of reinforcing agenda-laden categories that ignore local concerns. We must begin questioning the discursive othering that occurs in the dominant narrative by shifting focus from that narrative and instead focusing on the stories told by those typically identified as Other.

The regional specificities informing media culture in Southeast Asia differentiate it from that of the West in important ways. Tien Hoang Le's work highlights these specificities, particularly raising the concern that "mass media campaigns operated by government agencies do not reach a wide range of high risk people and localities"[28] because of language barriers, educational barriers, and a deficiency of use of television, radios, newspapers, and internet in remote areas. The lack of translation from national languages to local dialects represents a particularly unique problem not seen in the homogenized context of the English-speaking West.

Acknowledging the limited reach of government-approved media portrayals of human trafficking, are there forms of media in Southeast Asia that reshape and reinterpret these Western models in uniquely and more locally informed Southeast Asian ways? The answer, I think, is decidedly yes. In a review of media across Southeast Asia, I have identified a number of locally generated media campaigns addressing human trafficking. In Cambodia, Thailand, and Vietnam, locally informed nongovernmental media campaigns complicate the Western narrative frame that we see in government-approved campaigns like A21's "Can You See Me?" Run directly by local nonprofits, these campaigns are at the epicenter of producing awareness films, internet resources, and print media with homegrown narrators and multilingual translations.

In Cambodia, for example, the Phnom Penh–based organization Cambodia ACTs routinely produces and disseminates film and print media on human trafficking related topics. The organization produced a short documentary titled *Together on the Move to Save Children* (2014). While the production quality is subpar and sometimes raw, the footage is real and not staged, the content is delivered in Khmer and tribal languages with English subtitles, and instead of voyeuristic displays of violence the film focuses on the spoken narratives of actual people who experienced exploitation. To pursue the goal of local awareness in and on local terms and to help others do the same, such media productions move beyond a framework in which their narratives are connected only to concepts of victimhood and survivorship. Indeed, the centerpiece of the film is the extended storytelling of individuals who were trafficked; they tell their stories, in their own voices, in their own language, in their own words, and on their own terms. Importantly, they speak less about the trauma of being trafficked and more about the process of healing and renewal. Not unlike African American, Chicana, Indigenous, and Queer women writers and activists who find themselves silenced, ignored, and written out of culturally dominant narratives in the West, those in Southeast Asia who attempt to combat the issue of human trafficking via media productions like that of *Together on the Move to Save Children* are engaged in an ongoing effort to rid themselves of labels that assign to them the value of being the sexualized other who is to be voyeuristically displayed through stand-in actors. In opposition to this predominantly Western portrayal, they instead redefine "themselves by their humanity, their human dignity, and their rights to justice, equality, and empowerment within the human enterprise."[29] For them, this process of redefining identity and shifting away from the Western lens of scripted media portrayal and high-value media production designed for consumption is rooted in a process of recognizing themselves in a way that transcends the Western labels so commonly affixed to them, thereby transforming their stories and communities to be rendered through localized rather than globalized cultural discourse to formulate solutions to the problem of increasing awareness.

And, yet, while these local media productions resist the oversimplifications of the dominant narrative seen in the West, we still see them using the language of the dominant narrative to tell stories. As such, they exhibit a discursive in-betweeness, or liminality, that they tactically navigate in telling stories about human trafficking. For example, Daughters Rising—a nonprofit organization in Chiang Mai, Thailand, creates films not only to generate awareness but to invite viewers to directly engage in its mission. In the informational film titled *How an Ecolodge Empowers Women to Fight Trafficking* (2018) the viewer is presented with a continual shifting of language that is both self-regulatory and moves transgressively within and between narrative frames and discursive spaces. The scenes shift from footage from nearby villages to the facilities run by the organization, and from narratives delivered by English-speaking advocates to trafficking survivors telling their stories in Thai. Interestingly, within these locally driven narratives exists an inherent tension between how they encourage others to view the issue in relation to identity and community and how they use language still reflective of the dominant Western paradigm. In *How an Ecolodge Empowers Women to Fight*

Trafficking, the introductory sequence reflects the ideal victim narrative as a Western woman describes the threats that faceless and vulnerable female foreigners face by being on the streets and not in school. But, as the footage moves forward, the viewer is introduced to four survivors of trafficking who each tell their stories, in their own voices, in their own language, and in their own words. Persistently aware of liminal situatedness, this type of media campaign on human trafficking in Southeast Asia shares information that aligns with the dominant narrative while drawing that narrative into question through the storytelling of interviewed survivors. In other words, their liminality is rooted in both perception and performance: they reject the language of the dominant narrative while also appropriating that same language throughout their stories because that is what is expected.

In Hanoi, Vietnam, the Blue Dragon Children's Foundation runs a media production arm that encompasses print, videos, and radio and podcasts. In its video titled *Coming Home: Fighting Trafficking in Vietnam* (2011) Blue Dragon introduces the viewer to two child labor trafficking survivors who speak in tiếng Việt with English subtitles. The production value is low, and the grainy images are combined with amateurishly emotive piano music. Yet the video's poor production is compensated by the compelling imagery—all of it locally shot footage—and the close-ups of these children sharing their experiences in excruciating detail. Like the other examples, this video invokes aspects of the dominant narrative—in this case, the rhetorics of rescue and liberation—while demonstrating individual voices, providing locally based storytelling, using real people instead of actors, and portraying an underdiscussed aspect of human trafficking by focusing on labor trafficking. But instead of recapitulating the tragic "caught in between two worlds" stereotype, these child narrators demonstrate the promises of occupying the liminal, where they can negotiate the distance between several discourse communities.[30] This is precisely what we see happening in localized Southeast Asian media productions around human trafficking: in effect, they use their liminality to transgressively travel between domains of knowledge, between East and West. It is in this discursive shifting—from their own language, to the language of the dominant narrative—that we see a distinctly Southeast Asian reimagination and refiguring of the tropes of the dominant narrative. This use transforms each story within the colonizing discourse of human trafficking narratives into a fully acknowledgeable presence, instead of an absence or merely a voiceless human interest story.

The media campaigns of Cambodia ACTs, Daughters Rising, and Blue Dragon deploy English and local languages, and they adeptly engage in tactical refigurings in which media producers simultaneously consume, deploy, and reject dominant narratives about human trafficking, which in turn allows them to "maintain their difference in the very space" occupied by the dominant narrative.[31] Their approaches push against the apparent stability and fixity of the dominant narrative, instead employing a distinctly Southeast Asian approach that blends language, moves between discursive spaces, and is defined by embodied, relational rhetoric that often centers on the identification of self in relation to community. This transgressive travel between discursive spaces allows productions to maintain control over their stories and exert a sense of community, while not ceding it to the larger forces of the West. In doing so, such productions rewrite how communities impacted by trafficking understand themselves in relation to broader discursive spaces, while also garnering credibility for a wider cultural audience.

The media campaigns do not describe their rhetorical moves in this particularized language, but I see their practice—specifically as it relates to the West—as a proclamation of presence that acknowledges the intricate connections between local status, local needs, and local recognition of the status and needs of others like them.[32] In this sense, they function in a way that is boldly at odds with the normative discursive frame of human trafficking. Indeed, by grounding their stories in the idea and language of human dignity, they prioritize the humanity, the presence, and the subjectivity of their audiences. This isn't merely bearing witness, it isn't merely testifying, rather it is an act of human connection, one that finds no place or comparison in the Western-dominant narrative.

These theaters of action present potential for the possibility of change within the stories told, yet they also structure "journeys and actions [that] are marked by the 'citation' of the places that result from them or authorize them."[33] From the maps offered in such localized media productions, we can compare local stories against broader narratives. Such comparison is not merely disruptive but also generative, insofar as it can be tactically used to build connections and cross bridges between East and West. Importantly, this traversal of terrain reveals how localized Southeast Asian media productions about human trafficking exist in a rhetorically liminal space. This liminality requires rhetorical transference and, as such, these stories are constructed in both legitimate and exterior spaces created through the practice of specific and shifting constructions of consciousness, identity, and place to create spaces of tactical use. Or, in the words of Sandra Pannell, "more than just reproducing and preserving what is perceived as already given," we might see these "stories as forms of the 'productive imagination' [that] also pave the way for an exploration of the possible and of the possibility of change."[34] While such media productions may exist in a rhetorically liminal state, they are able to negotiate systems of knowledge productively, in ways that both serve their respective local constructions of identity and community and connect those constructions of identity and community to different discourse communities to make meaning. The value of making these connections is, for them, clear: with each telling, with each connection, they open up important new spaces to seriously contemplate—and to help others contemplate—the ways in which Southeast Asian media collide and constellate with global issues of human rights, media narrative circulation, and power.

Notes

1 The United Nations, in *Protocol to Prevent, Suppress and Punish Trafficking in Persons, Especially Women and Children*, defines trafficking as "the recruitment, transportation, transfer, harbouring or receipt of persons, by means of the threat or use of force or other forms of coercion, of abduction, of fraud, of deception, of the abuse of power or of a position of vulnerability or of the giving or receiving of payments or benefits to achieve the consent of a person having control over another person, for the purpose of exploitation. Exploitation shall include, at a minimum, the exploitation of the prostitution of others or other forms of sexual exploitation, forced labour or services, slavery or practices similar to slavery, servitude or the removal of organs." For more, see UN General Assembly, *Protocol to Prevent, Suppress and Punish Trafficking in Persons, Especially Women and Children, Supplementing the United Nations Convention Against Transnational Organized Crime.* November, 15 2000, 2, https: www.refworld.org/docid /4720706c0.html.

2 John T. Gagnon, "How Cultural Rhetorics Can Change the Conversation: Towards New Communication Spaces to Address Human Trafficking," *Poroi: An Interdisciplinary Journal of Rhetorical Analysis and Invention* 12, no. 2 (2017): 3–4.

3 Ibid., 4.

4 Tryon Woods, "Surrogate Selves: Notes on Anti-trafficking and Anti-blackness," *Social Identities* 19, no. 1 (2013): 126.

5 Rachel Austin, "Human Trafficking in the Media: A Content Analysis on Human Trafficking Frames in Documentaries, Movies, and Television Episodes" (PhD diss., Northeastern University, 2016), 10.

6 John Gagnon, "Review of *Policing Sexuality: The Mann Act and the Making of the FBI*," *Journal of Interdisciplinary Humanities* 33, no. 2 (2016): 182.

7 Austin, "Human Trafficking," 25.

8 Ibid., 29.

9 Some of the more recent scholarship on media portrayals of human trafficking includes Silvia Rodríguez-López, "(De)Constructing Stereotypes: Media Representations, Social Perceptions, and Legal Responses to Human Trafficking," *Journal of Human Trafficking* 4, no. 1 (2018): 61–72; Jessica Reichert, Jaclyn Houston-Kolnik, Amanda Vasquez, and Emma Peterson, "News Reporting on Human Trafficking: Exploratory Qualitative Interviews with Illinois News Journalists," *Journal of Human Trafficking* 4, no. 1 (2018): 6–20; Jaclyn Houston-Kolnik, Christina Soibatian, and Mona M. Shattell, "Advocates' Experiences with Media and the Impact of Media on Human Trafficking Advocacy," *Journal of Interpersonal Violence* (2017): 1–25; Dina Francesca Haynes, "The Celebritization of Human Trafficking," *ANNALS of the American Academy of Political and Social Science* 653, no. 1 (2014): 25–45; Sarah Steele and Tyler Shores, "Real and Unreal Masculinities: The Celebrity Image in Anti-trafficking Campaigns," *Journal of Gender Studies* 24, no. 4 (2015): 419–435; Girish Gulati, "News Frames and Story

Triggers in.the Media's Coverage of Human Trafficking," *Human Rights Review* 12, no. 3 (2011): 363–379; Austin, "Human Trafficking."

10 Andreas Scholoenhardt, Paris Astill-Torchia, and Jarrod M. Jolly, "Be Careful What You Pay For: Awareness Raising on Trafficking in Persons," *Washington University Global Studies Law Review* 11, no. 2 (2012): 415.

11 Altheide D. L., *Qualitative Media Analysis* (Newbury Park: Sage, 1996).

12 John Gagnon, "Rhetoric Matters: Race and 'Slavery' in the Trafficking Victims Protection Act," *Present Tense: A Journal of Rhetoric in Society* 5, no. 3 (2016): 1–7.

13 Jacqueline Jones Royster and Molly Cochran, "Human Rights and Civil Rights: The Advocacy and Activism of African-American Women Writers," in *Human Rights Rhetoric: Traditions of Testifying and Witnessing*, ed. Arabella Lyon and Lester Olson (New York: Routledge, 2012), 18.

14 Shelley Wright, *International Human Rights, Decolonization, and Globalization: Becoming Human* (New York: Routledge, 2001), 214.

15 Inés Hernandez-Avila, "Relocations upon Relocations: Home, Language, and Native American Women's Writings," in *Reading Native American Women*, ed. Inés Hernandez-Avila (New York: Altamira Press, 2005), 174.

16 Ibid.

17 Erin Michelle Kamler, "Negotiating Narratives of Human Trafficking: NGOs, Communication and the Power of Culture," *Journal of Intercultural Communication Research* 42, no. 1 (2013): 2.

18 Michel Foucault, *The Archaeology of Knowledge* (New York: Vintage, 2010).

19 Tien Hoang Le, Kerry Carrington, Thanh Hung Tran, Thanh Phuc Nguyen, Trung Kien Le, and Ngoc Ha Bui, "Inter-agency Cooperation to Raise Awareness on Human Trafficking in Vietnam: Good Practices and Challenges," *Asian Journal of Criminology* 13 (2018): 251–274.

20 Meghan Sobel, "Chronicling a Crisis: Media Framing of Human Trafficking in India, Thailand and the USA," *Asian Journal of Communication* 24, no. 4 (2014): 315–332.

21 "Can You See Me? Thailand Campaign Launch," A21, accessed January 1, 2019, https://www.a21.org/content/can-you-see-me-thailand/goahmg.

22 Ibid.

23 Ibid.

24 Ibid.

25 The similarities can be witnessed through comparing the A21 video and my analysis of two U.S. case studies in "How Cultural Rhetorics Can Change the Conversation: Towards New Communication Spaces to Address Human Trafficking," *Poroi: An Interdisciplinary Journal of Rhetorical Analysis and Invention* 12, no. 2 (2017), 1–21.

26 Julie Cruikshank, "Oral History, Narrative Strategies, and Native American Historiography: Perspectives from the Yukon Territory," in *Clearing a Path: Theorizing the Past in Native American Studies*, ed. Nancy Shoemaker (New York: Routledge 2002), 7.

27 David Spurr, *The Rhetoric of Empire: Colonial Discourse in Journalism, Travel Writing, and Imperial Administration* (Durham, NC: Duke University Press, 1993), 1.

28 Le, "Inter-agency Cooperation," 252.

29 Royster and Cochran, "Human Rights," 16.

30 Gloria Anzaldua, *Interviews/Entrevistas,* ed. AnaLouise Keating (New York: Routledge, 2000), 268.
31 Michel De Certeau, *The Practice of Everyday Life* (Berkeley: University of California Press, 1984), 32.
32 Royster and Cochran, "Human Rights," 16.
33 Certeau, *The Practice of Everyday Life,* 120.
34 Sandra Pannell, "From the Poetics of Place to the Politics of Space: Redefining Cultural Landscapes on Damer, Maluku Tenggara," in *The Poetic Power of Place: Comparative Perspectives on Austronesian Ideas of Locality,* ed. James Fox (Canberra: Australian National University Press, 2006), 164.

Bibliography

Altheide, D. L. *Qualitative Media Analysis.* Newbury Park: Sage, 1996.

Anzaldua, Gloria. *Interviews/Entrevistas.* Edited by AnaLouise Keating. New York: Routledge, 2000.

Austin, Rachel. "Human Trafficking in the Media: A Content Analysis on Human Trafficking Frames in Documentaries, Movies, and Television Episodes." PhD diss., Northeastern University, 2016.

"Can You See Me? Thailand Campaign Launch." A21. Accessed January 1, 2019. https://www.a21.org/content/can-you-see-me-thailand/goahmg.

Cruikshank, Julie. "Oral History, Narrative Strategies, and Native American Historiography: Perspectives from the Yukon Territory." In *Clearing a Path: Theorizing the Past in Native American Studies,* edited by Nancy Shoemaker, 3–28. New York: Routledge, 2002.

De Certeau, Michel. *The Practice of Everyday Life.* Berkeley: University of California Press, 1984.

Foucault, Michel. *The Archaeology of Knowledge.* New York: Vintage, 2010.

Gagnon, John. "How Cultural Rhetorics Can Change the Conversation: Towards New Communication Spaces to Address Human Trafficking." *Poroi: An Interdisciplinary Journal of Rhetorical Analysis and Invention* 12, no. 2 (2017): 1–21.

———. "Review of *Policing Sexuality: The Mann Act and the Making of the FBI.*" *Journal of Interdisciplinary Humanities* 33, no. 2 (2016): 179–182.

———. "Rhetoric Matters: Race and 'Slavery' in the Trafficking Victims Protection Act." *Present Tense: A Journal of Rhetoric in Society* 5, no. 3 (2016): 1–7. https://www.presenttensejournal.org/volume-5/rhetoric-matters-race-and-slavery-in-the-trafficking-victims-protection-act/.

Gulati, Girish. "News Frames and Story Triggers in the Media's Coverage of Human Trafficking." *Human Rights Review* 12, no. 3 (2011): 363–379.

Haynes, Dina Francesca. "The Celebritization of Human Trafficking." *ANNALS of the American Academy of Political and Social Science* 653, no. 1 (2014): 25–45.

Hernandez-Avila, Inés. "Relocations upon Relocations: Home, Language, and Native American Women's Writings." In *Reading Native American Women,* edited by Inés Hernandez-Avila, 171–188. New York: Altamira Press, 2005.

Hesford, Wendy. "Human Rights Rhetoric of Recognition." In *Human Rights Rhetoric: Traditions of Testifying and Witnessing,* edited by Arabella Lyon and Lester Olson, 80–87. New York: Routledge, 2012.

Hoang Le, Tien, Kerry Carrington, Thanh Hung Tran, Thanh Phuc Nguyen, Trung Kien Le, and Ngoc Ha Bui. "Inter-agency Cooperation to Raise Awareness on Human Trafficking in Vietnam: Good Practices and Challenges." *Asian Journal of Criminology* 13 (2018): 251–274.

Houston-Kolnik, Jaclyn, Christina Soibatian, and Mona M. Shattell. "Advocates' Experiences with Media and the Impact of Media on Human Trafficking Advocacy." *Journal of Interpersonal Violence* (2017): 1–25.

"If You See Something, Say Something." Department of Homeland Security. Accessed February 9, 2019. https://www.dhs.gov/see-something-say-something.

Jones Royster, Jacqueline, and Molly Cochran. "Human Rights and Civil Rights: The Advocacy and Activism of African-American Women Writers." In *Human Rights Rhetoric: Traditions of Testifying and Witnessing*, edited by Arabella Lyon and Lester Olson, 11–28. New York: Routledge, 2012.

Kamler, Erin Michelle. "Negotiating Narratives of Human Trafficking: NGOs, Communication and the Power of Culture." *Journal of Intercultural Communication Research* 42, no. 1 (2013): 1–18.

Pannell, Sandra. "From the Poetics of Place to the Politics of Space: Redefining Cultural Landscapes on Damer, Maluku Tenggara." In *The Poetic Power of Place: Comparative Perspectives on Austronesian Ideas of Locality*, edited by James Fox, 163–172. Canberra: Australian National University Press, 2006.

Reichert, Jessica, Jaclyn Houston-Kolnik, Amanda Vasquez, and Emma Peterson. "News Reporting on Human Trafficking: Exploratory Qualitative Interviews with Illinois News Journalists." *Journal of Human Trafficking* 4, no. 1 (2018): 6–20.

Rodríguez-López, Silvia. "(De)Constructing Stereotypes: Media Representations, Social Perceptions, and Legal Responses to Human Trafficking." *Journal of Human Trafficking* 4, no. 1 (2018): 61–72.

Scholoenhardt, Andreas, Paris Astill-Torchia, and Jarrod M. Jolly. "Be Careful What You Pay For: Awareness Raising on Trafficking in Persons." *Washington University Global Studies Law Review* 11, no. 2 (2012): 415–435.

Sobel, Meghan. "Chronicling a Crisis: Media Framing of Human Trafficking in India, Thailand and the USA." *Asian Journal of Communication* 24, no. 4 (2014): 315–332.

Spurr, David. *The Rhetoric of Empire: Colonial Discourse in Journalism, Travel Writing, and Imperial Administration*. Durham, NC: Duke University Press, 1993.

Steele, Sarah, and Tyler Shores. "Real and Unreal Masculinities: The Celebrity Image in Anti-trafficking Campaigns." *Journal of Gender Studies* 24, no. 4 (2015): 1–17.

UN General Assembly. *Protocol to Prevent, Suppress and Punish Trafficking in Persons, Especially Women and Children, Supplementing the United Nations Convention Against Transnational Organized Crime*. November, 15, 2000. https: www.refworld .org/docid/4720706c0.html.

Woods, Tryon. "Surrogate Selves: Notes on Anti-trafficking and Anti-blackness." *Social Identities* 19, no. 1 (2013): 120–134.

Wright, Shelley. *International Human Rights, Decolonization, and Globalization: Becoming Human*. New York: Routledge, 2001.

6

Addressing Transnational Legacies of Colonialism in East Asia

■■■■■■■■■■■■■■■■■■■■■■■■■■

Cases from Contemporary Japanese Art

HIROKI YAMAMOTO

This chapter examines the contested legacies of colonialism in East Asia through examples of contemporary Japanese art. Whereas the problematic legacies of colonial domination, albeit in different forms, can be found around the globe, it is particularly significant to work through the issues of historical injustice related to Japan's colonialist past in East Asia. Japan was a former imperial power that invaded neighboring countries and regions from the late nineteenth century to World War II (WWII). Its territorial enlargement in East Asia was driven by Japan's desire to be the modern nation that could compete with its Euro-American counterparts. The Empire of Japan, which existed from 1868 to 1947, colonized Taiwan in 1895 as a result of the first Sino-Japanese War. It also annexed Korea in 1910 by means of military power. The colonial legacies in East Asia, therefore, are essentially transnational and have their roots in the assimilation policies and destructive activities conducted by the Imperial Japanese Government and Army. Since the conclusion of WWII, moreover, the legacies of Japanese militarism in East Asia have left many unsettled conflicts and disputes that are still dividing the region.

Japan's war of aggression finally extended its geographical scope to almost the entire Asia-Pacific region at its climax in the late 1930s and early 1940s. The remaining legacies of Japanese colonialism, therefore, can be identified transnationally throughout the whole of East Asia. In a similar vein, the unresolved problems derived from Japan's wartime wrongdoings in East Asia can neither be considered nor addressed properly within the framework of one single nation. The issue of so-called comfort women, which became conspicuous in the 1990s, is a concrete example that illustrates this point. Contested issues concerning the women, who were forced or deceived into providing sexual services to Japanese soldiers, are particularly affecting current Japan–Korea relations. This postcolonial agenda, however, is equally vital to Japan's relationships not only with other East Asian counterparts, such as Taiwan and China, but also with Southeast Asian countries, including the Philippines and Indonesia.

While the language barrier has always been a crucial problem in discussing sensitive war-related subjects among the people of East Asia, visual art as a tool for nonverbal communication could be an effective alternative means of thinking and speaking about such issues. The Japanese artists discussed in this chapter have addressed, albeit through different approaches, controversial legacies deeply linked to Japan's imperial history. In doing so, they throw themselves into the realm in which their own positionality is critically interrogated.

While the modalities of colonialism's legacy in the contemporary world, be they material (e.g., monuments built during the colonial period) or immaterial (e.g., traumatic experience of colonial rule), vary greatly, this chapter focuses on facilities, buildings, and statues that are connected with Japanese colonial history and mobilize the concept of site. The term "site-specificity" has been a keyword in the field of art history and critique since the 1960s, with the emergence of "minimalism" and "public art" in the United States. These artistic trends, in spite of their difference in appearance, are characterized by the "exchanges between the work of art and the place in which its meanings are defined."[1] Hundreds of artists, who contributed to the development of the two genres, were aware of the visible and invisible features (shape, scale, climate, and so forth) of an exhibition space, be it a gallery room or an outdoor location, in the production of artworks.

There was, however, a remarkable watershed in the history of site-specific art practices. In the 1990s, more and more artists began paying attention to the social, political, and historical implications embedded in the particular spaces around which they worked. Art historian Miwon Kwon illustrates this shift exquisitely. Rather than considering the places in which artworks are installed as replaceable, Kwon reframes the concept of site-specificity as "the cultural mediation of broader social, economic, and political processes that organize urban life and urban space."[2] In line with her reconceptualization, this chapter explores possibilities of cultural strategies seeking to intervene in politically charged sites in East Asia related to Japanese colonialism, referring to recent examples of contemporary art practices in Japan.

Two Different Approaches to Contentious Locations: Motoyuki Shitamichi's *Torii* (2006–2012) and Mitsuhiro Okamoto's *The Reconstruction of Japanese Stone Lantern* (2004–2005)

I will compare two long-term projects concerned with religious facilities erected in the territories colonized by Japan: *Torii* and *The Reconstruction of Japanese Stone Lantern*. While the former is a photographic project conducted by Motoyuki Shitamichi between 2006 and 2012 in many places, including Japan's ex-colonies in East Asia, the latter is Mitsuhiro Okamoto's art project in Kaohsiung, a port city on the southern tip of Taiwan, which was launched in 2004 and eventually completed the following year.[3] These projects greatly differ in their aesthetic styles and approaches to their objectives, although they are similar in that both targeted the same type of colonial ruins and required a relatively long time to complete.

After graduating from an art university, Shitamichi traveled all over Japan and started to take pictures of the scenery he encountered and the people and places he encountered along the way. In 2005, he published *Bunkers*—a collection of his photographs capturing various war relics that remain in Japan. Okamoto, on the other hand, has participated in numerous artist-in-residency programs in different countries and initiated a large number of community art projects involving local residents since the late 1990s. Okamoto's projects dealing with politically sensitive topics have triggered controversies and oppositions.

Shitamichi started his *Torii* project in 2006. In this project, he took pictures of *toriis*, a traditional Japanese gate commonly found at the entrance of a Shintō shrine, built outside Japan. Shintō is the name of the traditional religion of Japan, which traces its roots back to ancient Japan. The Japanese government built Shintō shrines throughout its colonies and forced those colonized to worship the religion to assimilate them culturally. During the war, Japan adopted assimilation policies to rule its colonies efficiently. The shrines and their torii remain in the former Japanese colonies of East Asia transnationally and are symbols of Imperial Japan's assimilationism, exercised, for instance, as the enforcement of standard Japanese language and culture.

FIG. 6.1 "Taichung, Taiwan" from the *Torii* series by Motoyuki Shitamichi, 2006–2012. Original in color. (Courtesy of the artist.)

In *Torii*, Shitamichi's special interest lay in portraying contemporary—and continuously evolving—forms of a colonial residue. In this sense a morphological interest, as well as a political one, substantially underpins his project. To be more precise, these concerns are inseparably entwined in Shitamichi's works. In my view, he tries to discover a political connotation in a morphological transformation regarding ongoing legacies of colonialism. One of the photographs in the series taken in Taichung City, Taiwan, captures a massive stone torii inside a park, which is now used as a "public bench" by many residents of the area (fig. 6.1). We can easily identify, in this eye-catching picture, that the colonial object has been reused, appropriated, and transformed in a local context. Another photograph that Shitamichi took in Sakhalin, in stark contrast, impressively depicts a tiny torii standing alone in a vast grassy place, as if alluding that it is sinking into the profound oblivion. Moreover, no actual torii appears in the images taken in South Korea, as almost everything relevant to the three-and-a-half-decade period of Japanese rule has been destroyed in the country. In this picture, the viewers can only recognize very faint traces of religious facilities built during the colonial era.

Poetically recording the shapes and uses of torii that have been changed divergently in each site after the war, Shitamichi's project shows us the lasting ruins of colonial cultural homogenization in a new light. The seemingly discrete photographs produced throughout the project, as a consequence, foreground an unacknowledged connectivity linking geographically remote postcolonial sites together. This visualized connectivity could only be rendered perceivable by employing a transnational comparative approach in the field of art. This artistic transnationalism, therefore, might be able to broaden our understanding of the largely unknown interconnectedness among the legacies left behind by colonialism.

Whereas Shitamichi's photographic project tries to capture the present status of colonial legacies somewhat objectively, Okamoto's art project, *The Reconstruction of Japanese Stone Lantern*, is a more direct interventional activity in a contestable postcolonial location. Beginning with a chance encounter with old photographs of a shrine taken during Taiwan's colonial period, the project attempted to rebuild a stone lantern that appeared in the photographs with the help of the local people. Okamoto started this project by specifying the accurate position where the lantern stood in the precinct of the now abandoned shrine, successfully restoring it in November 2005 (fig. 6.2).

The project's aim is, as Okamoto himself iterated, not to glorify the age of imperialism in East Asia but to enable the re-emergence of something that can serve as a "witness" to the site's colonial history.[4] Perhaps owing to its straightforward manner of intervention, however, the *Reconstruction* project invoked tensions and controversies that involved local authorities. The incident also attracted considerable media attention, and Okamoto's project was picked up by a number of newspapers in Taiwan and China.

It would be worthwhile here to refer to the criticism of the rise of "participatory art" proposed by architect Markus Miessen. He polemicizes that the seemingly "democratic" structures of participatory art projects occasionally result in the reaffirmation of sham consensuses that simply maintain the existing order, and thus, in such a tenuous regime of "failed" participatory practices, radical changes and meaningful dissent hardly take place.[5] On the contrary, Okamoto's provocative art project reckons the politically saturated site as an irreplaceable medium to unveil what Jacques Rancière calls dissensus—a potential catalyst for social amelioration and political reform.[6] Within the unique transformative space shaped by the project, the reconstituted transnational legacy of colonialism newly functions as an efficacious counter device against the fading memories regarding the enforced cultural assimilation.

Despite their distinctively different approaches, both Shitamichi and Okamoto recognize politically charged sites as an important medium of artistic expressions. In this sense, it can be argued that their artworks are substantiated by contested spaces. We should also notice that, on the other hand, their creative projects equally shape unique spaces in which a deeper understanding of our postcolonial world could be gained. These notable reciprocal dynamics between art and site remain understudied in the domain of contemporary art theory.

FIG. 6.2 *The Reconstruction of Japanese Stone Lantern* by Okamoto Mitsuhiro, 2004–2005. (Courtesy of the artist.)

The Air in a Disputed Territory: Meirō Koizumi's *Rite for a Dream (Today My Empire Sings)* (2016)

I would now like to take up *Rite for a Dream (Today My Empire Sings)*, a three-channel video installation created by Meirō Koizumi in 2016 (fig. 6.3). He, like Shitamichi and Okamoto, uses a highly contested site as an indispensable

FIG. 6.3 *Rite for a Dream (Today My Empire Sings)* by Meirō Koizumi, 2016. Installation view at VACANT. (Photo: Shizune Shiigi. Courtesy of the artist.)

material for this video piece. Although the subjects that Koizumi deals with in his works are diverse, he has scrutinized the military history of Japan and its consequences in the postwar Japanese society through art since the turn of the twenty-first century.

In his confrontation with Japan's wartime history and its repercussions, Koizumi has used controversial motifs, including *tokkōtai* (the group of suicide bomber pilots during WWII) and Showa Emperor (the wartime emperor known more commonly as Emperor Hirohito in the West) in his artistic production. It should be noted that these topics have been treated as untouchable cultural taboos in the Japanese art world, and artists have been under the pressure of censorship exercised by the government and other authorities. In fact, for instance, *Enkin o Kakaete* (Holding perspectives), created by Japanese artist Nobuyuki Ōura between 1982 and 1985, a series of collage piece containing the images of the emperor, was censored twice, in 1986 and 2009.[7]

Before starting to create *Rite for a Dream (Today My Empire Sings)*, Koizumi made works of art in his series titled Air (*Kūki*), his investigation of the status of the emperor in contemporary Japan. The paintings in the Air series depict the figures of the present and erstwhile emperors and the imperial family members. Koizumi rendered these figures invisible and thus made them disappear in the paintings (fig. 6.4). The title "Air" is quite suggestive, touching upon the core of the works in the series. I will try to elucidate the meaning of this enigmatic title later in relation to my interpretation of *Rite for a Dream (Today My Empire Sings)*. In 2016, Koizumi proposed to display a part of the Air series in an exhibition held at The Museum of Contemporary Art Tokyo. In response to the museum's request to avoid dealing with politically delicate matters, however, he eventually decided to remove the Air paintings from the

FIG. 6.4 *Air #1* by Meirō Koizumi, 2016. (Photo: Shizune Shiigi. Courtesy of the artist.)

exhibition, leaving the caption alone on the blank wall as an imprint of self-regulation. The withdrawn pieces were, after all, made public in his solo show (also entitled *Air*) at MUJIN-TO Production, a contemporary art gallery located near The Museum of Contemporary Art Tokyo. In May 2017, with the aid of the gallery, Koizumi had another solo show at VACANT, an alternative space in the Harajuku area. This was the first time *Rite for a Dream (Today My Empire Sings)* was shown in Japan.

Rite for a Dream (Today My Empire Sings) can be divided into two parts, excluding the two short scenes at the beginning and ending that function as prologue and epilogue. The film starts with a shot of the Imperial Palace (*kōkyo*), setting the mood of a nationalistic atmosphere. The shot is followed by a scene of a male actor standing in the middle of the street and looking at a sheet of paper, which seems to be an instruction. Subsequently, Koizumi himself appears in the film to give the actor some instructions and to check his microphones. After Koizumi exits from the scene, the actor slowly lifts up his right hand as if signaling that he is ready. It may be worthwhile to consider why Koizumi inserted the "backstage" scenes into the beginning part. These unusual scenes seem to emphasize the constructedness (or, at least, the constructed nature) of what will happen in the film, suggesting that the artist facilitated the situation intentionally. This characteristic enables the film to astutely destabilize the clear-cut boundary between reality and fiction, opening up a new way of recollecting the contested history of war in the past and understanding its ramifications in the present.

The first part consists of a long monologue in which the artist talks in an almost inaudible voice about a dream he actually had when he was a child. The dream, according to the voice-over narration, was the one that "was invaded by the Empire." In the dream, the artist's father was about to be taken away by police officers for some unknown reason. His small son—that is, Koizumi himself—was trying hard to restrain him while crying with tears, "Please don't go!" The father, responding to his child, said, "I have got to go" because "there isn't enough chicken feed to go around and somebody has to be fed to the chickens." And the father added that he was "chosen" for the role.

It might be reasonable, when we look back on the war history of modern Japan, to read this first part in conjunction with philosopher Tetsuya Takahashi's conception of "the system of sacrifice." By employing this concept, Takahashi sheds light on the resemblance between the current situation of Okinawa, where there are many U.S. military bases, and that of Fukushima, which embraces a large number of nuclear power plants. In both places, an individual or a certain group of individuals undergo unbearable hardships on behalf of the interests of broader communities.[8] The Empire of Japan was maintained, upheld, and defended by the similar system of sacrifice. The presence of the kamikaze pilots, who conducted "self-sacrificing" suicide attacks, is an example that unambiguously shows this.[9] A plethora of individuals, who died on behalf of the Empire of Japan, have been enshrined in the Yasukuni shrine— the targeted site in which Koizumi attempts to intervene through the creation of *Rite for a Dream (Today My Empire Sings)*.

The Yasukuni shrine is an extremely controversial Shintō shrine located in central Tokyo. It was founded in 1869 and commemorates those who died in the service of the Empire of Japan, including a great number of convicted war criminals. Due to its enshrinement of individuals sentenced to be WWII criminals, other East Asian countries, such as China and South Korea, have denounced Japanese prime ministers' visits to the shrine, especially since the mid-1980s around the end of the Cold War. Even though the shrine itself is located in Japan, the imperial history of Japan associated with it entails a trans-Asian nature. This is why the phenomena happening around the place have inevitably attracted considerable attention and interest in East Asia as a whole.

The second part of the film opens with a scene of a male actor walking in the street that leads to the Yasukuni shrine. Although there is no explicit sign that indicates where the scene is taking place, the artist encloses visual clues that allow viewers to specify the location. For instance, he inserts short shots of Kudan Station, the station closest to the shrine, and a group of several males holding the flag of the Imperial Japanese Army and Navy (*kyokujitsu-ki*, the Rising Sun Flag), which symbolizes Japan's wartime militarism. The actor's hands are securely tied behind his back, and he is surrounded by a crowd of police officers. The viewers, in addition, witness the indecent words, such as "Get out of Japan" and "We don't need you in Japan," and hear insulting angry voices shouting back and forth.

What is filmed in the second part is a chauvinistic demonstration staged by Japanese ultranationalists around the Yasukuni shrine. As is pointed out by cultural anthropologist Tomomi Yamaguchi, right-wing political movements, which assail citizens with other nationalities or ethnic backgrounds in the country, have become prominent in Japan since the mid-2000s.[10] This is saliently exemplified in the activities of Zaitokukai set up in 2006. This xenophobic association that represents the rightward shift in recent Japan has strenuously organized the demonstrations demanding that foreign residents (particularly ethnic Korean residents) should move out of the country.

I would like to contend that it is of significance, as I stated before, to unearth Koizumi's *Rite for a Dream (Today My Empire Sings)* in connection with the word "air"—the title of his preceding series of paintings, which directly led to the production of the work.[11] "Air" (*kūki* in Japanese), unlike in English usage, refers to "contexts by which one is surrounded" or "moods in which one is embedded" in Japan.[12] In *Rite for a Dream (Today My Empire Sings)*, Koizumi astutely visualizes the "air" surrounding the Yasukuni shrine in the context of a recent surge of nationalist enthusiasm, capturing the exclusive mood widespread in the contemporary Japanese society. In line with this interpretation, the enigmatic phrase "It is swallowing me up," repeated twice by the actor in the second half of the video, can be read as an expression of fear of being uncritically dictated and swept by the mood of the time. This phrase seems to be a gesture toward resistance against a loss of critical subjectivity in a community at large.

"How much one can see, what one can see, and in what way one can see or be seen are," as Gil Hochberg asserts, "all outcomes of specific visual arrangements," and thus the (in)visibility of things is determined by a complex set of national, ethnic, racial, religious, gender, sexual, and many other factors.[13] By manipulating the degree of visibility through artistic intervention, Koizumi reveals intangible postcolonial (or neocolonial) forms of violence that encircle the Yasukuni shrine and that are directed at other ethnic groups across borders. The capacity of visual art to generate powerful narratives, well demonstrated in this work, deserves special attention here. Koizumi merges Japan's current political climate and his strange childhood memory, creating an idiosyncratic narrative that uniquely interprets Japan's postcoloniality. This unparalleled narrative invented through the process of artistic amalgamation could serve as a new sensory language that can help us to expand our view of the contemporary manifestations of deep-rooted colonialist sentiment. This sort of sensory contribution of art, which bypasses linguistic differences, might deepen the discussion on transnational postcolonial issues in East Asia.

The Appropriation of a Contested Space: Yoshiko Shimada's *Becoming a Statue of a Japanese Comfort Woman* (2012–)

The final case study is *Becoming a Statue of a Japanese Comfort Woman*, a performance art project that has been developed since 2012 by the renowned feminist artist Yoshiko Shimada. Shimada's series of performances I shall now discuss differs from the aforementioned three artistic practices. That is, her work can be interpreted as a creative appropriation of disputed places relative to East Asia's colonial history, rather than a direct use of them.

Shimada has actively tackled various issues concerning Japan's war responsibility, especially from a feminist perspective, through her artistic practices since the early 1990s. One of the important backgrounds of her commitment to the subject is that three former Korean "comfort women" filed lawsuits against the Japanese government to demand an official apology and individual compensation in 1991. Their public testimony compelled the Japanese to face the ineffable reality experienced by the women of the colonized territories. Nevertheless, as an art historian Hiroko Hagiwara emphasizes, "there are very few artists in Japan who take up the issue of military comfort women" in their works and projects.[14] More generally speaking, "political expression in art—especially art with an identifiably feminist edge, was largely shunned in the Japanese art world where a focus on aestheticism was, and in many ways still is, accepted as the dominant vision."[15] Considering these facts, Shimada's artistic activity over the comfort women issue turns out to be exceptional and thus significant in the contemporary Japanese art world.

In 1993, Shimada created an etching suggestively entitled *A House of Comfort* in order to, in the words of Fran Lloyd, "question the idea of whose home or nation, whose comfort and at what price."[16] In this politically charged artwork, Shimada places at the top of the photograph a "comfort station" (*ianjo*), the state-sponsored brothel for Japanese soldiers and officers, and a snapshot of Asian comfort women at the bottom, respectively. In the center, on the other hand, appears a blurred picture of an undressed female figure (fig. 6.5). *A House of Comfort*, through the careful juxtaposition of the found images, aimed to bring to light the largely neglected historical issue of the wartime system of sexual slavery.

Shimada has equally scrutinized the little known issue of war responsibility regarding Japanese women during WWII through the creation of artworks, reflexively self-critiquing her own positionality as a Japanese woman born after the war. *White Aprons*, another etching she created in 1993, illuminates the

FIG. 6.5 *A House of Comfort* by Yoshiko Shimada, 1993. (Courtesy of the artist.)

FIG. 6.6 *White Aprons* by Yoshiko Shimada, 1993. (Courtesy of the artist.)

contrasting but essentially related roles of Japanese women in wartime, by juxtaposing three photographs of women in *kappōgi*—the traditional "white
apron" that women wear to protect the kimono while doing housework. In this
work, we can see the startling picture of a woman with a pistol as she learns
from male soldiers how to shoot. This photo is placed between two other photos: a housewife cooking in the kitchen on the left and members of Kokubō
Fujinkai (National Defense Women's Association) sending male soldiers off on
the right (fig. 6.6). Kokubō Fujinkai was a female organization set up in the
1930s to provide a wide variety of support for the military and its soldiers. The
organization, as is epitomized in its favorite slogan "kokubō wa daidokoro kara"
("national defense starts from the kitchen"), aimed to prop up Japan's wars of
aggression by politicizing varied domestic activities.[17] Hence *White Aprons* can
be reckoned as a visual rendition, envisaged by Shimada, of Japanese woman's
actual—and even subjective—participation in the war. As Laura Hein and
Rebecca Jennison suggest, Shimada's noteworthy self-critical attitude stems
from the very absence of a personal war experience: "Shimada feels a responsibility to revisit the war precisely because she did not herself experience it and
so cannot be confident that she would have behaved ethically."[18]

In 2012, while undertaking her doctoral studies in London, Shimada conducted a performance of sitting in front of the Japanese Embassy in London
for approximately an hour (fig. 6.7). In this performance, Shimada wore a Japanese kimono and painted her skin bronze. This made its direct reference to
the statue commemorating comfort women. The first comfort women statue,
a bronze statue of a young girl wearing the traditional Korean *hanbok* and

FIG. 6.7 *Becoming a Statue of a Japanese Comfort Woman* performance by Yoshiko Shimada in London, 2012. (Courtesy of the artist.)

sitting next to an empty chair, was erected in front of the Embassy of Japan in Seoul (since 1992, the survivors and their supporters have staged demonstrations demanding an apology and compensation from the Japanese government outside the Japanese embassy every Wednesday at noon). It was established as a protest against Japan's collective amnesia about the history of sexual enslavement, exemplified in far-right politicians' denial of the comfort women issue. Shimada's performance at the Japanese Embassy in London was envisioned as an artistic appropriation of this protest.

While the performance in London was originally titled *Missing*, Shimada carried out the same performance in several different sites in Japan, such as the aforementioned Yasukuni shrine and the National Diet, under the name of *Becoming a Statue of a Japanese Comfort Woman*. In each place, Shimada, wearing a kimono and having her face painted like the comfort women statue, was just sitting there without saying one single word. While performing, she always taped her own mouth closed, as if indicating that the victims of the wartime sexual crimes are still forced into silence. Whereas a large number of the passers-by who saw the performance ignored her presence, according to the artist, some of them stopped in front of her and thought over what she was trying to convey.[19] Shimada told me that some spectators started discussions on the comfort women issue. This rarely happens in Japan where, as was explained earlier, any topics related to its colonial history tend to be avoided in public spaces. In this regard, through her performative reenactment, Shimada transplanted a contested space surrounding the comfort women issue to different sites transnationally and forged multiple platforms for facilitating meaningful discussions.

In *Becoming a Statue of a Japanese Comfort Woman*, Shimada intervenes in the vibrant disputes over the comfort women statue through the artistic appropriation of contested spaces. In doing so, she tries to negotiate her own positionality and identity, and recollects the memory of the victims of wartime sexual abuse. Additionally, and equally importantly, she also intends to cast light on the barely known presence of Japanese comfort women by dressing herself in the Japanese kimono. In fact, Japanese women were also forced to serve as comfort women during the war. Their presence, however, has been marginalized for a long time after the war.[20]

Becoming a Statue of a Japanese Comfort Woman tactically generates and then multiplies, in a literally performative manner, a contested site inseparable from colonial history. In this idiosyncratic discursive space crafted by the artist, people are urged to look at and think about the otherwise forgotten historical problem of gender and sexuality in close connection with their own positionality. In this visually compelling performance, Shimada draws out and exploits art's underacknowledged potential as a critical "weapon" for promoting wider and deeper social understanding of unresolved transnational legacies in the postcolonial world.

Conclusion

In this chapter, I have discussed several recent practices of Japanese artists wrestling with geographical sites as enduring colonial legacies in the contemporary world. In doing so, I have paid particular attention to the visual, sensory, and representational ways that the artists aim to intervene in the contested spaces and territories intricately tied up with the history of Japanese imperialism and colonialism. Art's ability to visualize transnational connectivity, as I have argued, is instrumental to dissecting the vexing territoriality configured through the cross-border expansions of Imperial Japan in East Asia.

The common thread running through the case studies is that all artists regard a contested site per se as an integral medium for art making. Another commonality is the mutually beneficial relationship of visuality and spatiality in their artworks. A visually intriguing nature is shaped by a contested space, and it in turn contributes to shaping a productive space that might spawn new insights. Thus their artistic works and projects turn out to be viable strategic interventions in the political debates concerning those polemical locations.

These interventional artistic strategies are surprisingly diverse and sometimes enormously different, if not mutually opposed. Such a notable orientation toward methodological diversity, I believe, is a positive characteristic underlying the domain of art. To acknowledge artistic diversity, nevertheless, does not necessarily mean that all sociopolitical practices should be equally appreciated and valued. This is exactly what art historian Claire Bishop pointed out when she criticized the recent tendency of "socially engaged art." As for the marked "social turn" in the post-2000s art world, Bishop problematizes that politically oriented practices "are all perceived to be equally important *artistic* gestures of resistance"; thus there can be, in theory, no failed or low-quality works in the related terrains.[21] Furthermore, she asserts that socially engaged art frequently puts so much emphasis on the ameliorative effect of works and projects that it is inclined to either disregard or overlook the visual aspect, writing that today's art "tends to value what is invisible."[22] The case studies I examined in this chapter, however, persuasively demonstrate that in spite of the anticipated difficulty, these two elements—that is, the social and the aesthetic—are not always incompatible but can be amalgamated significantly in the artwork or artistic practice.

Notes

This chapter is based on an oral presentation given at a panel in the AAS-In-Asia Conference in New Delhi, India, July 2018. I would like to thank Ma Ran (Nagoya University) and Pan Lu (The Hong Kong Polytechnic University), the two panel organizers, for giving me the opportunity to start thinking about the theme.

1. Nick Kaye, *Site-Specific Art: Performance, Place and Documentation* (London: Routledge, 2000), 1.
2. Miwon Kwon, *One Place after Another: Site-Specific Art and Locational Identity* (Cambridge, MA: MIT Press, 2002), 3.
3. Okamoto, when he works as an artist overseas, uses "OKAMOTO Mitsuhiro" as an official description of his name.
4. Mitsuhiro Okamoto, interview by the author, Kyoto, June 22, 2018.
5. Markus Miessen, *The Nightmare of Participation* (Berlin: Sternberg Press, 2010), 43–45, 120.
6. See Jacques Rancière, *Dissensus: On Politics and Aesthetics* (London: Continuum, 2010).
7. For more details, see Toyama Kenritsu Kindai Bijutsukan Mondai o Kangaeru Kai [Group to think about the issue of Toyama Prefectural Museum of Modern Art], ed., *Toyama kenritsu bijutsukan mondai zenkiroku: Sabakareta tennō korāju* [A complete chronicle of the issue of Toyama Prefectural Museum of Modern Art: The emperor tried] (Tokyo: Katsura Shobō, 2001) and Okinawa Kenritsu Bijutsukan Ken'stsu Kōgi no Kai [Group to protest against the censorship by Okinawa Prefectural Museum of Art], ed. *Āto, ken'etsu, soshite tennō: "Atomikku*

sanshain" in Okinawa ten ga inpē shita mono [Art, censorship, and the emperor: What the "Atomic Sunshine" in Okinawa exhibition concealed] (Tokyo: Shakai Hyōron Sha, 2011).

8 See Tetsuya Takahashi, *Gisei no shisutemu: Fukushima, Okinawa* [The system of sacrifice: Fukushima, Okinawa] (Tokyo: Shūeisha Shinsho, 2012).

9 Koizumi once dealt with the issue of the kamikaze fighters in his video work *Portrait of a Young Samurai*, produced in 2009. This implies that for a long time, he has been interested in the relationship between an individual and a community in respect to the system of sacrifice.

10 See Tomomi Yamaguchi, "Xenophobia in Action: Ultranationalism, Hate Speech, and the Internet in Japan," *Radical History Review* 117 (2013): 98–118.

11 Naoya Fujita, a literary critic in Japan, also relates the concept of *kūki* to his stimulating and insightful reading of Koizumi's *Rite for a Dream (Today My Empire Sings)*. In this chapter, however, I adopted a different approach. Whereas he mainly explored the sociopolitical and historical contexts in which the work is considered of grave importance, I am more interested in analyzing the representations themselves that appear in the work. See Naoya Fujita, "Jiyū he no yume o umu tame no gishiki: Koizumi Meirō sakuhin no kūki to yume to bōryoku" [The ritual for creating a dream toward freedom: Atmosphere, dream, and violence in Meirō Koizumi's works], in *Koizumi Meirō ten: Teikoku wa kyō mo utau* [The exhibition of Meirō Koizumi: Today my empire sings], ed. Meirō Koizumi (Tokyo: MUJIN-TO Production, 2017), 18–21.

12 Shichihei Yamamoto, in his ground-breaking book *"Kūki" no Kenkyū* [A study of "air"], succinctly analyzes the vital role the presence of *kūki* took in many irrational policy decisions made by the imperial Japanese government during WWII. See Shichihei Yamamoto, *"Kūki" no kenkyū* [A study of "air"], 2nd ed. (Tokyo: Bunshun Bunko, 1983 [1977]).

13 Gil Z. Hochberg, *Visual Occupations: Violence and Visibility in a Conflict Zone* (Durham, NC: Duke University Press, 2015), 5.

14 Hiroko Hagiwara, "Comfort Women, Women of Conformity: The Work of Shimada Yoshiko," in *Generations and Geographies in the Visual Arts: Feminist Readings*, ed. Griselda Pollock (New York: Routledge, 1996), 259.

15 Eliza Tan, "Yoshiko Shimada: Art, Feminism and Memory in Japan after 1989" (PhD diss., Kingston University, 2016), 104.

16 Fran Lloyd, "Strategic Interventions in Contemporary Japanese Art," in *Consuming Bodies: Sex and Contemporary Japanese Art*, ed. Fran Lloyd (London: Reaktion, 2002), 86.

17 For more on *Kokubō Fujinkai* and its "politics of kitchen," see especially Mikiyo Kanō, *Onna tachi no "jūgo"* [Women's "homefront"], 2nd ed. (Tokyo: Inpakuto Shuppankai, 1995 [1987]).

18 Laura Hein and Rebecca Jennison, "Against Forgetting: Three Generations of Artists in Japan in Dialogue about the Legacies of World War II," *Asia-Pacific Journal: Japan Focus* 9, no. 1 (2011), http://www.japanfocus.org/-Laura-Hein/3573.html.

19 Yoshiko Shimada, interview by the author, Tokyo, October 9, 2018.

20 Chizuko Ueno, *Nationalism and Gender*, trans. Beverley Yamamoto (Melbourne: Trans Pacific Press, 2004), 69–72.

21 Claire Bishop, *Artificial Hells: Participatory Art and the Politics of Spectatorship* (London: Verso, 2012), 13, emphasis in original.

22 Ibid., 6.

Bibliography

Bishop, Claire. *Artificial Hells: Participatory Art and the Politics of Spectatorship.* London: Verso, 2012.

Fujita, Naoya. "Jiyū he no yume o umu tame no gishiki: Koizumi Meirō sakuhin no kūki to yume to bōryoku" [The ritual for creating a dream toward freedom: Atmosphere, dream, and violence in Meirō Koizumi's works]. In *Koizumi Meirō ten: Teikoku wa kyō mo utau* [The exhibition of Meirō Koizumi: Today my empire sings], edited by Meirō Koizumi, 18–21. Tokyo: MUJIN-TO Production, 2017.

Hagiwara, Hiroko. "Comfort Women, Women of Conformity: The Work of Shimada Yoshiko." In *Generations and Geographies in the Visual Arts: Feminist Readings,* edited by Griselda Pollock, 253–265. New York: Routledge, 1996.

Hein, Laura, and Rebecca Jennison. "Against Forgetting: Three Generations of Artists in Japan in Dialogue about the Legacies of World War II." *Asia-Pacific Journal: Japan Focus* 9, no. 1 (2011). http://www.japanfocus.org/-Laura-Hein/3573.html.

Hochberg, Gil Z. *Visual Occupations: Violence and Visibility in a Conflict Zone.* Durham, NC: Duke University Press, 2015.

Kanō, Mikiyo. *Onna tachi no "jūgo"* [Women's "homefront"]. 2nd ed. Tokyo: Inpakuto Shuppankai, 1995 [1987].

Kaye, Nick. *Site-Specific Art: Performance, Place and Documentation.* London: Routledge, 2000.

Kwon, Miwon. *One Place after Another: Site-Specific Art and Locational Identity.* Cambridge, MA: MIT Press, 2002.

Lloyd, Fran. "Strategic Interventions in Contemporary Japanese Art." In *Consuming Bodies: Sex and Contemporary Japanese Art,* edited by Fran Lloyd, 69–108. London: Reaktion, 2002.

Miessen, Markus. *The Nightmare of Participation.* Berlin: Sternberg Press, 2010.

Okinawa Kenritsu Bijutsukan Ken'stsu Kōgi no Kai [Group to protest against the censorship by Okinawa Prefectural Museum of Art], ed. *Āto, ken'etsu, soshite tennō: "Atomikku sanshain" in Okinawa ten ga inpē shita mono* [Art, censorship, and the emperor: What the "Atomic Sunshine" in Okinawa exhibition concealed]. Tokyo: Shakai Hyōron Sha, 2011.

Rancière, Jacques. *Dissensus: On Politics and Aesthetics.* London: Continuum, 2010.

Takahashi, Tetsuya. *Gisei no shisutemu: Fukushima, Okinawa* [The system of sacrifice: Fukushima, Okinawa]. Tokyo: Shūeisha Shinsho, 2012.

Tan, Eliza. "Yoshiko Shimada: Art, Feminism and Memory in Japan after 1989." PhD diss., Kingston University, 2016.

Toyama Kenritsu Kindai Bijutsukan Mondai o Kangaeru Kai [Group to think about the issue of Toyama Prefectural Museum of Modern Art], ed. *Toyama kenritsu bijutsukan mondai zenkiroku: Sabakareta tennō korāju* [A complete chronicle of the issue of Toyama Prefectural Museum of Modern Art: The emperor tried]. Tokyo: Katsura Shobō, 2001.

Ueno, Chizuko. *Nationalism and Gender.* Translated by Beverley Yamamoto. Melbourne: Trans Pacific Press, 2004.

Yamaguchi, Tomomi. "Xenophobia in Action: Ultranationalism, Hate Speech, and the Internet in Japan." *Radical History Review* 117 (2013): 98–118.

Yamamoto, Shichihei. *"Kūki" no kenkyū* [A study of "air"]. 2nd ed. Tokyo: Bunshun Bunko, 1983 [1977].

Part II

Single-Nation Approach
■■■■■■■■■■■■■■■■■■■■■■■■■■

7

Media, Narrative, and Culture

■■■■■■■■■■■■■■■■■■■■■■■■■

Narrativizing and
Contextualizing Korean
Mukbang Shows

HYESU PARK

A medium can be defined in multiple ways. Most simply put, it is, as *Oxford Dictionary* explains it, a means by which something is communicated or expressed. It is also the material or form used by an artist, composer, or writer. Likewise, we can interpret and analyze the communication, information, and expression produced by a specific medium by focusing on, among other things, the technologies, policies, genres, workers, audiences, or environment, as media constitute and are constituted by these various factors.[1] What interests me the most, however, is the relationship between media and narrative, namely, how media structure narrative meaning and influence the audience's narrative experience. Scholars have considered for a long time questions regarding the intrinsic properties of the medium and how they inform both the narrative meaning and the experience. Marie-Laure Ryan, for instance, posits that "different media filter different aspects of narrative meaning. . . . [T]he shape imposed on the message by the configuration of the pipeline affects in a crucial way the construction of the receiver's mental image."[2] The media–narrative relation, however, deserves fresh new light, especially given the emergence of new media, including, for instance, digital media and media based on sensory channels, that are reconfiguring both the production and consumption of media and narrative in many significant ways.

Therefore this chapter explores how media shape and affect narrative and narrative experience by using Korean *mukbang* shows as case studies. Mukbang, meaning in Korean "eating and broadcasting," is an online audiovisual broadcast in which a host eats food in front of a camera while either interacting or not interacting with online viewers. Mukbang shows are usually done using a streaming platform, such as YouTube or AfreecaTV, and they became popular in South Korea in the 2010s. It is important to note that there are two kinds of mukbang. The first type, which I call silent mukbang in this chapter, features hosts dining alone silently without interacting with viewers. This kind of mukbang has no chat room and hence no obvious way for viewers to respond to their host. The other kind, which I term interactive mukbang, however, is drastically different, as hosts in these shows frequently talk to their audience through online chat rooms. Interactive mukbang hosts also eat abnormally large amounts of food to entertain viewers and provoke more dramatic responses from them. Many mukbang hosts find ways to generate revenue by accepting donations from their viewers or partnering with advertising networks.[3] The increasing popularity of online mukbang shows has caught mainstream media's attention as well, leading to numerous television shows, dramas, and commercials using variations of the same "eating and broadcasting" concept.

What kinds of information, communication, or expression do these mukbang shows deliver? How do they shape narrative meaning and inform viewers' narrative experience? Of course, mukbang shows, especially the silent ones without apparent verbal, linguistic, and textual markers, differ from other language-based media and lack "the code, the grammar, and the synthetic rules necessary to articulate specific meanings."[4] However, having less or even no "narrative" in its limited, conventional sense (a textual act of representation, that is, script) does not equal to having no "narrativity" (capacity to evoke such a script). Ryan, for instance, argues that although language with its ability to articulate "the logical structure of a story" has the privilege as a medium for summaries, this does not mean that media based on other sensory channels cannot make "unique contributions to the formation expressed visually or musically than verbally, and these meanings should not be declared a priori irrelevant to the narrative experience."[5] Considering how mukbang shows with their particular medial configurations contribute to the formation of meanings and influence media recipients cognitively, emotionally, aesthetically, ethically, and psychically is to join the ongoing effort to move beyond the language-oriented definition of narrative.[6] It is also to acknowledge mukbang shows' interpretive and analytical potentials and shed light on the interesting and precise ways in which viewers of mukbang shows make sense of what may otherwise be considered as another new media trend happening in this rapidly changing digital era. With the relation between media and narrative in mind, I contend in the rest of the chapter that the specific ways in which Korean mukbang shows communicate to their viewers need to be approached at multiple levels with careful narratological, technological, and cultural considerations.

The broad consensus about narratives is that they represent "worlds that are populated with characters and situated in space and time."[7] Narrative scholars have paid close attention to these "world(s)" evoked by narratives and coined the term "storyworld." Storyworlds, according to David Herman in *Story Logic* (2002), are "mental models of who did what to and with whom, when, where, why, and in what fashion in the world to which recipients relocate."[8] Although Marie-Laure Ryan has said that storyworld requires "narrative content, so the applicability of the concept of storyworld to lyric poetry is questionable,"[9] Herman considers the term and what triggers it more broadly, pointing out that storyworld can be simulated either implicitly or explicitly by narrative, "whether that narrative takes the form of a printed text, film, graphic novel, sign language, everyday conversation, or even a tale that is projected but never actualized as a concrete artifact."[10] In other words, storyworld is truly a transmedial concept. What is relevant in the context of media studies, then, is the question about how do media with their different forms and configurations influence viewers' mental models of these storyworlds and affect their narrative experience more generally? This question is especially pertinent when it comes to the silent mukbang shows in Korea, as they lack apparent narrative cues (written, audiovisual, verbal, nonverbal, and so forth) that may help viewers' construction of storyworlds, which they either relocate to or keep a critical distance from depending on how immersed they are in their narrative experience. One may also wonder, rightly so, why anyone would watch someone else dining alone quietly in front of a camera. Given the wide popularity of these shows, however, it is worth investigating what elements of these shows prompt viewers' cognitive and emotional engagement with them.

For instance, *O'live*, a television channel in Korea that airs a variety of lifestyle programming, including food and cooking, broadcast a silent mukbang show called "Quiet Dining" in 2016. As the title of the show indicates, "Quiet Dining" features numerous hosts, ranging from celebrities to ordinary people, as they dine alone in various usual and unusual settings—restaurant, classroom, inside a cave, under a bridge, campsite, gym, office, and so forth. This show was simultaneously streamed on YouTube and was subscribed to by 127,000 YouTube viewers. Each episode of the show starts with a full, establishing camera shot of a host with his or her food already prepared and set on a table. The host starts eating without saying anything and remains quiet throughout the episode. Each episode lasts for about seven minutes (fast-forwarded) and ends silently once the host finishes the meal. One particular episode, taking place on a railway track, presents a middle-aged male actor, Oh Kwang Rok, and *samgye-tang*, warm soup with a whole young chicken filled with garlic, rice, jujube, and ginseng especially popular in South Korea for hot summer days.[11]

One way to interpret this particular episode and viewers' engagement with it is to look into the components contributing to the making of its storyworld. Scholars of narrative have raised questions about the content of storyworld. Jan-Noël Thon, for instance, points out that storyworld consists of "existents, events, and characters" as well as "the spatial, temporal, and causal relations between them."[12] Marie-Laure Ryan, on the other hand, adds a few more components, such as setting (a space within which the existents are located), physical laws (principles that determine what kind of events can and cannot happen in a given story), social rules and values (principles that determine the obligations of characters), and events, physical as well as mental (the character's reactions to perceived or actual states of affairs).[13] While different theorists may take different approaches to conceptualize storyworld, it is generally agreed that these elements of storyworld together trigger cognitive and emotional activities of narrative recipients and help them construct and simulate in their minds mental images of narrative and its storyworlds.

Viewers of the railway track episode of "Quiet Dining" may recognize very few storyworld components at first glance: a single character (the host), a few existents (food, dinnerware, and dining table), a rather unusual setting for the occasion (railway track), and a minimal degree of event/action (the process of having a meal fast-forwarded by the editing of the episode). The lack of storyworld components in this episode has notable implications on how viewers comprehend the episode and its storyworld. For one thing, it leads to a lower degree of narrativity. The lower degree of narrativity, on the other hand, may interrupt the process of simulations in viewers' minds, which storyworld elements help to activate, and could impact viewers' immersive narrative experience more generally. Thon, however, points out that "narrative representations of storyworlds and these storyworlds themselves are necessarily incomplete, but recipients use their (actual as well as fictional) world knowledge to "fill in the gap," to infer aspects of the storyworld that are only implicitly represented."[14] The railway track episode with its limited range of storyworld components hence requires that viewers consider the spatial, temporal, and causal relations between storyworld components, and not only the components themselves, in order to comprehend the episode and explore its storyworld. That is, understanding these relations and making inferences through them help viewers "fill in the gaps" and complete aspects of the storyworld that are, as Thon says, "necessarily incomplete."

In the railway track episode, however, this process of gap-filling and inferencing faces some significant challenges, because the relations between storyworld components defy physical laws of the real world that viewers inevitably turn to in order to make sense of the episode and its storyworld. Storyworlds require that narrative recipients reorient themselves from the real world that they live in to the worlds constructed by narrative by "project[ing] upon these worlds everything [they] know about reality, [making] only the adjustments dictated by the text."[15] Kendall Walton calls this process of projection "the reality principle" and explains that when a text includes an object "that exists in reality, all the real-world properties of this object can be imported into the storyworld unless explicitly contradicted by the text."[16] Part of the difficulty of the episode, then, arises from the fact that the objects in the episode and the relations between them contradict some of the common principles of reality, complicating the "adjustment" and importation of real-world knowledge that are necessary for viewers to make sense of the episode and its actions and events. Railway tracks in a real-life situation, for instance, neither lead to an act of eating ("causal relations") nor offer the spatial setting for a dining table ("spatial relations"). While dining alone is highly mimetic and happens in real life as well, once it is staged for viewing in front of a camera and situated specifically on a railway track, viewers must reevaluate what they already know about these acts and objects in the actual world that they belong to.

It is thus interesting to note that while the episode and its storyworld content violate physical laws of the real world, these elements are oriented toward triggering more profound emotional responses from viewers, consequently allowing for a highly empathetic and affective viewing experience. Narratives, as David Miall points out, are intended to "entertain, to excite interest, and to arouse various types of affective response."[17] Affect, in other words, plays a significant role in understanding and experiencing narratives, governing the cognitive processes of narrative comprehensions. When readers/viewers of narrative face an unfamiliar narrative situation with no coherent schema to follow, then narrative recipients' affective responses help reshape their interpretive strategies and guide them through a narrative. Importantly, too, affect in narrative comprehension is self-referential, enabling "cross-domain linking" and occurring when recipients identify with one or more of the characters in a narrative. This is why characters' motives and goals are important in any narrative. Just as it is possible in social situations to identify with those whose physical traits are different, narrative recipients are concerned more with characters' motives than with their appearance or behavior, as "motives explain behavior, that is, what characters do as actants and why."[18] Once narrative recipients adopt characters' motives, they can more readily identify with them, respond affectively, and comprehend a narrative no matter how unfamiliar the characters and their circumstances and actions in the narrative may be.

The railway track episode indeed focuses on establishing this affective relationship between viewers and the episode by directing viewers to the motives and thoughts of the host, although they are never explicitly narrated. The episode unfolds with quiet, soothing music and a short caption that reads, "Oh Kwang Rok who wishes to eat samgye-tang on a railway track." Both the music and the caption disappear after a close-up shot of the food, and only the silence and a full shot of the host eating his meal fill the screen. Miall asserts that affect, crucial for narrative comprehension, occurs when narrative recipients can identify with one or more of the characters in a narrative by sharing with them their motives. The caption at the beginning of the episode, while hinting at the motive of the host ("wishes"), is highly ambiguous and portrays only a partial picture of exactly what the intent of the host may be and why he wishes to have his meal on a railway track. Nevertheless, being the only obvious linguistic cue of the episode and appearing at the very beginning, the caption succeeds in drawing viewers' attention to the unsaid motive of the host as an ambiguity to be filled in and helps provoke viewers' curiosity. The ambiguity and curiosity in viewers' minds are important. As Thon asserts, "Narrative representations across media commonly employ ambiguity to such an extent that more than one storyworld can be intersubjectively constructed, and, at least in some cases, there may be no way to decide which of these constructs is more plausible, "mandated," or "authorized.'"[19] The ambiguity surrounding the motive of the host, then, engages viewers to more actively participate in the narrative and suggests that viewers make sense of the episode by intersubjectively constructing multiple plausible storyworlds that they can explore and relate to. Rather than obstructing viewers' interpretive strategies and identification with the episode, the unsaid motive in the episode liberates viewers and generates multiple interpretations of the episode and constructions of its storyworld.

The episode is especially successful in encouraging these intersubjective constructions and keeping viewers' interest in the host thanks to its overall lyric quality.[20] Although the episode includes some sense of change (the process of starting and ending a meal), this change is never foregrounded in the episode. There are no significant actions or conflicts involved in the episode that cause any meaningful transformation in the course of the narrative, either. In other words, the episode focuses not on what happens, but what is, including the host's quiet meditation on the particular food and place of his choice. This lyric quality significantly influences viewers' attitude and position toward the host and their narrative experience more generally. Jim Phelan, for example, explains that in lyric progressions, "our judgments and emotions focus not on character's choices and what they mean for what does and does not happen to them but rather on the progressive revelation of characters and their static situations."[21] Moreover, in some lyric progressions, "judgment drops out of our response to be replaced by sympathetic identification: rather than viewing the speaker from an observer position, we take on his or her perspective."[22]

The same can be said about the progression of the railway track episode. The episode starts quietly with the host seated at a dining table, while the railway track offers a seemingly unusual setting for his dining experience. During the brief progression of the narrative, viewers notice hardly any change from the beginning except for the food that is consumed by the host little by little in silence. The physical setting and situation of the episode remain static, but the show frequently offers close-up shots of the host's face, capturing subtle changes in his facial expression. The host first appears excited, but soon becomes increasingly pensive, reminiscent, and thoughtful. While viewers are still unable to access exact details of his interiority, these camera shots together reveal and translate to the minds of viewers the overall mood of stasis and pensiveness. The subsequent effect is the representation of the sheer depth of the host's perspective in its relation to the current circumstances in the episode. Even as the total silence and lack of other storyworld components still maintain the overall ambiguity and opaqueness of the episode, the gravity of the unsaid perspective and thoughts of the host is foregrounded in the episode against the static background, situating viewers within the host's vantage point. Consequently, viewers are likely to become more affectively engaged with the host and his circumstances, take on his perspective, and attempt to share with the host his thoughts, beliefs, and attitudes by simulating in their own minds multiple plausible scenarios and interpretations about them. It is no longer important for viewers to judge and understand precisely the host's action and reasons for his action, and whether they make any logical sense at all.

Once this affective relationship is established between viewers and the episode, and viewers become emotionally invested, mental events, "the character's reactions to perceived or actual states of affairs,"[23] become more prominent than physical events in the episode. Furthermore, viewers' interest in these mental events leads to a highly imaginative (albeit speculative) and empathetic narrative experience—the silent host's reactions and perceptions are implicit and have to be inferred, thereby requiring that viewers join a higher degree of metacognitive activity, that is, thinking about thinking, which is particularly prone to empathy. Following this affective and empathetic interpretive strategy, then, viewers can reevaluate and reexperience some of the existing storyworld components in the episode. The seemingly illogical choice of the setting, for instance, can trigger a more immersive narrative experience for viewers. Ryan points out that "spatial immersion is not only a matter of experiencing space through movement; it can also consist of an emotional attachment to a certain location."[24] This feeling attached to a particular location is called "sense of place" and influences significantly one's experience and relationship with the location. A railway track as the setting for a quiet meal may defy the obvious physical law of the real world. However, the episode with its overall lyric quality and emphasis on mental events engages viewers affectively and guides them to revisit the setting by considering what "emotional attachment" the host may have to this particular location of his choice. It is worth noting in this regard that the final close-up shot of the camera reveals the glint of a tear in the host's eyes. No details about his mental state are offered, but attentive viewers comprehend the episode and its setting through the "sense of place" rather than through some preexisting physical law or logic about it. Importantly, too, as viewers simulate and hypothesize in their minds the interiority of the host, they, too, are likely to foster the very sense of place and to be taken to places that matter to them, thereby experiencing the spatial immersion that Ryan speaks of. Viewers join this quiet mukbang show empathetically by feeling, thinking, and imaging with the silent host, and making sense of its storyworld, which is, in fact, not too far apart from their own world.

Although the semiotic (narrative elements) and technological (use of caption, camera shots, and so forth) approaches are useful to illuminate the narrative power of silent mukbang, these approaches need to be contextualized culturally as well. After all, culture informs behaviors and beliefs of both the media users and the producers. Likewise, "Quiet Dining" can be understood as a response to the changing cultural and social landscape of the South Korean society. One recognizable consumption pattern of most mukbang shows, for instance, is that most of the subscribers to these channels and programs live by themselves. Asian society in the era of neo-Confucianism has undergone drastic transformations, and South Korea is not an exception in this regard. Individualism, or individualized lifestyle, for instance, no longer belongs exclusively to the Western or Anglo-American society. It is now a distinct characteristic of urban life in Korea. According to the Korean Statistical Information Service's 2017 statistics, one-person households represent 27.2 percent of the entire 20,170,000 households in South Korea.[25] The sense of oneself as an independent, "freely choosing individual,"[26] however, was never a part of the Korean cultural tradition. As a result, individualism in Korea comes with interesting ambivalence and irony—a yearning for the emancipatory, Western lifestyle on the one hand and a desire for connection and belonging on the other hand. Mukbang shows target those viewers who live and dine alone and help them establish, albeit virtually, this very connection that they may be missing in their lives. As viewers watch these shows with hosts dining alone, they are likely to feel an empathetic affiliation with the host's aloneness and simultaneously become acquainted with them. After all, someone dining alone is not an unusual scene to most viewers, and viewers reach out to mukbang shows in order to fill a void in their heart.

Interactive mukbang shows, where viewers directly communicate with their host through online chat rooms, capitalize on this need for connection among viewers by offering them an opportunity not only to watch the host dining alone but also to interact with the host during the meal. The remainder of the chapter analyzes closely one of these interactive mukbang shows with a focus on how it engages viewers. While continuing to pay close attention to the narratological and technological properties of the show in my analysis, I will attempt to shed more light on the situatedness of media production and consumption—that is, how does the cultural and social environment, within which a specific media text is situated, further impact both the making and perceiving of media in meaningful ways? Benzz, one of the most popular interactive mukbang hosts in South Korea, for instance, is known for the massive amounts of food that he consumes all in one setting in front of a web camera that he sets up for a live-streaming broadcast. His YouTube broadcasting channel has 2.9 million subscribers, and masses of people gather in the online chat room of his channel to watch him eat and talk. With the popularity of his show, Benzz has been featured in various mainstream media in Korea and interviewed by Western media, which describe him as one of the leading figures of the Korean mukbang culture, "a unique and strange phenomenon trending throughout the country."[27] In one particular episode, Benzz eats four whole cakes and drinks a half-gallon of regular milk, as well as two kinds of flavored milk—chocolate and vanilla—in slightly smaller containers.[28]

There are a few standard features of these interactive mukbang shows. Hosts usually eat so-called junk food, including fried chicken, instant noodles, and a wide range of desserts, to name a few. They also devour abnormally large amounts of food. A typical interactive mukbang episode starts with a host enumerating food items placed before him or her on a table, either large quantities of a single item or five or six (or even more) double-portion dishes. These interactive mukbang shows also have online chat rooms that enable live interactions between the host and viewers. Although mukbang is a recent, "strange" occurrence, food television, whose form Korean mukbang shows have adapted and transformed, has been a long-standing phenomenon globally. In the United States, for instance, there were already several cable channels dedicated to food and cooking by the 1940s, starting with the 1946 cooking show by the famous chef James Beard.[29] Pauline Adema contextualizes the popularity of food television in America within the ambiguity of contemporary American society, where the desire for "clear and solid values to live by" and the desire "to embrace the limitless possibilities of modern life and experience that obliterates all values" co-exist.[30] Food and cooking shows allow viewers to keep a delicate balance between these two opposing kinds of desire by incorporating "the vicarious pleasures of watching someone else cook and eat; the emulsion of entertainment and cooking; the jumbling of traditional gender roles; and the ambivalence toward cultural standards of body, consumption, and health."[31] Viewers of food television can have limitless options of all kinds of scrumptious food and vicariously enjoy them while not having to worry about the consequences of excessive eating.

Similarly, interactive mukbang shows in Korea epitomize the irony of contemporary Korean society, confounding, as discussed earlier, desires for individualism and connection on the one hand and the issues of control and excess on the other hand. The interactive mukbang show is a particularly apt channel for viewers to manage between excess and control. It makes possible the vicarious pleasure of eating and not eating food at the same time, while also allowing viewers to interact with the host who does the eating for them. Benzz, for instance, while leisurely indulging himself in four whole cakes, repeatedly says, "I feel so happy. Is this the sugar that makes me so happy?" As if these cakes are not enough for him, Benzz happily gulps all his milk (and he turns his regular milk into chocolate milk by melting chocolates in it). In the meantime, viewers directly ask him questions about his foods—how do they taste? Which one do you like better? Does the cake taste better with vanilla milk or chocolate milk? Can you bring the cakes closer to the camera so that we have a more unobstructed view of them? It is almost as though viewers try to eat these cakes by watching Benzz consuming them and having him eat in the way that they would have liked to if they were free from the virtue of control and cultural standards of body and beauty. Indeed, viewers seem to choose to watch these mukbang shows as a way of virtually and imaginatively consuming food without consequences.

While the anxiety about food consumption, especially for women, is by no means an exclusively South Korean phenomenon, "lookism," a term referring to the attitude of privileging physical attractiveness, is especially prevalent and deeply rooted in modern South Korean society.[32] According to the 2015 survey by Nielsen Korea, conducted online with 3 million people from sixty different countries, six out of ten Koreans responded that they believed that they were overweight, marking higher (60 percent) than the global average of 49 percent. This was despite the fact that Korea has the lowest overweight rate among all OECD (the Organisation for Economic Co-operation and Development) nations. Likewise, 50 percent Koreans are actually on a diet, rigorously controlling their daily food consumption.[33] Food anxiety and body dissatisfaction lead to other more severe problems, such as eating disorders and excessive bodybuilding and exercises, but a safer and newer way to benefit from the comfort and pleasure inherent in food seems to be to increase consumption vicariously, by ingesting media related to food and cooking. The extreme lookism in Korea, coupled with the ubiquity of mobile devices aided by the world's fastest internet that makes possible easy and quick access to any streaming show, facilitates the perfect environment for the production and consumption of mukbang shows in Korea.

Another aspect of these interactive mukbang shows that deserves closer attention is the dynamics between host and viewers, as the particular relationship between them makes it possible to watch the show in the first place. Viewers of interactive mukbang not only watch the show, they also listen to the show—that is, noises made by the host while he or she eats: the swallowing, slurping, chewing, and so forth. In order to make these noises more vivid, interactive mukbang hosts often use elaborate and advanced sound equipment. These noises, of course, provoke viewers' sensory channels and create an illusion that helps viewers feel as though someone is dining with them, right next to them. However, these intimate "mouth noises" could also be, quite frankly, rather unpleasant and even repulsive to some viewers, especially given that in Korea, one is supposed to eat without making any noise. Moreover, interactive mukbang hosts' tendency to consume unhealthy foods in such abnormally large quantities can appear to be self-abusive and destructive, causing some viewers to frown with discomfort and disgust. Hyejin Kim, for instance, points out that the increasing number of mukbang shows[34] and the severe competition among them have led mukbang hosts to find ways to draw attention from their viewers by becoming more "provocative, sensational, and self-abusive."[35] Kim notices that many popular interactive mukbang hosts select food that is extremely spicy or hot. They also openly express pains and agonies by consuming large quantities of food within a very short time frame. In other words, what happens in interactive mukbang shows can be utterly unappealing, unpleasant, and aversive, but certainly not unwatchable, and it can rather be amusing and entertaining simultaneously, as the continuing popularity of these shows indicates. Why and how do viewers watch someone whose behavior is likely to provoke unpleasant feelings? The viewer–host relationship in these shows hence requires further consideration.

The consumption of mixed feelings, or the concurrence of pleasure and displeasure, has been a long-standing interest in emotion research. Some researchers view them as mutually exclusive because, as Ulrich Schimmack points out, they describe different quantities along a single dimension, "just like 'short' and 'tall' are opposing labels for different heights."[36] According to these researchers, just as one cannot be short and tall simultaneously, opposite feelings along a single dimension, such as pleasure and displeasure, cannot occur concurrently. Other researchers, on the other hand, argue that these two conflicting feelings could occur at the same time, and consequently, are "at best represented by two unipolar dimensions" rather than a single bipolar dimension.[37] Recent developments in functional magnetic resonance imaging (fMRI) offer a compelling ground for this two-unipolar, coactivation approach. The mapping of the emotional brain through fMRI scans, for instance, has shown the amygdala as the main neural correlate for fear and other likely negative emotions, whereas happiness and other likely positive emotions usually require prefrontal cortex participation, among other areas.³⁸ With the evidence from fMRI scans, it seems safe to conclude that pleasure and displeasure, represented by two unipolar dimensions, are indeed mutually in-exclusive and can occur simultaneously.

What is most interesting about the coactivation approach to opposing feelings is that the concurrence of mixed feelings is most likely to occur when viewers take a distant observer position from what seems unpleasant and repulsive. Scott Hemenover and Ulrich Schimmack, for instance, conducted an experiment where participants watched a disgusting-humorous scene from the movie *Pink Flamingos* (1973), in which the main character eats dog feces in a funny manner. Participants in the experiment were divided into two groups. Some were given a role of an insider and read the following instruction: "Imagine that you are this main character doing, thinking, and feeling what this character does. Put yourself in the frame of mind so that you are responding as you would if it was actually you experiencing the situation as the main character."³⁹ The other participants, on the other hand, were invited to take a position of an outsider: "Imagine you have no connection to what is happening and that what is happening cannot impact you in any way. You are simply observing and reacting to the events as they unfold."⁴⁰ Participants completed a consent form before watching the clip and answered questionnaires after the clip assessing their emotional responses between amusement and disgust. In order to measure mixed feelings, ratings were made on a 5-point scale ranging from 0 (not at all) to 4 (extremely). According to their answers, participants who watched the scene from a protagonist position (the character who eats dog feces) reported disgusting feelings, whereas those who took an outsider's position reported mixed feelings of disgust and amusement. This experiment reveals two significant findings: the co-occurrence of two conflicting feelings (disgust and amusement, displeasure and pleasure) is indeed possible, and taking an outsider's point of view enhances the experience of mixed feelings, allowing viewers to tolerate and even take pleasure in watching something that is distasteful and disagreeable.

It is important to consider, then, how interactive mukbang shows facilitate the experience of mixed feelings to entertain viewers with what can be potentially unpleasant and aversive. Interestingly, interactive mukbang shows incorporate elements that both push and pull viewers. Importantly, too, this push-pull effect can be best understood when one takes into account technological, narratological, and cultural elements of the shows simultaneously. One defining characteristic of popular culture is the "interactive relationships between consumer and producer, rejecting the mass culture approach that accepted the audience as passive receptors."⁴¹ The wide and rapid development of the internet in South Korea has further accelerated and enhanced these "interactive relationships" of popular culture using a digital platform. Users of the internet, thanks to its mobility and high penetration rate in South Korea, are freed from physical and temporal constraints and can access media content at any time and in any place.[42] Interactive mukbang shows in particular are especially suited for pulling viewers and encouraging them to move beyond the role of "passive receptors," as viewers of mukbang can make specific requests through online chat rooms and significantly inform and even change the course of the shows. These chat rooms, coupled with the advanced sound equipment, versatile use of camera shots, and the fast and easy access to the internet, engage viewers to actively participate in the making of mukbang.

Nevertheless, these technological properties of interactive mukbang shows, while actively engaging viewers and encouraging their participation, do not lead to developing fully formed empathy between viewers and host. Empathy, the sharing of emotion that often leads to identification with others, arises from our physical and social awareness of one another. This awareness can be simulated by emotional contagion, "the tendency to automatically mimic and synchronize facial expressions, vocalizations, postures, and movements with those of another person."[43] While technological advancements of interactive mukbang shows, such as close-up camera shots, sound, and chat rooms, may more readily provoke emotional contagion between viewers and host, thereby leading to empathy, empathy is also a contextual experience, as "our personal histories and cultural contexts affect the way we understand automatically shared feelings."[44] Personal histories and cultural contexts of individuals regulate the automatic sharing of emotion and help reshape how one feels and responds emotionally. This is important to note, especially given the cultural context of Korea, where extreme lookism has become the norm of modern life. Even as viewers automatically mimic facial expressions and feelings of mukbang hosts who overeat and overindulge, most viewers certainly do not identify with these hosts and take their position due to the pressure of the society, which demands control over excess. Viewers watch these interactive mukbang shows so that they do not have to do what these hosts do—to overeat and to overindulge—in the shows.

Likewise, online chat rooms, while making possible intimate and direct interactions between viewers and host, shape the viewer–host relationship hierarchically rather than horizontally. That is, most viewers use the chat rooms in order to make specific requests and demand certain actions from their host. This hierarchical relationship is especially evident when viewers pay money to their host in the form of "star balloons," a type of proprietary virtual currency that can be converted into regular cash, to show that their demands are met satisfactorily. Some of the top-ranked interactive mukbang hosts in Korea make as much as $10,000 a month through viewer donations alone.[45] Viewers of interactive mukbang shows choose to be vicariously gratified and yet suppress their desire to eat by not taking the position of the host and instead becoming an intimate and yet somewhat superior, disciplined, and detached observer/patron. Moreover, by doing so, viewers can enjoy watching something that they will not possibly mimic, something that is in fact quite repulsive and disagreeable.

Although Western media have called mukbang "a unique and strange phenomenon trending throughout the country,"[46] the narratological, technological, and cultural investigations of mukbang help make sense of its production and consumption. Mukbang is a phenomenon that actively capitalizes on viewers' capacity and tendency to construct mental models of narrative, even as these models (i.e., storyworlds) are only implicitly simulated by narrative with seemingly scarce storyworld components and a lower degree of narrativity— the silent mukbang shows in Korea are a good example. Interactive mukbang shows, on the other hand, are equipped with technology that helps accommodate the cultural sentiment of South Korea that demands vicarious consumption of food among other things. These shows also position viewers in such a way that they become intimate and yet detached observers, taking pleasure in viewing something that can be potentially repulsive, and regulate their empathetic relationship with mukbang hosts. Ultimately, the bridging of narrative, culture, and technology adds depth to our understanding of the why and how of media, while the use of Korean cultural precepts and concepts as theoretical and interpretive lenses makes possible a localized approach to media and narrative studies. Adaptations of mukbang across national borders, on the other hand, raise multiple intriguing questions to consider further. Whereas globalization has been long understood as a mediated Western cultural force, "Asian media have emerged as new players for transnational consumption, changing the dynamics of the media landscape in the region."[47] American mukbang,[48] inspired by Korean mukbang and started by a longtime YouTube user, Trisha Paytas, who uploaded her own mukbang video on YouTube in late April 2015, is an example where an Asian media product is changing not only the media landscape within the region but also beyond the region. It is also an indication that culture and cultural identity, which inform and are informed by media, are no longer restricted by geographical and national boundaries—media and their digital circulation are further reinforcing the adaptive and transformative nature of culture.

Narratologically, adaptations of Korean mukbang across the globe allow us to think more deeply about the author/producer and reader/audience relationship, as well as the existing theories of reader response that, as Brian Richardson points out, center around the "monist" and "relativist" approaches.[49] The monist notion proposes models that conceptualize a particular kind of "ideal" reader. Wayne Booth, for instance, posits that the "author creates, in short, an image of himself and an image of his reader . . . and the most successful reading is one in which the created selves, author and reader, can find complete agreement."[50] Relativist notion, set forth by theorists such as Norman Holland,

Roland Barthes, and Jacques Derrida, on the other hand, supports "indeterminate, subjective, or relativistic criticism" and denies in theory "the possibility of any model, ideal, or authorial reading."[51] The advent of digital media with their highly circulatory and participatory nature, however, suggests that readers are no longer conceived primarily in their relationship to the author. Rather than merely interpreting narratives as designed and given by the author, readers now actively reconstruct and reproduce the narratives—the ways in which viewers of interactive mukbang shows communicate with their hosts through online chat rooms highlight this point. Also, circulation and adaptations of mukbang across borders indicate that media and their narratives are already inherently potent with multiple and diverse meanings, authors, and audiences, but simultaneously not indeterminate and relativistic, as these meanings, authors, and audiences are ultimately bound by time and place once they cross borders and are situated within a certain context (i.e., Korean mukbang vs. American mukbang). The strange phenomenon called mukbang, then, is a key to understanding multiple facets of how and why we produce and consume media, and how their narratives inform us and others across boundaries.

Notes

Portions of this chapter appeared in "Joy of Ugly Feelings: Korean "Bad Taste" Webtoons as a Case Study," *Studies in 20th & 21st Century Literature* 42, no. 1 (2017). http://doi.org/10.4148/2334-4415.1960.

1 See Toby Miller and Marwan M. Kraidy, *Global Media Studies* (Malden, MA: Polity Press, 2016).
2 Marie-Laure Ryan, *Narrative across Media: The Language of Storytelling* (Lincoln: University of Nebraska Press, 2004), 17.
3 According to an NPR article, some top-ranked Mukbang hosts earn up to $10,000 a month. See Elise Hu, "Koreans Have an Insatiable Appetite for Watching Strangers Binge Eat," NPR, March 24, 2015 (3:36 A.M. ET), https://www.npr.org/sections/thesalt/2015/03/24/392430233/koreans-have-an-insatiable-appetite-for-watching-strangers-binge-eat.
4 Ryan, *Narrative*, 10.
5 Ibid., 12.
6 To understand better how narrative theorists are broadening the definition of narrative and its applicability across media, see Marie-Laure Ryan and Jan-Noël Thon's edited volume *Storyworlds across Media: Towards a Media-Conscious Narratology* (Lincoln: University of Nebraska Press, 2014), Jan-Noël Thon's *Transmedial Narratology and Contemporary Media Culture* (Lincoln: University of Nebraska Press, 2016), and David Herman's *Narratology beyond the Human* (Oxford: Oxford University Press, 2018).
7 Thon, *Transmedial Narratology*, 35.
8 David Herman, *Story Logic* (Lincoln: University of Nebraska Press, 2002), 9.
9 Marie-Laure Ryan, "Story/Worlds/Media: Tuning the Instruments of a Media-Conscious Narratology," in *Storyworlds across Media: Towards a Media-Conscious*

Narratology, ed. Marie-Laure Ryan and Jan-Noël Thon (Lincoln: University of Nebraska Press, 2014), 32.

10 David Herman, *Basic Elements of Narrative* (Oxford: Wiley-Blackwell, 2009), 106.

11 "Quiet Dinning," YouTube, July 28, 2016, https://www.youtube.com/watch?v=pv -ewDoNnOs&t=3s.

12 Thon, *Transmedial*, 46.

13 For detailed explanations about each component, see Ryan, "Story/Worlds /Media."

14 Thon, *Transmedial*, 46.

15 Marie-Laure Ryan, *Possible Worlds, Artificial Intelligence, and Narrative Theory* (Bloomington: Indiana University Press, 1991), 51.

16 Kendall Walton, *Mimesis as Make-Believe: On the Foundations of the Representational Acts* (Cambridge, MA: Harvard University Press, 1990), 145.

17 David Miall, "Affect and Narrative: A Model of Response to Stories," *Poetics* 17, no. 3 (1988): 261.

18 Ibid., 270.

19 Thon, *Transmedial*, 55.

20 James Phelan defines "lyricality" rhetorically, meaning (1) "somebody telling somebody else (who may or may not be present to the speaker) or even himself or herself on some occasion for some purpose that something is—a situation, an emotion, a perception, an attitude, a belief" or (2) "somebody telling somebody else (who may or may not be present to the speaker) or even himself or herself on some occasion about his or her meditations on something." For more details, see James Phelan, *Living to Tell About It* (Ithaca, NY: Cornell University Press, 2005), 161.

21 Ibid., 10.

22 Ibid.

23 Ryan, "Story/Worlds/Media," 36.

24 Marie-Laure Ryan, "From Narrative Games to Playable Stories: Toward a Poetics of Interactive Narrative," *Storyworlds* 1 (2009): 54.

25 KOSIS, Korean Statistical Information Service, accessed January 11, 2019, http://kosis.kr/eng/index/index.do.

26 Youna Kim, "Media Globalization in Asia," in *Media Consumption and Everyday Life in Asia*, ed. Youna Kim (New York: Routledge, 2008), 12.

27 Amy McCarthy, "This Korean Food Phenomenon Is Changing the Internet," Eater.com, April 19, 2017, https://www.eater.com/2017/4/19/15349568/mukbang -videos-korean-youtube.

28 Benzz, "Benzz Mukbang, Cake Special," YouTube, October 31, 2018, https://www .youtube.com/watch?v=m5L8t6g6UfE&t=98s.

29 Pauline Adema, "Vicarious Consumption: Food, Television and the Ambiguity of Modernity," *Journal of American Culture* 23, no. 3 (2000): 113–123.

30 Ibid., 120.

31 Ibid., 113.

32 The term "lookism," a discriminatory treatment toward people considered physically unattractive, was first coined in the 1970s and used in the *Washington Post* magazine in 1978. The word now appears in several major English language dictionaries.

33 "South Korea Has the Lowest Overweight among All the OECD Nations, But!" (my trans.), Joongang Ilbo online, last modified January 23, 2015, https://news .joins.com/article/17010069.

34 In 2015, there were 3,000 active Mukbang hosts in Korea with one or more shows regularly updated. The number has most likely increased since then. See Hu, "Koreans."

35 Hyejin Kim, "Investigation of Mukbang as a Lowbrow Cultural Phenomenon as Well as Food Pornography" (my trans.), *Journal of Humanities Studies* 50 (2015): 441.

36 Ulrich Schimmack, "Pleasure, Displeasure, and Mixed Feelings: Are Semantic Opposites Mutually Exclusive?" *Cognition and Emotion* 15, no. 1 (2001): 81.

37 Ibid., 82.

38 Eduardo Andrade, and Joel Cohen, "On the Consumption of Negative Feelings," *Journal of Consumer Research* 34, no. 3 (2007): 286.

39 Scott Hemenover and Ulrich Schimmack, "That's Disgusting! . . . , But Very Amusing: Mixed Feelings of Amusement and Disgust," *Cognition and Emotion* 21, no. 5 (2007): 1106.

40 Ibid.

41 Adema, "Vicarious Consumption," 114.

42 According to the 2016 statistics by Business Insider, Korea ranks second in the world when it comes to the fiber optic penetration rate. "Korea Ranks 2nd in the World for the Fiber Optic Penetration Rate" (my trans.), Chungnyun Ilbo online, last modified February 23, 2016, https://m.post.naver.com/viewer/postView.nhn?volumeNo=3648723&memberNo=25584196&vType=VERTICAL.

43 Elaine Hatfield, John Cacioppo, and Richard Rapson, *Emotion Contagion: Studies in Emotion and Social Interaction* (New York: Cambridge University Press, 1994), 81.

44 Suzanne Keen, "A Theory of Narrative Empathy," *Narrative* 14, no. 3 (2006): 209.

45 Hu, "Koreans."

46 McCarthy, "This Korean."

47 Kim, "Media," 3.

48 It is also important to note that American mukbang videos are quite different from their Korean inspiration. For instance, while the hosts in Korean interactive mukbang shows focus on talking about the food they eat, American mukbang hosts talk more frequently about themselves, what they think and how they feel. For more details, see McCarthy, "This Korean."

49 Brian Richardson, "The Other Reader's Response: On Multiple, Divided, and Oppositional Audience," *Criticism* 39 (1997): 32.

50 Wayne Booth, *The Rhetoric of Fiction* (Chicago: University of Chicago Press, 1983), 138.

51 Richardson, "The Other Reader's Response," 32.

Bibliography

Adema, Pauline. "Vicarious Consumption: Food, Television and the Ambiguity of Modernity." *Journal of American Culture* 23, no. 3 (2000): 113–123.

Andrade, Eduardo, and Joel Cohen. "On the Consumption of Negative Feelings." *Journal of Consumer Research* 34, no. 3 (2007): 283–300.

"Benzz Mukbang, Cake Special." YouTube. October 31, 2018. https://www.youtube.com/watch?v=m5L8t6g6UfE&t=98s.

Booth, Wayne. *The Rhetoric of Fiction*. Chicago: University of Chicago Press, 1983.

Hatfield, Elaine, John Cacioppo, and Richard Rapson. *Emotion Contagion: Studies in Emotion and Social Interaction*. New York: Cambridge University Press, 1994.

Hemenover, Scott, and Ulrich Schimmack. "That's Disgusting! . . . , But Very Amusing: Mixed Feelings of Amusement and Disgust." *Cognition and Emotion* 21, no. 5 (2007): 1102–1113.

Herman, David. *Basic Elements of Narrative*. Oxford: Wiley-Blackwell, 2009.

———. *Narratology beyond the Human*. Oxford: Oxford University Press, 2018.

———. *Story Logic*. Lincoln: University of Nebraska Press, 2002.

Hu, Elise. "Koreans Have An Insatiable Appetite for Watching Strangers Binge Eat." NPR. March 24, 2015 (3:36 A.M. ET). https://www.npr.org/sections/thesalt/2015 /03/24/392430233/koreans-have-an-insatiable-appetite-for-watching-strangers -binge-eat.

Keen, Suzanne. "A Theory of Narrative Empathy." *Narrative* 14, no. 3 (2006): 207–236.

Kim, Hyejin. "Investigation of *Mukbang* as a Lowbrow Cultural Phenomenon as Well as Food Pornography" (my trans.). *Journal of Humanities Studies* 50 (2015): 433–455.

Kim, Youna. "Media Globalization in Asia." In *Media Consumption and Everyday Life in Asia*, edited by Youna Kim, 1–24. New York: Routledge, 2008.

"Korea Ranks 2nd in the World for the Fiber Optic Penetration Rate" (my trans.). Chungnyun Ilbo online. Last modified February 23, 2016. https://m.post.naver .com/viewer/postView.nhn?volumeNo=3648723&memberNo=25584196&vType =VERTICAL.

KOSIS (Korean Statistical Information Service). Accessed January 11, 2019. http:// kosis.kr/eng/index/index.do.

McCarthy, Amy. "This Korean Food Phenomenon Is Changing the Internet." Eater .com. Last modified April 19, 2017. https://www.eater.com/2017/4/19/15349568 /mukbang-videos-korean-youtube.

Miall, David. "Affect and Narrative: A Model of Response to Stories." *Poetics* 17, no. 3 (1988): 259–272.

Miller, Toby, and Marwan M. Kraidy. *Global Media Studies*. Malden, MA: Polity Press, 2016.

Phelan, James. *Living to Tell about It*. Ithaca, NY: Cornell University Press, 2005.

"Quiet Dinning." YouTube. July 28, 2016. https://www.youtube.com/watch?v=pv -ewDoNnOs&t=3s.

Richardson, Brian. "The Other Reader's Response: On Multiple, Divided, and Oppositional Audience." *Criticism* 39 (1997): 31–53.

Ryan, Marie-Laure. "From Narrative Games to Playable Stories: Toward a Poetics of Interactive Narrative." *Storyworlds* 1 (2009): 43–59.

———. *Narrative across Media: The Language of Storytelling*. Lincoln: University of Nebraska Press, 2004.

———. *Possible Worlds, Artificial Intelligence, and Narrative Theory*. Bloomington: Indiana University Press, 1991.

———. "Story/Worlds/Media: Tuning the Instruments of a Media-Conscious Narratology." In *Storyworlds across Media: Towards Media-Conscious Narratology*, edited by Marie-Laure Ryan and Jan-Noël Thon, 25–43. Lincoln: University of Nebraska Press, 2014.

Schimmack, Ulrich. "Pleasure, Displeasure, and Mixed Feelings: Are Semantic Opposites Mutually Exclusive?" *Cognition and Emotion* 15, no. 1 (2001): 81–97.

"South Korea Has the Lowest Overweight among All the OECD Nations, But!" (my trans.). Joongang Ilbo online. Last modified January 23, 2015. https://news.joins .com/article/17010069.

Thon, Jan-Noël. *Transmedial Narratology and Contemporary Media Culture*. Lincoln: University of Nebraska Press, 2016.

Walton, Kendall. *Mimesis as Make-Believe: On the Foundations of the Representational Acts*. Cambridge, MA: Harvard University Press, 1990.

8

Construction, Consumption, and Representation of White Supremacy in Sri Lankan Advertisements

■■■■■■■■■■■■■■■■■■■■■■■■■

Living White while
Being Non-White

ASANTHA U. ATTANAYAKE

The postcolonial dependent mentality and the tendency to imitate other mostly Western cultures are the two traits that plague young Sri Lankans today. Sri Lankans, for instance, hardly identify themselves primarily as Sri Lankans. They tend rather to identify with their ethnicity and/or religion as Sinhalese Buddhists, Sinhalese Christians, Tamil Hindus, Tamil Christians, or Muslims.[1] Hence there is no shared view of what it is to be a Sri Lankan. Some trace the roots of this issue of a weak national identity to the political agenda after independence. In 1956, Sinhala, the language of the majority (79 percent of the total population), was made the only official language of the country. This was a move to undermine English, the colonial master's language, and also to appeal to the majority for political advantages and gains. However, this resulted in marginalizing the minority groups whose mother tongue was Tamil, thus making them feel excluded from the country. Nipunika Lecamwasam's explanation of citizenship, in its first aspect as stated below, may shed some meaningful light on the origin of the problem of Sri Lankans' tendency to identify with their ethnicity rather than with one unified nation: "From a socio-political perspective, citizenship can be understood in relation to two aspects. (1) The legal framework that stipulates rights and duties for citizens. (2) The creation of an overarching cultural identity for the citizenhood of a particular state. In democracies that entertain an array of differing opinions, it is of crucial importance to sustain both elements because the idea of citizenship rests upon the attitudes of diverse political subjects whose differing opinions do not ideally affect their identification with the state as its constituent members."[2]

When Tamil, the mother tongue of both Tamils and Muslim minority groups, was not given equal status, the legal framework that stipulated citizens' rights ended up failing to encompass minority rights. Under such a scenario, culture, the strongest carrier of which is language, is not allowed to develop as an overarching cultural identity, but as a subservient one. By the same token, when the mother tongue of the majority defines the legal framework, it is the label of the majority that becomes the dominant identification marker of citizenship. Consequently, there arise divided identities within one nation.

Nevertheless, Sri Lanka, when compared to its South Asian neighbors, stands out in many respects: (1) Sri Lanka introduced a free education policy in 1941 and eliminated illiteracy decades ago, whereas most of the neighboring countries are still struggling with high illiteracy rates;[3] (2) Sri Lanka's strict law prohibiting child labor, where no child under the age of fourteen can be employed, contributes to the country's high literacy rate. As a result, Sri Lankans are more open to and knowledgeable about the world outside Sri Lanka; (3) Sri Lanka opened up its economy in 1977, decades before other South Asian neighbors opened up to the world market, and probably before Sri Lanka's own market was mature enough to handle the impacts of free trade; (4) Sri Lanka has never had the same degree of trouble in regard to gender issues, especially when compared to other South Asian nations such as India and Pakistan. This is likely due to the fact that Sri Lankan women obtained the franchise as early as 1931, almost as soon as women in England were able to vote. The resulting climate may even have contributed to Sri Lanka's producing the world's first female prime minister, Mrs. Sirimavo Bandaranaike, in the 1960s; and (5) Sri Lankans have longer life expectancies than those in other South Asian nations[4] owing to the free health care provided by the state.

If one looks at all these accomplishments, one would think that Sri Lanka has created a very positive, promising future for its people. However, the reality is far less positive. Sri Lanka seems to have set the standard in South Asia in terms of education, entertainment, health care, lifestyle, and so forth, even matching the norms of the developed Western nations. However, on the other hand, Sri Lanka is a poor imitation of these Western societies, and Sri Lankans have created their own pseudo-Western society that elevates the white ideal while devaluing their own Sri Lankan culture. This chapter examines the role of newspapers and other media in Sri Lanka in creating and propagating seemingly Western values that are, in reality, only a superficial exaltation of whiteness. First, I will generally provide and review examples of white supremacy found in Sri Lankan newspaper and other advertisements. I will then discuss theories concerning identity formation and linguistic imperialism to make sense of the prevalence and power of white supremacy in Sri Lanka today.

Examples of White Supremacy in Advertisements in Sri Lanka

While the ideal of a gentleman is often and generally represented by his dress, it is invariably the European outfit that is given the pride of place in Sri Lanka. In advertisements for male clothing, one will rarely see the Sri Lankan traditional national dress, which consists of a long, white kurtha-type shirt (a loose, collarless shirt) and a white sarong (a large tube of fabric wrapped around the waist). Wearing national dress is never promoted by anyone other than politicians who would wear it in public as a symbol of pseudonationalism. For most, European attire, despite its utter impracticality in Sri Lanka's tropical climate, is seen as the symbol of gentlemanliness, a legacy transmitted from the days of colonial rule. Similarly, most Sri Lankan women wear skirts or trousers and blouses, all of which are very Western in their aesthetics. Sri Lanka underwent significant social and cultural changes during the Portuguese, Dutch, and British colonial eras, which together lasted for more than four hundred years. For instance, P. M. Wickramarachchi notes how the costume of the Sinhalese women changed with the arrival of the Portuguese in 1505 as a result of "the widespread adoption of Christianity and the free social intercourse which existed between the Portuguese and Sinhalese of the upper classes."[5] These changes included Sri Lankan upper class women wearing the Portuguese long-sleeved jacket with a V-neckline in front. The fact that it was the Sinhalese of the upper class who started wearing the Portuguese dress indicates the clear symbolic value that Western dresses in general represent in Sri Lanka.[6] Not surprisingly, then, most tailors in Sri Lanka use European dress in their advertisements. Notably, too, most of these advertisements feature white men and women wearing the clothes. It was observed that the central advertisement in a popular tailoring shop in Colombo actually pictured a group of clean-shaven white men wearing well-cut European suits while sporting cowboy hats.

The idea of looking white in the primary sense, that is, having fair skin, is another area that Sri Lankan media painstakingly promote in order to encourage and meet the demand for skin-lightening products. The desire to look white is not confined to skin care in Sri Lankan society, especially in its upper echelons. Looking white has also crossed into the territory of hair care. Many Sri Lankan women with brown skin bleach their hair in an effort to approximate the idealized beauty of Western blondes. For instance, the marriage proposals section of a popular Sunday newspaper in Sri Lanka, the Sunday Observer, features images of Western clad white brides and grooms.[7] Of course, all proposals listed in this section are actually seeking well-educated, professional Sri Lankan (Sinhala Buddhist or Christian) brides and grooms, although the images posted on the website say otherwise. It is interesting to note that India shares the same white skin syndrome that Sri Lanka has. Itisha Nagar in her 2018 article on the skin-color bias in Indian arranged marriages concludes that the color of the skin, fairness in this case, can overpower other traits, such as general competency and physical attractiveness.[8]

The idea of speaking white is another aspect of this discussion. The Sri Lankan constitution recognizes three main languages. Sinhala and Tamil are both National and Official languages, whereas English is the Link language. It is compulsory for all students in the country to pass their mother tongue (Sinhala or Tamil) at the General Certificate of Education (Ordinary Level) to further their education. English is taught as the second language from grade three onward as a compulsory subject in the school curriculum. In terms of the utility value, however, English, especially spoken English, is deemed higher than the two mother tongues, Sinhala and Tamil. English is an essential component for upward social mobility. Being able to speak English means that one is presenting oneself as educated, belonging to a higher class and as a member of the intellectual community without having to prove it by writing in English.[9] Speaking English in Sri Lanka includes speaking posh English with a made-up accent presumed to sound either American or British. It is also common for upper class Sri Lankans not to be able to speak their own mother tongue properly (or pretending to be unable to speak it fluently). In short, Sri Lankan society seems to have given an increasingly prominent place to the way one speaks English (the how) than to what is spoken in the former colonial master's tongue.

For instance in Sri Lanka, if people speak English with an accent that sounds Western, their social class is immediately identified as high, thanks to their perceived proximity to the Western world. This attitude leads lower- and middle-class parents to send their children to elocution classes designed for their children to learn to put on an accent, but not necessarily to actually learn to speak English properly. One can see an incalculable number of advertisements, both in newspapers and open cut-outs in major cities, for these elocution classes to learn to speak like an American or an English person. For instance, when searching the internet for "list of elocution classes in Sri Lanka," about 297,000 results pop up.[10] The irony, however, is that none of the local varieties taught in these elocution classes actually matches any standard American or British accent. This is due to two reasons: one, there is no singular American or British accent since numerous varieties of English are spoken in both countries; and two, what the local elocution teachers teach is an artificial accent that sounds vaguely Western to Sri Lankans. These elocution classes are also usually advertised with an image of a Sri Lankan person in Western dress or, more commonly, a white person. There is little resistance to the association between English and higher social class/intellect propagated through such images—Sri Lankan society has already internalized standards of white superiority.

The promise of being able to speak white does not end there. It also allows one to ridicule other Sri Lankans, usually those from a rural or semirural background, based on unilaterally imposed measures, consequently exacerbating divisions among people within the nation. As I have identified in my earlier work,[11] Language Attitude Anxiety (LAA) stems from the prejudices of the society against speakers of English whose accent and elocution fall outside the arbitrarily set standards of how spoken English should sound. This LAA creates a lack of confidence among English language learners, manifested in a fear of ridicule, which is one of the main causes for many Sri Lankan learners' inability to use English. To further explain this phenomenon, the fear, shyness, and uncertainty that inform one's ability to speak in English are produced by social attitudes that generate a lack of confidence in English language learners. This lack of confidence to speak English may in turn lay the ground for learners to develop a set of negative attitudes toward their own speaking ability. This may even be projected onto their entire English language learning process, thus resulting in their further poor performance in learning English, including writing and reading, as a whole.

The desire to study white is predominant in the education section of every newspaper, especially when it comes to higher education. There are limited opportunities in the state universities for higher education in Sri Lanka because there are only fourteen state universities that can recruit about 5 percent of the total student population who sit for the university entrance examination in a given year. As a result, there is a very lucrative potential market for private higher education (local or foreign), with about 95 percent of Sri Lankan students being unable to get into a state university. One can see that private higher education institutes, in their advertising images, use young people (whether brown and local or white and foreign) in Western dress. These images are of females in miniskirts and coats and males in well-pressed European suits, representing the ideal elites who resemble those in Western societies. In addition, almost all of these advertisements are for private educational institutes and highlight seemingly promising opportunities for further education in countries such as the United States, United Kingdom, Canada, Australia, New Zealand, and so forth. All of these are predominantly Western countries. Also, almost all of these local private institutes have Western, especially British names—Oxford, Cambridge, Sussex, and Royal, for instance.

The buy white domain encompasses all kinds of household items (furniture, electrical items, kitchenware, and so forth) and personal items (clothes, handbags and wallets, shoes, and so forth). In Sri Lanka one will often hear phrases such as "I bought this from England when I visited there last summer." "This is my son's gift, from America." "This is imported, not the local, I think from the UK." Advertisements for household and personal items, therefore, are often headlined with phrases such as "imported from UK," "made in America," and "exclusively from Italy." These advertising phrases attract local customers almost immediately. For instance, an online advertisement for an import shop in Colombo describes the shop in the following manner: "The Import shop is known for its high quality food and cosmetic products imported from USA."[12] This particular shop imports goods from America exclusively and has high customer recommendations: "best place on earth," "authentic stuff."[13] In a nation dominated by the buy white mentality, local products are devalued and looked down upon as substandard. Locals regard and hence favor imported goods as more valuable and as the sign of higher social class.

The act white side of the narrative is reflected in the practices of individuals in many areas of the society. Celebrations of imported consumer holidays like Halloween, Valentine's Day, Mother's Day, Father's Day, and so forth are also some of the clear examples of white supremacy in Sri Lanka. These occasions do not belong to Sri Lankan culture but are concepts and practices imported predominantly from the Western societies. For instance, Sri Lankan media grab every opportunity to advertise occasions like Valentine's Day by giving mega publicity to these holiday celebrations. Sri Lankan youth are attracted to these concepts and the practices associated with them. For instance, advertisements published by local hotels for Valentine's Day celebrations usually propagate the idea of "dance and romance" and invite people to "wine and dine." All these activities are the symbols of Western high society while Valentine's Day itself is borrowed from the West. And of course, all these advertisements are written in English, reinforcing the tendency to speak white.

This attraction is soon seen to spread to all social strata, but its reach is still more prevalent at the higher social level. One sees the lower-income class trying to follow suit when the upper class sets these new standards. However, there is a vast gap in financial affordability between the manifestations of acting white in different classes. The income gap in Sri Lanka is widening, and even the middle class itself is complex, with many layers within it. A study done to investigate the structure of the contemporary middle class of Sri Lanka indicates that lower middle class is the "dominant sub-class within the Sri Lankan middle class, with its share at 55 percent of the middle class." Middle-middle class, on the other hand, accounts for 41 percent, while the upper middle class "accounts for a meager 4 percent."[14] Nevertheless, the standards that are set with the aid of representations of white supremacy invariably percolate down to the lower level and are reflected in various ways among the people in the lower class.

Unfortunately, most of these act white activities conflict with local standards at the moral, philosophical, and social levels in Sri Lankan society. Nevertheless, they persist. For instance, Mother's Day and Father's Day, where one is expected to celebrate one's parents by doing something special, were not popular ideas in Sri Lanka even a decade ago. Sri Lankan society has always considered filial piety and looking after parents to be the important social and moral values. From the time of the socialization processes of early childhood, these values are inculcated in children as part of their future duties and responsibilities. Therefore, the need to take parents out for a meal and give presents to them on a particular day of the year does not resonate in Sri Lankan culture and values. However, as a result of foreign practices creeping into the society and those practices being considered superior and more civilized, the concept of taking care of parents seems to be undergoing a significant paradigm shift in Sri Lanka. Reviewing and problematizing these practices leads us to question what is causing the construction, consumption, and representation of white supremacy in Sri Lanka. The next section discusses the culture and psychology of white supremacy in Sri Lanka.

Understanding the Culture and Psychology of White Supremacy in Sri Lanka

Two theories on identity/identity change, social identity theory (SIT)[15] and identity theory (IT),[16] can perhaps help us make sense of Sri Lankans' motivation to conform to a Western identity while detaching themselves from their local one. SIT contends that (1) "category traits and their comparisons in intergroup relations act as contexts of motives for identity change"[17]; (2) "categories establish expectations of and for behavior, and even suggest a narrative history of group membership"[18]; and (3) category labels can reflect notions of status, permanence, size, and other meanings that influence the actor's motive to improve his or her situation.[19]

IT, on the other hand, proposes that (1) personal, day-to-day relationships act as an immediate context that defines the salience of particular roles[20]; (2) the idea of competing memberships in varying contexts causes actors to encounter competing group demands, changing identity hierarchy; and (3) prominent network positions that an individual holds also influence identity formation.[21] Unlike the SIT, IT argues that individuals "seek external endorsement or mutuality between their notion of self and that which others hold of them."[22] Sri Lankans' choice to look and act white, then, may be due to the appealing nature of the developed Other in the context of the less powerful local counterforces that place competing demands on Sri Lankans. It may also be because of Sri Lankans' identity position in the perennially developing or third world category for over seventy years after independence in 1948, something that Sri Lankans cannot be proud of.

The IT analysis seems to explain the speak white tendency in Sri Lanka where individuals are reluctant to speak English due to the fear of being ridiculed in the larger society. Moreover, the desire for elocution classes to acquire an accent that is considered to be more Western is also embedded in the definite influence of external endorsement. At the same time, the set ideal self discussed in SIT, in this case an ideal self speaking in perfect English with an American or British accent, is associated with the West. The identity change in this case is hence simulated by the desire to be a better self than what the local culture attributes to the individual, both in terms of their perceptions of an ideal self as well as what they want others to see themselves as. By the same token, the other instances of white supremacy, all of which contribute to the ideal of looking and acting white, can be located in the same theoretical concept. It is significant to note that individuals seek memberships and interactions which verify the view they hold of themselves.

Another concept that aids discussion of the matter at hand is the idea of situated identities. Situated identities can be described as "the attributions that are made about participants in a particular setting as a consequence of their actions. Not only is this situated identity essential as a basis for initiating interaction, it is crucial for guiding and anticipating the course of that interaction."[23] For people to choose a particular behavior that is expected with external associations, such as the choice of attire, personal belongings, manner of speaking, and so forth that will help them stand out as the ideal among others, is to conform to an identity that is an extension of a situated identity. As "different response patterns produce differentially desirable social selves, and people choose among them so as to obtain the most favorable identity outcomes,"[24] Sri Lankans try to associate themselves with whiteness with apparent favorable experiences. The cognitive mechanism at work is the actor's perception of an inconsistency that leads the person to change their self-conception.[25] This inconsistency in the case of Sri Lankans discussed so far is associated with not being satisfied with the compared, which is the local, thereby selecting over an available hierarchy of category traits and network associations, that is, the whiteness.

The argument the situated identity theory posits is that "the relevant cues in the behavioral setting are first translated into identity potentials, and that these potential identities provide the basis for specific behavioral choices."[26] These identities collectively contribute to how people behave (to act, speak, buy, and dress white). The most desirable social selves are Western associated as they bestow one with the most favorable identity outcomes linked to Western powers. We can see a clear merging of SIT and IT in the case of Sri Lanka to construct these white-associated selves. On the one hand, it is the social status, which the individual perceives as higher with its affiliation to certain category traits, that results in Sri Lankans' tendency to eat, buy, and speak white. On the other hand, the positive feedback of the social network that individual receives as a result of imitating the white reinforces Sri Lankans' identity choice to be the arbitrarily constructed Western selves rather than the local ones. In both instances, the choice is between one other alternative, the local. Also, as per the situated identity principles, the potential identities that provide the basis for specific behavioral choices in specific contexts are not associated with those of the local, but essentially Western related in the Sri Lankan scenario.

It is also important to note the fact that Sri Lankans' identity construction to be the white seems to occur so frequently and with such a degree of willingness. For instance, there are always more Western-dressed women than women in traditional Sri Lankan attire. There are more English names than Sri Lankan names for private education institutes. There are more people who speak English (or English words mixed with Sinhala or Tamil) than those who speak their mother tongue, especially in urban centers of the country. Why do these occasions of identifying oneself with the white happen so frequently? Why does it seem very easy for Sri Lankans to adopt their particular identity? Whether Sri Lankans choose to move closer to the Western world or not is no longer the question. The important matter now is to understand better how and why Sri Lankans are able to select and reinforce the version of an ideal self, associated with whiteness and the West, so readily, quickly, and frequently.

My argument is that the power of English as a global language and the linguistic imperialism the English language enjoys are extended to a cultural imperialism as well. According to David Crystal, a certain language becomes a global language for one chief reason: the political power of its people, especially their military power.[27] When the British Empire collapsed, the United States took over as the world power. As the language of the two powerful nations, then and now, English remains the most powerful language. With the Western language, that is, English, the prominence of Western culture is inevitable. Thus, Western cultural artifacts, be they American or British, represent the ideal and the powerful to most Sri Lankans. Even though language and culture are intertwined, the latter exists even without the former. The best example is of the Western cultural representations, such as dress patterns, food habits, and other commodities, that are existent even when the English language is not present. In other words, even when the language is not being used, or not used in its fluent and accurate form, the culture it represents is alive in many other forms as discussed. In rural Sri Lanka, one would not find many people who speak English in a coherent manner. However, they are the subjects (or victims) of the aforementioned instances of whiteness and white supremacy, leading them to try to look and act white.

The theoretical framework of linguistic hegemony is closely related to linguistic imperialism. Robert Phillipson argues that English achieved its dominant position as the principal world language because it has been actively promoted as an instrument of foreign policy of the major English-speaking states.[28] The language policies that third world countries reproduce as a result of colonization serve the first and the foremost interests of Western powers and contribute to preserving existing inequalities between countries and what Phillipson calls English linguistic imperialism. With linguistic imperialism, cultural imperialism creeps in with its various manifestations. With English as the most powerful language today, the culture it represents attributes power so as to create a definite cultural imperialism.

Another theoretical attribute that can be used in this instance is, as cited in Jackson Lears, Antonio Gramsci's cultural hegemony. "Cultural hegemony" refers to the "spontaneous consent given by the great masses of the population to the general direction imposed on social life by the dominant fundamental group; this consent is historically caused by the prestige which the dominant group enjoys because of its position and function in the world of production."[29] This analysis matches well with the Sri Lankan context where the masses seem to embrace Western cultural artifacts, even when they are unable to speak the language of the dominant group, who are the West-worshiping Sri Lankan elites who speak good English. This is done by the common man with zero resistance to letting go of local cultural artifacts to embrace the Western ways and means. In addition, Sri Lankans' eager acceptance of the cultural artifacts seems to compensate for not being able to speak in English. The power of English as the global language and the linguistic imperialism it represents make everything that is associated with the language and its culture very appealing. Thus the culture that represents the West is classy and superior in the minds of Sri Lankans. To add to that, Western culture represents the developed nations while the local is developing, something that many Sri Lankans seem to be either not proud of or ashamed of.

My reading of the dress white, buy white, speak white, and act white is twofold, associated with the ability or inability to speak English well. For those who are unable to speak English well, looking and acting white may be a desperate attempt to be on par with the people who do speak English or to show off a class that is otherwise not present. For those who speak English fluently and therefore do not need to show off a class that is not present, the appealing nature of consumerism, attractive individualism as opposed to communalism, and the fast spread of and easy access to pop culture attract Sri Lankans to Western manifestations. This, of course, applies to those who are unable to speak English as well.

While all of these aspects show the undeniable desire to draw closer to the developed Other, the fast and vast spread of acting white with all the other attributes is partly due to the weak local counterforces. This argument can be supported by observing the situation in India, another South Asian nation. India is a country in which powerful local cultures are still strong and very much present in the society. This may be a consequence of the high illiteracy rate, large population, lack of access to education for all, and so forth, with the result that a large segment of the Indian population is not exposed to the broader world. In Sri Lanka, the opposite is true, as almost everyone can read, has access to education, and is therefore exposed to the outside world. This exposure enables an individual to aspire to an ideal self, to be influenced by external forces, or to seek external endorsement to become a different, better self. This phenomenon may weaken the less impressive and common local cultures, unless role models and visionaries posit strong cultural embodiments. This is evident in the case of India, where the influence of visionaries such as Mahatma Gandhi remains extremely significant, even in the twenty-first century.[30]

Conclusions

The identity change that Sri Lankan society has embraced is manifested in society through social and cultural artifacts pertaining to the lifestyle of its people. The motive to act and look white, with all the examples presented in this chapter, is the result of the two dimensions in which an individual perceives his or her ideal self on the one hand, while catering to how they want others to perceive them on the other hand. The influence of Western culture on an Asian society like Sri Lanka is due to the influence of the power of the collective West, particularly England and the United States, stretching from the colonial past to the capitalistic present. The South Asian outlook forces us to observe the weakness in the local counterforces resulting in the cultural rootlessness of Sri Lankan society, a nation confused.

Notes

1 Celina Cramer, "The Struggles of Identity in Sri Lanka," groundviews.org, accessed September 13, 2019, https://groundviews.org/2012/11/24/the-struggles-of-identity-in-sri-lanka/.
2 Nipunika Lecamwasam, "'United We Stand, Divided We Fall': A Case Study of Sri Lankan Youth in Citizenship Development," *International Journal of Adolescence and Youth* 20, no. 4 (2015): 443.
3 According to UNESCO Institute for Statistics reports in 2017, the literacy rate in Sri Lanka among people aged 15 and older is 91.9 percent. That of India, on the other hand, is 69.3 percent, whereas those of Bangladesh and Pakistan are 72.89 percent and 56.98 percent, respectively. For more details, see "Sri Lanka: Education and Literacy," UNESCO Institute for Statistics, accessed May 18, 2019, http://uis.unesco.org/country/LK.

4   Likewise, according to UNESCO Institute for Statistics reports in 2017, life expectancy at birth (years) in Sri Lanka is 75, whereas those of India, Bangladesh, and Pakistan are 69, 72, and 66, respectively. For more details, see "Sri Lanka: General Information," UNESCO Institute for Statistics, accessed May 18, 2019, http://uis.unesco.org/country/LK.

5   P. M. Wickramarachchi, "A Study on Social Meaning of 'Clothes' in Sri Lankan," Academia.edu, accessed May 22, 2019, https://www.academia.edu/10010445/A _study_on_social_meaning_of_Clothes_in_Sri_Lanka.

6   For more, see Nira Wickramasinghe, *Dressing the Colonised Body: Politics, Clothing, and Identity in Sri Lanka* (Telangana, Hyderabad: Orient Blackswan, 2003).

7   "Marriage Proposal," Sunday Observer online, last modified May 19, 2019, http://www.sundayobserver.lk/marriage-proposals.

8   Itisha Nagar, "The Unfair Selection: A Study on Skin-Color Bias in Arranged Indian Marriages," *Sage Open* 8, no. 2 (2018): 1–8, https://journals.sagepub.com /doi/full/10.1177/2158244018773149.

9   M. Samarakkody, "Motivation and Acquisition of English in Sri Lanka: A Linguistic and Social Psychological Study," in *Teaching English: Possibilities and Opportunities*, ed. David Hayes (Colombo: British Council, 2001), 37–47.

10 For a complete list of elocution classes in Sri Lanka as found on Google, please search "list of elocution classes in Sri Lanka."

11 Asantha U. Attanayake, *Post-colonial Curriculum Practices in South Asia: Building Confidence to Speak English* (London: Routledge, 2019).

12 "Where to Get Imported Goods in Sri Lanka," Pulse, last modified August 30, 2018, http://www.pulse.lk/everythingelse/where-to-get-imported-goods-sri-lanka/.

13 Ibid.

14 Ravi Bamunusinghe, "Today's Middle Class: An Insight into the Contemporary Middle Class of Sri Lanka," *Sunday Times*, December 7, 2014, http://www .sundaytimes.lk/141207/business-times/todays-middle-class-an-insight-into-the -contemporary-middle-class-of-sri-lanka-130841.html.

15 Henri Tajfel, "Social Stereotypes and Social Groups," in *Intergroup Behavior*, ed. John Turner and Howard Giles (Oxford: Basil Blackwell, 1981), 144–167.

16 Richard Serpe and Sheldon Stryker, "The Construction of Self and the Reconstruction of Social Relationships," *Advances in Group Processes* 4 (1987): 41–66.

17 Jan Stets and Peter Burke, "Identity Theory and Social Identity Theory," *Social Psychology Quarterly* 63 (2000): 226.

18 Kay Deaux and Daniela Martin, "Interpersonal Networks and Social Categories: Specifying Levels of Context in Identity Processes." *Social Psychology Quarterly* 66 (2003): 105.

19 Daniel McFarland and Heili Pals, "Motives and Contexts of Identity Change: A Case for Network Effects," *Social Psychology Quarterly* 68, no. 4 (2005): 291.

20 Ibid., 290.

21 Ibid.

22 Susan Harter, "Self and Identity Development," in *At the Threshold: The Developing Adolescent*, ed. Shirley Feldman and Glen Elliott (Cambridge, MA: Harvard University Press, 1990), 377.

23 C. Norman Alexander and Pat Lauderdale, "Situated Identities and Social Influence," *Sociometry* 40, no. 3 (1977), 225.

24 Ibid., 232.

25 McFarland and Pals, "Motives," 291.

26 Alexander and Lauderdale, "Situated," 232.
27 David Crystal, *English as a Global Language* (Cambridge: Cambridge University Press, 1997).
28 Robert Phillipson, *Linguistic Imperialism* (New York: Oxford University Press, 1992).
29 Jackson Lears, "The Concept of Cultural Hegemony: Problems and Possibilities," in *American Historical Review* (Oxford: Oxford University Press on behalf of the American Historical Association, 1985), 568.
30 About 1,040,000 results (0.55 seconds) popped up for my Google search on "Gandhian studies in modern India," https://www.google.com/search?q=gandhian+studies+in+modern+india&oq=Gandhian+studies+in+moder&aqs=chrome.1.69i57j33l5.22095j1j7&sourceid=chrome&ie=UTF-8.

Bibliography

Alexander, Norman, and Pat Lauderdale. "Situated Identities and Social Influence." *Sociometry* 40, no. 3 (1977): 225–233.

Attanayake, Asantha U. *Post-colonial Curriculum Practices in South Asia: Building Confidence to Speak English*. London: Routledge, 2019.

Bamunusinghe, Ravi. "Today's Middle Class: An Insight into the Contemporary Middle Class of Sri Lanka." *Sunday Times*, December 7, 2014. http://www.sundaytimes.lk/141207/business-times/todays-middle-class-an-insight-into-the-contemporary-middle-class-of-sri-lanka-130841.html.

Cramer, Celina. "The Struggles of Identity in Sri Lanka." groundviews.org. Accessed September 13, 2019. https://groundviews.org/2012/11/24/the-struggles-of-identity-in-sri-lanka/.

Crystal, David. *English as a Global Language*. Cambridge: Cambridge University Press, 1997.

Deaux, Kay, and Daniela Martin. "Interpersonal Networks and Social Categories: Specifying Levels of Context in Identity Processes." *Social Psychology Quarterly* 66 (2003): 101–117.

Harter, Susan. "Self and Identity Development." In *At the Threshold: The Developing Adolescent*, edited by Shirley Feldman and Glen Elliott, 352–388. Cambridge, MA: Harvard University Press, 1990.

Lears, Jackson. "The Concept of Cultural Hegemony: Problems and Possibilities." In *American Historical Review*. Oxford: Oxford University Press on behalf of the American Historical Association, 1985.

Lecamwasam, Nipunika. "'United We Stand, Divided We Fall': A Case Study of Sri Lankan Youth in Citizenship Development." *International Journal of Adolescence and Youth* 20, no. 4 (2015): 442–456.

"Marriage Proposal." Sunday Observer online. Last modified May 19, 2019. http://www.sundayobserver.lk/marriage-proposals.

McFarland, Daniel, and Heili Pals. "Motives and Contexts of Identity Change: A Case for Network Effects." *Social Psychology Quarterly* 68, no. 4 (2005): 289–315.

Nagar, Itisha. "The Unfair Selection: A Study on Skin-Color Bias in Arranged Indian Marriages." *Sage Open* 8, no. 2 (2018): 1–8. https://journals.sagepub.com/doi/full/10.1177/2158244018773149.

Phillipson, Robert. *Linguistic Imperialism*. New York: Oxford University Press, 1992.

Samarakkody, M. "Motivation and Acquisition of English in Sri Lanka: A Linguistic and Social Psychological Study." In *Teaching English: Possibilities and Opportunities*, edited by David Hayes, 37–47. Colombo: British Council, 2001.

Serpe, Richard, and Sheldon Stryker. "The Construction of Self and the Reconstruction of Social Relationships." *Advances in Group Processes* 4 (1987): 41–66.

"Sri Lanka: Education and Literacy." UNESCO Institute for Statistics. Accessed May 18, 2019. http://uis.unesco.org/country/LK.

"Sri Lanka: General Information." UNESCO Institute for Statistics. Accessed May 18, 2019. http://uis.unesco.org/country/LK.

Stets, Jan, and Peter Burke. "Identity Theory and Social Identity Theory." *Social Psychology Quarterly* 63 (2000): 224–237.

Tajfel, Henri. "Social Stereotypes and Social Groups." In *Intergroup Behavior*, edited by John Turner and Howard Giles, 144–167. Oxford: Basil Blackwell, 1981.

"Where to Get Imported Goods in Sri Lanka." Pulse. Last modified August 30, 2018. http://www.pulse.lk/everythingelse/where-to-get-imported-goods-sri-lanka/.

Wickramarachchi, P. M. "A Study on Social Meaning of 'Clothes' in Sri Lankan." Academia.edu. Accessed May 22, 2019. https://www.academia.edu/10010445/A_study_on_social_meaning_of_Clothes_in_Sri_Lanka.

Wickramasinghe, Nira. *Dressing the Colonised Body: Politics, Clothing, and Identity in Sri Lanka*. Telangana, Hyderabad: Orient Blackswan, 2003.

9

A Liminal Bengali Identity
■■■■■■■■■■■■■■■■■■■■■■■■■■■■

Film Culture in Bangladesh

SABIHA HUQ

This chapter reviews the history of the Bangladeshi film industry and analyzes a few significant Bangladeshi films screened in Bangladesh from the earliest of its records to current days to elucidate cinema's impact on the formation of national ideologies. The entertainment industry by and large plays the role of a mass deceiver. Max Horkheimer and Theodor W. Adorno, for instance, note that "films and radio no longer need to present themselves as art. The truth that they are nothing but business is used as an ideology to legitimize the trash they intentionally produce."[1] It is generally believed that a film has the power to transform viewers' conceptual realms, and film directors and producers try to meet the public demand by targeting particular classes or groups of audiences. The problem, however, is that the public demand itself is a vague concept. Since viewers' need is seen from the subjective and materialistic rationality of the industry, it is difficult to connect the doctored visual world of a film to the actual demand of the viewers. Nevertheless, in Bangladesh, there have been efforts to (re)position a national cultural identity through national cinema, although these efforts have been facing rampant winds of beguiling in a sort of internationalism that tends to obfuscate any true national culture. As Adorno and Horkheimer show, the faculties of imagination and spontaneity of viewers are crippled by commercial interests in films. Consequently, a fake image of national culture is produced in Bangladesh.

My proposition is that the film industry in Bangladesh has been suffering not from the lack of technological prowess or logistics but, rather, from the decline of its clientele. Viewers may feel that this has happened largely due to the paucity of quality films, while directors/producers allege that if people do not come to the theaters, it is difficult for them to keep on producing films and incurring cumulative losses. My contention is not against the globalization or commercialization of the Bangladeshi film industry. Rather, I share the apprehension about the current status of the film industry in Bangladesh. I hence posit that fancy (fantasy) devoid of imaginative potential, the absence of clear policies on how to evolve a national imaginary, and the lack of a vision of the future constitute a triad of forces that leads to the production of a hotchpotch Bengali culture that does no good for any stakeholder in the long run.

Nation Formation and Bangladeshi Cinema

Bangladesh means the land of the Bengalis or the land of Bangla, both emphasizing the language aspect of the culture. The eponymous naming of the nation has quite a long history. There are many facets of subaltern uprising that culminated in the emergence of the independent nation of Bangladesh. In 1947 when the British colonizers divided India into India and Pakistan, the then East Pakistan, with the majority of people speaking Bangla, protested against the linguistic colonization by the dominant Western center of political power, the Urdu-speaking West Pakistan.[2] The people's Bhasha Andolan (movement to establish the right and sanctity of Bangla as their mother-tongue)[3] gave the world its first ever martyrs for the cause of linguistic rights as five young men laid down their lives in the city of Dhaka on February 21, 1952. Today being a Bengali in Bangladesh means embracing a syncretic identity that derives from complex postcolonial ramifications—that is, assimilating identity markers beyond the Orientalist perceptions of religious denominations and geographical boundaries of ascribing nationhood. The inklings of Bengali nationalism in the modernist sense of the term were first palpable after the partition of Bengal in 1905 in British India. The Bengali nationalism has since then passed through several historic phases, each with its own ideological bases, until Bangladesh finally emerged as an independent nation-state in 1971.

The first crucial blow on the imaginary of a united Bengal was witnessed in 1947 when along with the whole of India, Bengal, too, was divided along religious lines. This divide left people in East Pakistan constantly baffled by the subordination of their ethnic identity as Bengali Muslims. They could neither erase religious differences nor embrace the linguistic commonalities imposed upon them by West Pakistan. As a racial group defined by their language, people in East Pakistan, unfazed by religious identities and consisting largely of civilian armies pitted against neocolonial state forces, indomitably fought back against chronic body blows that lasted for over two decades under a semblance of pseudoindependence.

During these years of intense struggle for Bangla as the state language, the ideal of Bengaliness witnessed a linear development in Bangladesh. However, since the 1980s, after the assassination of Bangabandhu Sheikh Mujibur Rahman, commonly known as the Father of the Nation, ideological state apparatuses (ISAs) have systemically subverted visual and other media in the country. This unfortunately led to the erasure of the history of struggle for Bengali language and culture. Globalization and multicultural flows that are the order of the day have further convoluted the situation. As the youth force of today stands in Bangladesh, they are largely unaware of what constitutes a quintessential Bengali identity. In the public domain, it is unsettling to note that Bengali identity seems still undefined in the visual media of the country. This is not to deny the role of national television programs and films that still try to preserve the history and culture of the nation. But due to the jumble of ideological issues as well as commercial stakes reflected in the Bangladeshi film industry, there is a gap between what is understood as Bengali when posited against the history of the nation, and what is represented as Bengali in popular media. The influence of Hollywood and of Indian cinema, which significantly impacts Bangladeshi commercial films, is a convergence that needs to be critically examined if one sincerely wishes to figure out what constitutes the film culture for a present-day Bangladesh.

A Brief History of Bangladeshi Films

The Bengali film industry in Bangladesh has a short and yet struggling history. While at present, there are the Film Development Corporation (FDC), the only government organization, and three private studios for making films, the first films made in Bangladesh did not have the support from such organizations. A short silent film titled *Sukumari* (The noble virgin)[4] and a full-length silent film titled *The Last Kiss* were released in 1928 and 1931, respectively, in Dhaka in the then undivided Bengal under British rule. A documentary on Muhammad Ali Jinnah's visit to East Pakistan in March 1948, titled *In Our Midst* and released in the same year, is the first film made in independent East Bengal.[5] In 1953, Nazir Ahmed made *Salamat*, another documentary on Dhaka as a growing city. In this documentary, Ahmed uses the persona of Salamat, a mason, whose intent and awestruck vision perceives the newly built constructions of the city and compares them with the declining old city. The effort was highly praised by government officers, intellectuals, and distributors. The success of the film led to the award of government funds for establishing a film laboratory in Dhaka in 1954, which later turned out to be the FDC.

Nonetheless, the story of FDC's journey in erstwhile East Pakistan was not meant to be smooth, which became visible in the very first attempt at producing *Mukh o Mukhosh* (The face and the mask) in 1956. The film has a story along the lines of a traditional morality play in which a small, injured boy is found by a group of bandits, who treat the boy with utmost cruelty. Finally righteous and courageous people fight against the bandits to save the boy. This story is based on a play, *Dakaat* (Robber), directed by the film's director Abdul Jabbar Khan. Produced by Iqbal Films, the film was released in East Pakistan on August 3, 1956. It simultaneously ran in Dhaka, Chattogram (Chittagong), Narayanganj, and Khulna.

The film was a challenge for its director, as the history of the film goes. The film industry in erstwhile East Pakistan did not exist. Moreover, local theaters showed only films made in either Kolkata (India) or Lahore (West Pakistan). In 1953 at a meeting of cultural activists, Indian producer F. Dossani remarked that the climate of East Pakistan was not suitable for making films, at which Abdul Jabbar Khan was much enraged and asked, "Several Indian-Bangla films have been partially shot here, then why would it be impossible to make our own films?"[6] He challenged that if no other director took the initiative, he would make films in East Pakistan. Eventually, that same year, Khan started working on the film with amateur casts who volunteered to work for free. During the making of the film, there were floods in the country for which the shooting was postponed more than once. Ultimately, it took about two years to complete the shoot. As there were no local film production studios, the negatives of the film were taken to Lahore for development. In Lahore, Khan had to face more troubles, as he writes in his journal: "I was about to get on board the plane from Lahore when the customs told me I could not take the prints of the movie to East Pakistan. Disheartened, I returned the plane ticket and went to Karachi by train. I didn't want to waste any time and met with the home minister of that time, Justice Abdus Sattar, regarding the snags I was facing."[7]

Khan could convince the minister that he was not trafficking the film to any foreign country, and since he was allowed to bring the negatives to Lahore from Dhaka, he should be able to take them back as well. The positive gain in this bargain was that Khan was asked to screen the film in Karachi for the Bengalis living there.[8] That was not the end of the struggle though. After his return, Khan faced difficulties as the distributors and theater owners were unwilling to screen the film. They argued that the movie was not "super hit" material and would not earn profitably.[9] At the end, the owner of Roopmahal Cinema in old Dhaka agreed to screen the film. In the midst of a flood, *Mukh o Mukhosh* was premiered with A. K, Fazlul Haque[10] as the chief guest of the event.

The following year in 1957, the East Pakistan Film Development Corporation (EPFDC) was established through the initiatives of Nazir Ahmed and the intervention of Sheikh Mujibur Rahman, the Father of the Nation, the then minister of Trade and Commerce of Pakistan.[11] With the production of *Mukh o Mukhosh* in 1956, the development of Bangla feature films under the banner of the FDC was a checkered story with its ups and downs. From then on, a number of films were produced each year, and more than 160 films can be credited to Bengali directors of the time. Several of the films were in Urdu and were commercially successful. Films in Urdu evidence the spontaneity of film producers living in a syncretistic tradition who were already aware of their linguistic assimilation with their West Pakistani brethren, even after the language movement in 1952. Expansion of cultural territory and commercial success in all of Pakistan were also the reasons for making films in Urdu. Indeed, some of the films produced during these years became very popular among the Urdu-speaking communities.

Some of these films discussed complexities of urban life and relations among the city dwellers—how a person has to struggle in a city to maintain a family, how cruel the city dwellers can be to each other, and how love and sympathy can exist despite the crude selfishness of city life. *Rajdhanir Buke* (In the capital city, 1960), *13 No Feku Ostagar Lane* (titled after a lane in old Dhaka, 1966), *Abirbhab* (Appearance, 1968), *Agontuk* (Stranger, 1969), and *Neel Akasher Niche* (Under the blue sky, 1969) can be referred to in this regard. Emotional turmoil of lovers was also popular subject matter in films during this period. Films such as *Harano Din* (Those lost days, 1961), *Surjosnan* (Bathing in the sun, 1962), *Knacher Deyal* (The glass wall, 1963), *Talash* (Search, 1963), *Dui Digonto* (Two horizons, 1964), *Sutorang* (Aftermath, 1964), which won the second prize at the Frankfurt Film Festival the same year, *Agun Niye Khela* (Playing with fire, 1967), *Moner Moto Bou* (The coveted wife, 1969), and *Anari* (Untidy, 1969) became famous for their handling of romantic love and complicated issues of social life.

Socialism also played a significant role and led to a large number of films that criticized class prejudice. *Jowar Bhata* (High and low tides, 1969), *Mayar Songsar* (The charm called family, 1969), *Dip Nebhe Nai* (The lamp still lights, 1970), *Dorpo Churno* (Fall of prejudice, 1970), *Pitch Dhala Ei Path* (This concrete road, 1970), *Swarolipi* (Notation, 1970), and *Taka Ana Pai* (Money money money, 1970) became very popular in this regard. Some films even concentrated on the subjugation of women and their unuttered feelings. *Asiya* (based on the female protagonist, Asiya, 1960) is a good example of this.

Adaptations of popular novels were also in practice. *Padma Nodir Majhi* (The boatman of the River Padma, 1969) indicates this trend, which continued through the postindependent years. These films are still remembered as milestones of Bangla cinema. They not only defined the philosophy of visual culture of the then East Pakistan but also forecasted the expectation of a Bengali nation. The first films did not concentrate on incorporating the idea of national struggle, and their focus was on the depiction of middle class urban life, as urbanization in the newly independent economy was a prime concern. A village lad's migration to *mahalla* or *para*[12] and meeting the complexities of life in the city vis-à-vis the idyllic village life were popular themes of cinema at that time. The urban–rural divide symbolized the paradoxical and discriminatory development of East and West Pakistan that created economic disparity between the territories.

Since the 1970s, the Dhaka-based film industry, which is frequently referred to as Dhallywood, and the Kolkata-based Tollygunge Film Industry called Tollywood, have significantly shaped and contributed to the production of Bengali films. Many talented film actors from Bangladesh made it to mainstream cinema in India. Mithun Chakrabarty,[13] for example, became very popular on screen in India, while retaining a credible acceptance in Bangladesh. Ferdous Ahmed, an actor of the present generation, has also become very popular after he acted in a Dhaka–Kolkata joint venture film *Hothat Brishti* (Sudden rain, 1998). Jaya Ahsan, a popular Bangladeshi actress, acts regularly in Tollywood films.

It is evident that Bengali films before and during the independence and until the death of the Father of the Nation in the 1970s combined indigenous folktales and stories akin to contemporary life. The folktale adaptation *Rupban* (Beautiful) was a commercial success. More realistic films depicted almost Dickensian heroes aspiring to become gentlemen, young university/college students falling in love and facing class conflicts while trying to unite in conjugality, and rural life presented in its rustic simplicity as well as in phases of transition. These themes and plots were presented with an overarching idea of morality pervading the world and appealed to viewers. Films of the 1960s and 1970s were based in reality, and people had a certain attraction to them. With the palpable realization of a virtually divided homeland and the garnering of popular political support around the cult identity of leaders like Bangabandhu (the Father of the Nation) and his associates, the communal identity of a shared Bengali culture was gaining deep roots. This communal Bengali identity was cumulatively reflected in cinema of the period that can be represented as the national cinema. After all, Catherine Masud defines national cinema as "an authentic reflection of a country's tradition, society, history and culture, in all its diversity and richness."[14] Not surprisingly, then, the most popular films during this period were those that depicted the language movement in 1952, mass movement in 1969, and Liberation War in 1971. These films include *Jiban Theke Neya* (Taken from life, 1970), *Arunodoyer Agnishakkhi* (Witness to sunrise, 1972), *Ora Egaro Jon* (Those eleven, 1972), *Abar Tora Manush Ho* (Be human again, 1973), and *Alor Michil* (Rally of light, 1974). Such films produced throughout the first half of the decade drew audiences to the cinema halls, which were nothing like today's multiplexes.

Film: A Product or a Producer?

Horkheimer and Adorno comment that the culture industry is actually the producer of viewers' taste, although it claims to be the product of that very taste: "Each single manifestation of the culture industry inescapably reproduces human beings as what the whole has made them. And all its agents, from the producer to the women's organizations, are on the alert to ensure that the simple reproduction of mind does not lead on to the expansion of mind."[15] We must acknowledge that the Kantian schematism[16] works in the mind of consumers and makes them internalize anything unnatural as natural. Furthermore, the continuous acceptance and naturalization of such products create a constant need for consumers. Film directors, producers, and critics in Bangladesh thus have a common question: what is the unique selling proposition that can draw the middle class audience, the emerging segment of population with purchasing power,[17] to movie theaters? Who set the standard for films and whether the standard itself creates film consumers are critical questions. In order to answer these questions, we need to look again at the history of the Bangladeshi film industry.

The history of *Mukh o Mukhosh* shows the pattern of creative minds working behind the emergence of a genre of Bangla films. The movie was received very cordially by viewers. Official records indicate that it earned a total of Rs. 48,000 (about USD575) during its initial run. Neither a corporate sponsor nor any state patron was behind the making and success of this first initiative of commercial film in Bangladesh. The credit goes to the patriot director and the enthused public who reciprocated each other's emotional needs. Establishing Bangladesh's film industry was a matter of pride for both the producer and the spectators. We can thus infer that the grounding of film culture in the preindependent country happened on a solid nationalistic base.

Today's situation is just the opposite as the film industry is already established with both mainstream and parallel cinemas produced by quite a number of directors. Parallel cinema or alternative cinema, inspired by Italian Neo-realism and French and Japanese New Waves, was introduced in India by internationally acclaimed filmmakers such as Satyajit Ray, Mrinal Sen, Ritwik Ghatak, and Tapan Sinha in the 1960s. It gained prominence in Bangladesh in the hands of a few determined directors, such as Tareque Masud, Tanvir Mokammel, Humayun Ahmed, and others. They stopped submitting to the demands of producers whose main intention was to profit from films by attracting viewers who sought simple entertainment. These directors either looked for patrons with sophistication or invested their own capital. Big budget and famous actors were not the selling factors in movies directed by them. Popular themes of these parallel movies include Partition of Bengal, Liberation War, alienation and other complexities of city life in modern times, and the psychological journey of characters. Humayun Ahmed, a popular novelist-cum-film director, has been one of the pioneers in this line. He directed *Aguner Parashmoni* (The fire touchstone, 1994), *Srabon Megher Din* (A cloudy day of Sraban, 2000), and *Shyamol Chhaya* (The green shade, 2004) that became very popular. *Shyamol Chhaya,* for example, was nominated the best contemporary film at the 6th Bangladesh Film Festival in London (2005) and was chosen by the Bangladesh Federation of Film Societies as the Bangladeshi submission to the 78th Academy Awards in the Foreign Language Film category.

Tareque Masud (1956–2011), on the other hand, is a role model in Bangladeshi alternative cinema. He experimented with short and full-length documentary and animation films. *Muktir Gaan* (Song of freedom, 1995) is Masud's great contribution to Bangla documentary films because it captures a special episode of the Liberation War in a truly transnational manner. In this film, Masud combines Lear Levin's[18] footage on the Liberation War with several other footages collected from different parts of the world. In *Muktir Katha* (Words of freedom, 1999), by highlighting people's reaction to *Muktir Gaan*, which was screened around the country and the stories of common people who participated in the Liberation War, Masud creates an important subaltern history of the war. These two are counted as important documentaries on the Liberation War. *Adam Surat* (The face of a human, 1989), *Matir Moyna* (The clay bird, 2002), *Antorjatra* (The inward journey, 2006), *Narsundor* (The barbershop, 2009), and *Runway* (2010) are some of the other remarkable films by him.

In *Matir Moyna,* Masud portrays life in preindependence Bangladesh in which life is mired in superstition, backwardness, and religious puritanism against which young people seem to revolt. This represents the eternal debate over Bengali Muslim identity. *Narsundor,* on the other hand, portrays a multidimensional discourse of the Liberation War, as Masud shows the sympathy of a non-Bengali character, Behari,[19] toward a Bengali freedom fighter in the film. By doing so, Masud wanted to break down the Muslim and non-Bengali villain archetypes and display a different view of Bengali nationalism. Parallel cinema gained popularity among the middle class educated citizens. Shihab Sarkar writes that two new trends in cinema actually managed to motivate the middle class to return to cinema halls to watch Bangla films. One is the "new-generation mainstream cinema" that has "outshone the long-predominant sentimentalised social entertainers." The other is the "new-generation producers and directors committed to making movies based on purely Bangladeshi realities." These movies, according to him, attracted "movie people belonging to the offbeat trends."[20]

While parallel cinema brought back more sophisticated, educated middle class audiences and those belonging to the "offbeat trends" to movie theaters, commercial films still retain their popularity among their main targets, the working class audiences. The socialist fabric of the nation envisioned by the Father of the Nation is thus challenged by the film culture that has its "base" and "superstructure"[21] in current circumstances. Moreover, the products of mainstream and parallel cinemas have now become markers of class difference. Categories like a box office hit and the critics' choice in film awards function as tools of differentiation, as the former represents commercial, mainstream success and the latter more sophisticated and nonmainstream choice of the intellectual class. If so, it is imperative to refer to Horkheimer and Adorno again: "The mentality of the public, which allegedly and actually favors the system of the culture industry, is a part of the system, not an excuse for it."[22] They observe that the culture industry simultaneously produces consumers and gives them the idea that whatever is produced must be taken as having factored in public demand. In the present context, then, it becomes relevant to take into account the remarkable absence of any guiding ideology of nation-building in the establishment of a nation's visual culture.[23]

After the independence in 1971, the first constitution of Bangladesh written in 1972 was based on an egalitarian and secular ideology. The Father of the Nation himself inspired everyone to work toward building a classless secular country that would be called "sonar Bangla."[24] Most artists and intellectuals of the time shared this idea. Filmmakers also concentrated on the theme of the war-devastated economy and inspired people to reconstruct it. The movie *Alor Michil* (Rally of light, 1974), for example, responds to this. Alo, one of the main characters of the film, is an innocent young girl who is shot dead. Meanwhile, the news comes that the West Pakistanis killed thousands of men and women and destroyed houses and properties. Alo's maternal uncle, the freedom fighter and the hero of the film, takes up her dead body and takes a vow that he will not let her sacrifice go in vain. Importantly, however, he chooses peace over violence, as his oath to rebuild the country is his revenge. Such a theme is readily identifiable in a large number of films of the time that depicted the war-devastated Bangladesh.

Apart from the Liberation War movies, Bengali films after the independence depicted social life in the time of transition with its numerous intricacies. Nazir Ahmed in his account of the EPFDC years comments that their intention was to produce creative films that were based on life.[25] However, this socially liable artistry did not continue so strongly in the film industry in the later years, especially after Bangabandhu's murder in 1975. Substance and quality of films in terms of themes, content, and methods of presentation declined in most commercial films of the 1980s and 1990s. In the 1980s, not only was the constitution clipped off its secular intent, but Islamic ethos of a more extreme type was also being implemented.[26] This turn in cinema seems to be very interesting. While the nation, politically and religiously, declared Islam as the state religion of Bangladesh, making a fundamental shift away from the original secular constitution of the country, the country became more open and liberal, so to speak, culturally. Scenes of violent action, sexual promiscuity, and even rape, and the rampant use of bed scenes that made audiences privy to voyeurism, started dominating films produced in Bangladesh. These scenes might have been an easy way to preoccupy audiences and distract them from more serious state affairs. A comment by Horkheimer and Adorno is applicable here: "The withering of imagination and spontaneity in the consumer of culture today need not be traced back to psychological mechanisms. The products themselves, especially the most characteristic, the sound film, cripple those faculties through their objective makeup. They are so constructed that their adequate comprehension requires a quick, observant, knowledgeable cast of mind but positively debars the spectator from thinking, if he is not to miss the fleeting facts."[27] The idea is that films would preoccupy the imagination of the public. On the one hand, the voyeuristic scopophilia[28] will keep consumers (film audiences) busy. On the other, viewers taken aback by these scenes would be busy protesting against the vulgarity in films. In the meantime, all may end up ignoring more serious social and political issues in the country.

Additionally, remakes of English films from Hollywood and Hindi films from the Bombay film industry (popularly known as Bollywood) started dominating the Bangladeshi film industry after the independence. Sajedul Awwal writes that "after the independence towards the end of the 70s and in the beginning of the 80s cinema was being made by copying and thus the film industry met its ruin and the number of film viewers declined."[29] However, some such remakes became popular too. For example, *Qeyamat theke Qeyamat* (From doomsday to doomsday, 1993), a remake of the Hindi film *Qayamat se Qayamat Tak* (From doomsday to doomsday, 1988), was quite popular as viewers appreciated the new faces that acted in the lead roles. The film's songs and visualization also suited the taste of the young local viewers. Given the political situation in Bangladesh in the 1980s after the independence, mass media as popular culture could have offered people an escape route from grim realities. Unfortunately, however, the film industry in Bangladesh did not contribute anything except to offer a new trend of following Hollywood and Bollywood in Bangla films.

There is a Bangladesh Film Censor Board (BFCB), a wing of the Ministry of Information and Technology, but there is no clear-cut policy against copying. According to Mohammad Ali Sarker, the secretary of BFCB in 2019, there is no policy against plagiarizing films, and there is a need for revising the codes for filmmaking as the last revision was made in 1985. In 2019 the Board already held meetings to rethink the codes, but there was no discussion on the preservation of national cinema and culture.[30] Ilias Kanchan, a popular actor of Bangladesh, called the Bangladeshi film industry "a neglected orphan" whose last guardian was Bangabandhu who "set regulations in place to protect the domestic film market [after the liberation]."[31] During an interview conducted on March 23, 2019, I asked Tanvir Mokammel, a renowned writer and filmmaker of Bangladesh, "From the ban on *Karnaphulir Kanna* in 2005 (Teardrops of Karnaphuli, 2005) to the Ekushey Padak in 2017,[32] what is your perception of the role of the State in Bangladeshi cinema?" He answered the question as follows: "Bangladesh state, with some minor exceptions here and there, is generally undemocratic, bureaucratic, communal and philistine. The spirits of the 1971 Liberation War, like secularism and equalitarianism, are long lost, especially after the killing of Bangabandhu Sheikh Mujib and the four national leaders in 1975. The present day Bangladesh state has made too many compromises with the utterly corrupt and super rich business cliques and with the regressive Islamic forces of this land. Not too many positive things, at least in culture, can be expected from the state of Bangladesh, as it is now."

The Present Scenario

In the present context the status of films in Bangladesh is complicated. Viewership of Bangladeshi films in general has dropped, and the industry is being criticized for producing low-quality melodramatic films.[33] In the meantime, viewers with different interests and tastes are left out, leading to a film industry that lacks diversity and balance. Except for the few alternative trends, the previously rich film industry in Bangladesh now suffers from a lack of imaginative directors and generous producers who are willing to support creative works that refuse to simply follow popular trends. This has caused the decline of Bangladeshi films in terms of both quality and quantity, and instead of making original films, remakes of Indian films have gained more popularity. A field study conducted by Benazir Rahman and Yeasmin Islam shows that the majority Bangladeshi audience (43.33 percent) think that distributors' preference for foreign films is affecting the progress of the Bangladesh film industry, while 18.33 percent feel that the foreign film industry has grabbed the local film market.[34]

After the Indian Partition in 1947 and before East Pakistan had its first film, the country was largely dependent on Indian films. Although this trend continues, the Bangladeshi film industry is now becoming more conscious about simply copying foreign films. Inwin Enterprise, for instance, imported three Hindi films, *Wanted*, *Don 2*, and *Three Idiots*, to Bangladesh in 2010. All commercial film producers in Bangladesh protested against this. Masud Parvez Sohel Rana, a popular Bangladeshi actor and film director, for instance, reacted to this in the following manner: "Bollywood is a big institution. Their production cost is 100 times more than our production cost. How can we compete with them? . . . It seems to me like you are asking a flyweight boxer to fight with a heavyweight boxer."[35] The decision enraged filmmakers, producers, and actors. As a result, the Bangladesh government had to declare that Indian films would not be imported anymore.[36] Such restrictions, however, can never be effective and sustainable and could lead to nondemocratic and dictatorial policies and control. Viewers will not stop watching Indian films unless Bangladeshi films are able to capture the vision of a wide range of viewers through diverse themes and styles.

Gender inequality and the objectification of women are other important issues that today's male-dominated Bangladeshi film industry needs to pay more attention to. Women constitute almost half of the population, and yet there are only a few filmmakers who could give women their due respect. It becomes evident if we look at the history of Bangladeshi films. A good-looking young man played the role of a heroine in the nation's first film titled *Sukumari*. In the second film, made in East Pakistan and titled *The Last Kiss,* Lolita and Charubala, both prostitutes in real life, acted in the female roles. These two female actresses were never considered significant. It is thus not surprising that their last names are not known, nor is it known what the film was about. The situation has not changed much today. At present actresses are not only paid less, they are often presented in uncomely attires in unnecessarily vulgar scenes. Zahidur Rahman writes that "in the name of glamour they [the women in Bangladeshi films] get themselves covered in bizarre attires."[37] Exposures of body parts, close ups of lips and breasts, raunchy gestures, pelvic thrusts, and in numerous other ways commoditization of the female body is noticed in films. One can always refer to the Bangladeshi film industry as a typically male enterprise. Most of these films are directed and produced by males. The uncomely attires of the females satisfy the typically Orientalist male gaze that voyeuristically objectifies women. Laura Mulvey can be referred to here to explain such objectification. Mulvey, for instance, remarks that mainstream cinema, which once "coded the erotic into the language of the dominant patriarchal order," has changed much over the years. However, it is still evident that "the presence of woman is an indispensable element of spectacle in normal narrative film, yet her visual presence tends to work against the development of a story line, to freeze the flow of action in moments of erotic contemplation. This alien presence then has to be integrated into cohesion with the narrative."[38]

In Bangladeshi commercial films, rape scenes or unnecessary presentations of female body parts are often used as the motivation for revenge or action. For example, in *Ammajaan* (Dear mother, 1999) directed by Dipjol, the mother is raped and her teenage son kills the rapist in the opening scene of the film. This constitutes the gangster career of the son who is the hero of the movie and whose love for his mother becomes illustrious in the film. The mother–son relationship is the subject matter of the film for which the rape scene seems necessary. However, the scene is overdramatized and emphasized in such a way that the female body is exploited in order to provoke and draw sensation from viewers. In the Liberation War–based films that are considered significant contributions to Bangladeshi cinema, rape scenes are claimed to be necessary to emphasize the cruelty of the war and sufferings of the people. However, the problem occurs when such presentations are overused and oversensationalized. Sajedul Awwal, for instance, charges some films with unnecessary presentations of rape scenes. These films include *Bagha-Bangali* (The heroic Bengali, 1972), *Roktakto Bangla* (Bloody Bengal, 1972), *Amar Janmabhumi* (My motherland, 1973), *Banglar 24 Bochor* (24 Years of Bengal, 1974), and *Ajo Bhulini* (Yet unforgotten, 1975).[39] It is evident that rape scenes were not necessary to highlight the oppression of the Pakistani soldiers and local compradors during the Liberation War in 1971, and direct presentation of rape scenes could be avoided in these films. Scarcity of female producers is an important reason for this problematic "male gaze" in the Bangla film industry, and until more female directors come forward with their dissenting and new ideas, the practice of misrepresentation of female bodies cannot be stopped.

Conclusion

There has been hardly any study on the existing visual culture in Bangladesh, and the paradoxes it entails. Apart from few books published on films, documentation of visual media itself is sparse. While it is a fact that the visual media presupposes strong roots in its Bengali identity and most cultural endeavors lead to the same vision of defining a Bengali identity, this conspicuous absence of any theoretical framework to map the culture industry is inherently problematic. Also related is the fact that globalization has made many people feel uneasy. This has necessitated the idea of revisiting tradition and introducing modernity in a coherent and relevant way. All of these leave one with a conundrum to ponder over—since both identity and its manifestations are ever-shifting categories, what relevant strategies can visual culture adopt to become a repository of Bengali identity in global times? Perhaps even more important is the answer to the question whether visual cultures promoted by corporate nationalism at all have the obligation to demarcate individualizing traits of Bengali culture, or if their interests lie in evolving homogeneous packages in tandem with global norms of universality through uniformity.

Notes

1   Max Horkheimer and Theodor W. Adorno, "The Culture Industry: Enlightenment as Mass Deception," in *Media and Cultural Studies: Keyworks*, ed. Meenakshi Gigi Durham and Douglas M. Kellner (Malden, MA: Blackwell Publishing, 2006), 42.

2 In 1947 the British colonizers divided India into India and Pakistan. Pakistan was formed with its Eastern and Western parts. West Pakistan was dominated by Urdu-speaking populations while the majority that lived in East Pakistan had Bangla as their mother tongue.

3 "Bhasha Andolan" literally means language movement. It specifically refers to the movement of East Pakistani Bengalis in 1952 against the declaration of the West Pakistan government that Urdu will be the state language of Pakistan. Student protest on February 21, 1952, against the linguistic oppression resulted in the death of five students. The day is observed worldwide as the International Mother Language Day.

4 *Sukumari*, literally meaning the noble virgin, was the first short film directed by Ambuj Gupta and produced through the initiatives of some enthusiasts of the Nawab family of Old Dhaka (1927–1928). In this film, Khwaza Nasirullah played the lead role while a young man named Abdus Sobhan acted as the heroine. It was not screened anywhere outside of the Nawab family circle. After the success of *Sukumari* Ambuj Gupta directed *The Last Kiss* in which another young man of the Nawab family, Khwaza Ajmol, acted the lead role and Lolita and Charuabala acted as the heroines of the film. Lolita and Charuabala are the first women film actors in Bangladeshi film history. Yet their last names are unknown, and it is not clear what the film was about. From the title it can be speculated that the film was in English. For more information, see Alam Qureshi, *Cholochitryer Nana Kotha* [Varied thoughts on films] (Dhaka: Adorn Publication, 2012), 29–30.

5 Anupom Hayat, *Muktijudder Cholochitro Abong Onnonno* [Films on the Liberation War and others] (Dhaka: Matribumi Prokashani, 2017), 20.

6 Fayeka Zabeen Siddiqua, "Talking about Our First Talkie," *Daily Star*, November 6, 2015, https://www.thedailystar.net/star-weekend/heritage/talking-about-our-first-talkie-167824.

7 Karim Waheed, "Celebrating 50 Years of Our Cinema: Remembering *Mukh O Mukhosh* and Abdul Jabbar Khan," *Daily Star*, August 12, 2005, http://archive.thedailystar.net/2005/08/12/d50812140197.htm.

8 Ibid. There were about 200 Bengalis living in Karachi at that time.

9 Ibid.

10 A. K. Fazlul Haque (Abul Kasem Fazlul Haque, 1873–1962) was a Bengali political figure and statesman in British India and later in Pakistan.

11 Sheikh Mujibur Rahman (1920–1975) is the father of the nation of Bangladesh as he was the driving force behind the independence of Bangladesh. He is popularly known as "Bangabandhu" or "Friend of Bengal." He was assassinated by miscreants in a military coup d'état in 1975.

12 A *para* or *mahalla* is a locality within which a few families live. Usually such localities have their own mosque, temple, library, and so forth.

13 Mithun Chakraborty is the stage name of the actor Gourang Chakraborty, who was born in Barisal, Bangladesh (then East Pakistan) in 1952. He migrated to India in his youth and became very popular in Bollywood and retained his mass popularity among the Bangladeshi audiences.

14 Catherine Masud is the wife and co-producer of late Tareque Masud, a renowned Bangladeshi film director. For her discussion of the elements of national cinema in Bangladesh, see "Bangladesh National Cinema in the Age of Globalization," *Star Weekend Magazine*, Accessed March 13, 2019, http://archive.thedailystar.net/magazine/2004/12/03/cinema.htm.

15 Horkheimer and Adorno, "The Culture Industry," 46.

16 Horkheimer and Adorno posit that the consumers must orient themselves with the production to rationalize their needs for it, and here Horkheimer and Adorno refer to Kant's concept of Schema that creates in the mind of consumers a sense and significance, that is, "the system of pure reason," that leads to the actual act of consumption. In the chapter titled "The Culture Industry: Enlightenment as Mass Deception" they argue that "according to Kantian schematism, a secret mechanism within the psyche [of the consumers] preformed immediate data to fit them [the products] into the system of pure reason." For more reference, see Horkheimer and Adorno, "The Culture Industry," 44.

17 Syed Mansur Hashin, "Bangladesh's Growing Middle Class," *Daily Star*, October 27, 2015, https://www.thedailystar.net/op-ed/politics/bangladeshs-growing-middle-class-162670.

18 Lear Levin is an American filmmaker who visited Bangladesh in 1971 and traveled with the artiste group Bangladesh Mukti Shangrami Shilpi Shangstha. This group used to travel to different refugee camps and different areas in Mukta Anchal (freed territories) to perform patriotic songs, arrange puppet shows, and stage dramas to inspire the freedom fighters. Tareque and Catherine Masud used the original footage by Levin in *Muktir Gaan* with other archival footages collected from India and England.

19 An inhabitant of Behar, Uttar Pradesh, India.

20 Shihab Sarkar, "Bangladesh Cinema: Keeping up the Tempo of Revival," *Financial Express*, June 8, 2017, https://thefinancialexpress.com.bd/views/bangladesh-cinema-keeping-up-the-tempo-of-revival.

21 Base and Superstructure are Marxian concepts and are the two parts of human society. The base includes the forces and relations to production while the superstructure includes culture, institutions, political power structure, and the state. The base determines the superstructure, and the superstructure often influences the base. The predominant base is the economic class. According to Antonio Gramsci, "the State appears to have its socio-political base among the ordinary folk and the intellectuals, while in reality its structure remains plutocratic and it is impossible for it to break its links with big finance capital." For more, see Antonio Gramsci, *Selections from the Prison Notebooks of Antonio Gramsci*, ed. Quintin Hoare and Geoffrey Nowell Smith (New York: International Publishers, 1992), 315.

22 Horkheimer and Adorno, "The Culture Industry," 42.

23 My Discussion with the Bangladesh Film Censor Board (BFCB) on February 24, 2019 is the source for this remark.

24 Sonar Bangla or the "golden Bengal" was a popular epithet used by Bangabandhu to describe a progressive and economically self-sufficient Bangladesh.

25 Hayat. *Muktijudder Cholochitro*, 24.

26 After Bangabandhu's murder there were military regimes; the first was established by Khondaker Mushtaq Ahmad in 1975. Ziaur Rahman took over the state in 1977 and till 1978 there was martial law in the country. The second and longer lasting military regime was established by Hussain Muhammad Ershad who served as the president from 1983 to 1990. He arranged for an election in 1986 which was a farce and his regime is considered as an era of military dictatorship. Ershad forced the parliament to declare Islam the state religion of Bangladesh. This was a fundamental move away from the original secular constitution of the

country. Ironically, in Bangladesh there were open alcohol trading and all kinds of non-Islamic activities during his time.

27 Horkheimer and Adorno, "The Culture Industry," 45.

28 Scopophilia actually means voyeurism.

29 Sajedul Awwal, *Cholochchitrochorjya: Understanding Cinema* (Dhaka: Journeyman Books, 2017), 148.

30 Live in-Discussion with the secretary of BFCB on February 24, 2019.

31 Faruque Ratul, "Bangladesh's Film Industry Is Like a Neglected Orphan," *Dhaka Tribune,* January 16, 2019, https://www.dhakatribune.com/showtime/2019/01/16/bangladesh-s-film-industry-is-like-an-orphan.

32 Mokammel's film *Karnaphulir Kanna* (Teardrops of Karnaphuli, 2005), a documentary film on the plight of the indigenous people of the Chittagong Hill Tracts, was banned in 2005 for depicting objectionable messages against the interests of the country as well as its people. Nevertheless, Mokammel received the Ekushey Padak in 2017 in the film category. Ekushey Padak is the second-highest civilian award in Bangladesh given to recognize contributions in a number of fields, including awards given posthumously for contributions in the language movement in 1952 and the Liberation War in 1971. For more information, please see "Mokammel Reacts Sharply at Ban of His Documentary Karnaphulir Kanna," BDNEWS, August 20, 2005, https://bdnews24.com/politics/2005/08/20/mokammel-reacts-sharply-at-ban-of-his-documentary-karnaphulir-kanna, as well as Pallab Bhattacharya, "Tanvir Mokammel Bags Ekushey Padak for 2017," *Daily Star,* February 16, 2017, https://www.thedailystar.net/arts-entertainment/tanvir-mokammel-bags-ekushey-padak-2017-1361587.

33 Helen Rowe, "Bangladeshis Reject 'Smutty' Bengali Films," Things Asian, April 22, 2004, http://thingsasian.com/story/bangladeshis-reject-smutty-bengali-films.

34 Benazir Rahman and Yeasmin Islam presented a paper, "Factors Affecting Progress of Film Industry in Bangladesh: Some Observations" at the "International Conference on Envisioning Our Common Future 2016" in Dhaka, Bangladesh. In this paper they presented their survey conducted in that year among the educated urban audiences of Dhaka city. The audiences' opinion is extracted from their report. For more, see https://www.researchgate.net/publication/326718689_Factors_Affecting_Progress_of_Film_Industry_in_Bangladesh_Some_Observations.

35 Anbarasab Ethirajan, "Bangladeshi Film Industry's Fight for Survival," *BBC News*, October 5, 2011, https://www.bbc.com/news/business-15178289.

36 Awwal, *Cholochchitrochorjya*, 134.

37 Zahidur Rahman, "Women in Bangladeshi Cinema," *Daily Observer*, May 27, 2016, https://www.observerbd.com/2016/05/27/153250.php.

38 Laura Mulvey, "Visual Pleasure and Narrative Cinema," in *Media and Cultural Studies: Keyworks*, ed. Douglas Kellner and M. Gigi Durham (Malden, MA: Blackwell, 2006), 837.

39 Awwal, *Cholochchitrochorjya*, 143.

Bibliography

Awwal, Sajedul. *Cholochchitrochorjya: Understanding Cinema*. Dhaka: Journeyman Books, 2017.

Bhattacharya, Pallab. "Tanvir Mokammel Bags Ekushey Padak for 2017." *Daily Star*. February 16, 2017. https://www.thedailystar.net/arts-entertainment/tanvir -mokammel-bags-ekushey-padak-2017-1361587.

Ethirajan, Anbarasan. "Bangladeshi Film Industry's Fight for Survival." *BBC News*. October 5, 2011. https://www.bbc.com/news/business-15178289.

Gramsci, Antonio. *Selections from the Prison Notebooks of Antonio Gramsci*. Edited by Quintin Hoare and Geoffrey Nowell Smith. New York: International Publishers, 1992. https://libcom.org/files/Gramsci%20-%20Selections%20from%20the%20 Prison%20Notebooks.pdf.

Haq, Fahmidul, and Pronab Bhowmik. *TarequeMasud, Jatiotbad O Cholochchitro* [Tareque Masud, Nationalism and Cinema]. Dhaka: Agamee Prakashani, 2014.

Hasan, Khondokar Mahmudul. *Muktijuddher Cholochchitro* [Films on the Liberation War]. Dhaka: Katha Prokash, 2015.

Hashin, Syed Mansur. "Bangladesh's Growing Middle Class." *Daily Star*. October 27, 2015. https://www.thedailystar.net/op-ed/politics/bangladeshs-growing-middle -class-162670.

Hayat, Anupom. *Muktijudder Cholochitro Abong Onnonno* [Films on the Liberation War and others]. Dhaka: Matribumi Prokashani, 2017.

Horkheimer, Max, and Theodor W. Adorno. "The Culture Industry: Enlightenment as Mass Deception." In *Media and Cultural Studies: Keyworks*, edited by Douglas Kellner and M. Gigi Durham, 42–52. Malden, MA: Blackwell Publishing, 2006.

Masud, Catherine. "Bangladesh National Cinema in the Age of Globalization." *Star Weekend Magazine*. Accessed March 13, 2019. http://archive.thedailystar.net /magazine/2004/12/03/cinema.htm.

"Mokammel Reacts Sharply at Ban of His Documentary Karnaphulir Kanna." *BDNEWS*. August 20, 2005. https://bdnews24.com/politics/2005/08/20 /mokammel-reacts-sharply-at-ban-of-his-documentary-karnaphulir-kanna.

"Mukh o Mukhosh." Pakistani Films. Accessed March 12, 2019. https://web.archive.org /web/20060512131717/http://pakistani_films.tripod.com/mukh_o_mukhosh.htm.

Mulvey, Laura. "Visual Pleasure and Narrative Cinema." In *Media and Cultural Studies: Keyworks*, edited by Douglas Kellner and M. Gigi Durham, 342–352. Malden, MA: Blackwell, 2006.

Qureshi, Alam. *Cholochitryer Nana Kotha* [Varied thoughts on films]. Dhaka: Adorn Publication, 2012.

Rahman, Benazir, and Yeasmin Islam. "Factors Affecting Progress of Film Industry in Bangladesh: Some Observations." Paper presented at the International Conference on Envisioning Our Common Future 2016 in Dhaka, Bangladesh. https://www .researchgate.net/publication/326718689_Factors_Affecting_Progress_of_Film _Industry_in_Bangladesh_Some_Observations.

Rahman, Zahidur. "Women in Bangladeshi Cinema." *Daily Observer*. May 27, 2016. https://www.observerbd.com/2016/05/27/153250.php.

Ratul, Faruque. "Bangladesh's Film Industry Is Like a Neglected Orphan." *Dhaka Tribune*. January 16, 2019. https://www.dhakatribune.com/showtime/2019/01/16 /bangladesh-s-film-industry-is-like-an-orphan.

Rowe, Helen. "Bangladeshis Reject 'Smutty' Bengali Films." Things Asian. April 22, 2004. http://thingsasian.com/story/bangladeshis-reject-smutty-bengali-films.

Sarkar, Shihab. "Bangladesh Cinema: Keeping up the Tempo of Revival." *Financial Express*. June 8, 2017. https://thefinancialexpress.com.bd/views/bangladesh-cinema -keeping-up-the-tempo-of-revival.

Siddiqua, Fayeka Zabeen. "Talking about Our First Talkie." *Daily Star*. November 6, 2015. https://www.thedailystar.net/star-weekend/heritage/talking-about-our-first -talkie-167824.

Waheed, Karim. "Celebrating 50 Years of Our Cinema: Remembering *Mukh O Mukhosh* and Abdul Jabbar Khan." *Daily Star*. August 12, 2005. http://archive .thedailystar.net/2005/08/12/d50812140197.htm.

10

Screening Southeast Asia

■■■■■■■■■■■■■■■■■■■■■■■■■■

Film, Politics, and the
Emergence of the Nation
in Postwar Southeast Asia

DARLENE MACHELL
DE LEON ESPENA

On May 18, 2015, I was sitting in the Screening Room of the Arts House in Singapore anticipating the showing of the Mexican movie *Enamorada* (A woman in love, 1946).[1] People from diverse ethnicities and nationalities filled the room, with Mexicans forming the majority. A part of me wondered how a Mexican staying in Singapore would react to the classic movie from home, created and released six decades ago. My curiosity was satisfied when, halfway into the film, a Mexican woman sitting beside me started to sing along to the religious composition, "Ave Maria," crooned by one of the movie characters. The music lasted for a good minute, and she was so enamored by the song that she was practically crying. When the music ended, she gesticulated to make the sign of the cross.

At that precise moment, I realized (perhaps with more clarity than before) how absorbing and captivating films could be. She was watching a movie that reminded her of home, no matter how obscure its features could have appeared in her imagination. More importantly, she was prompted to act—singing a song she found meaningful and then publicly expressing her religious beliefs by making the sign of the cross. That episode triggered more questions. What do we see when we watch films? What do films tell us about ourselves, the ones who made them, or societies, in general? Why do some films provoke us to act or to behave in a certain way?

This chapter adopts an alternative approach to understanding the history of Southeast Asia during the period of nation-building and decolonization following the Second World War. Departing from the traditional method of studying history through solely scrutinizing (and being partial to) written documents and manuscripts,[2] I reconstruct the past using and analyzing moving pictures in their historical contexts.[3] What were framed, what were excluded, and how were the films themselves products of culture and history? Rather than limiting myself to written historical sources, I focus more on what can be understood through national cinema.

Contrary to the belief that films should be regarded as secondary, if not weak, sources of history, I maintain that films narrate and make sense of human experiences.[4] Films are not produced only to entertain, to profit the production companies, and for filmmakers to make names for themselves. Filmmaking is ultimately an act of empathy. Films reflect as well as shape the concerns of societies. Filmmakers and actors take the lived experiences of their times and the past and turn them into perceptive and soulful works of art. Like Renaissance Italy's architecture, paintings, and sculptures, post-1945 Southeast Asian films offer insight into the spirit of the age and the mindsets of the societies that produced them.[5] Analyzing the history, themes, and dynamics of Southeast Asian national cinema thus helps us grasp how Southeast Asian states made sense of their decolonization experiences, their nationalist projects, and the processes that shaped their domestic as well as international political approaches.[6]

I further argue that Southeast Asian films are intricately embedded in the social, cultural, economic, and political history of the region. While films were introduced by the Europeans to Southeast Asians during the colonial period, Southeast Asians took it upon themselves to utilize films as a means of navigating their own nascent national identities. Films traveled across and within Southeast Asia, further intensifying the region's shared anticolonialist sentiment and collective nationalist experiences as well as imagination. Films afforded the locals a space not only to imagine but to construct their national (as well as regional) identities. The following sections trace the intersections among film, history, and politics in Southeast Asia by looking at different historical periods beginning from the terminal stage of European colonialism and the Japanese interlude up to the postwar nation-building and decolonization. The chapter ends with a brief discussion on contemporary Southeast Asian cinema and an outlook of the future of cinema in the region.

The Backstory: A Broad Overview of Cinema and Society under the Colonial Period

European rule profoundly influenced the development of Southeast Asia, shaping almost every aspect of the region's societies. In 1511, the Portuguese built a small settlement in Malacca[7] that served as a base of maritime commerce. By the sixteenth century, the Spaniards followed and secured their foothold in the Philippines. Soon after, other Europeans arrived, including the British, Dutch, French, and, eventually, the Americans. Each colonial power worked to protect its respective territories. They imposed their unique political systems, institutions, and ways of life on their colonies. Their presence consequently made inter-regional interaction difficult. Under European colonialism, Southeast Asia was disconnected (despite their shared experiences with colonialism and precolonial maritime trade). As the historian Nicholas Tarling notes, the colonial states "had little in common but their colonialism."[8] Southeast Asia under colonial rule was internally segmented, culturally heterogeneous, and economically linked to and even dependent on Europe.

By the second half of the nineteenth century, however, the region witnessed radical economic changes and profound shifts in society, culture, and colonial governance. As historian Russell Fifield explains, the region became vital as a production center of raw materials to fulfil Europe's needs.[9] Trade and commerce increased, and technological innovations from Europe percolated to Southeast Asia. Among these innovations, cinema arrived in the region. On December 5, 1900, the technology of cinema reached Indonesia (then called the Dutch East Indies) through a Dutch company, De Nederlandsche Bioscope Maatschappij (The Netherlands Bioscope Company). A little over a decade after the first screenings, film production started in Indonesia. Dutch, French, German, and other European filmmakers came to Indonesia to produce mostly documentary clips about the country's culture, society, and lifestyle. While the Europeans provided the technology, the capital was procured mostly from ethnic Chinese entrepreneurs. The locals, however, were uninterested in these films as they could not relate to the films' European-based storylines and images captured on screen.

In the Philippines, cinema was introduced by the Spaniards. According to the film historian Nick Deocampo, "Film was among the last—if not the very last—cultural legacy those colonial powers bequeathed their native vessels before the winds of change finally shook off their control over the region."[10] In 1897, the earliest known display of moving pictures in the Philippines took place in a movie house in Escolta owned by two Spanish businessmen, Messrs. Leibman and Peritz. With the use of Lumiere cinematography, they presented a series of shows with a live orchestra, which further enhanced the moviegoing experience.

The subsequent years were tumultuous in Philippine history, and filmmaking came to a halt. In 1896, Filipino revolutionaries declared war against Spanish colonizers, who were then defeated by the Americans during the Spanish-American War in 1898. Following American victory against Spain, relations between American officials and Filipinos turned sour. This resulted in the Philippine-American War from 1899 to 1902, which ended with the subjugation of the Philippines by the Americans. As the Americans consolidated their rule, the film industry had a new lease on life. American filmmakers and producers came to the country and started making and screening films. In 1905, Herbert Wyndham screened shorts of the Manila Fire Department's activity. In 1909, several new movie houses opened. Among them were Albert Yearsley's Empire Theatre and the Anda Theatre, located at the heart of Old Manila. Yearsely shot short films, including *The Cebu Typhoon of 1912*, *The Eruption of Taal Volcano*, *The 1912 Trip of the Igorots to Barcelona*, and *The Manila Carnival of 1910*. Filmmakers from the United States also produced short newsreel documentaries about the islands. The earliest film production and distribution companies began to appear, and slowly, film became one of the most dominant forms of entertainment in the Philippines. Toward the end of the 1920s, the film industry in the country was well established. As in Indonesia, however, filmmaking was mostly a foreign endeavor.

Similar to the cases of the Philippines and Indonesia, film also arrived in Malaya[11] via the Europeans. The film industry thrived, especially in Singapore. As Shariff Ahmad asserts, "Any discussion of the history of the Malay film industry must always start with Singapore."[12] As the most important entrepôt of the British in the region, Singapore, which was once a part of Malaya and subsequently of the Federation of Malaysia, served as the locus of the movie industry where local and international filmmakers congregated. The British brought films to the island in 1897 when British producer Robert William Paul brought projectors from Europe and screened the first film in Singapore at the Alhambra. Later that year, the first British-imported film, entitled *Edison's Projectoscope*, was shown in Kuala Lumpur, Malaya. In 1933, the first film in Bahasa Melayu (Malayan language) entitled *Laila Majnun* (Laila and Majnun) was produced, a collaboration between the India-born director Balden Singh Rajhans and the producer S. M. Chesty.

One of the most popular films produced in the Dutch East Indies during this time was *Terang Boelan* (Full moon, 1937), a collaboration between the Dutch-Indonesian filmmaker Albert Balink and the Wong Brothers, Othniel and Joshua, who were filmmakers from China working in the Dutch East Indies. *Terang Boelan* was an adaptation of the American film, *Jungle Princess* (1936) starring Dorothy Lamour. It revolves around the story of one couple, Rohaya and Kasim, who are forced to elope to Malacca when the former's father demands that she marry an opium dealer named Musa. In Malacca, they start a new life only to be discovered by Musa, who kidnaps Rohaya and takes her back to her village. The film ends after a fight between Kasim and Musa and Rohaya's father finally agrees to let the two stay together.

While the film follows a simple plot, it signifies a key juncture in filmmaking in Indonesia. On the one hand, it employed *keroncong* music[13] and appealed not just to the local Chinese but to Indonesians as well. On the other hand, it also utilized Indonesian language, which made it more accessible to the local audience. Due to the unprecedented success of the film, Balink's *Terang Boelan* became a template for other producers seeking to make the next successful movie. Although it started as an adaptation of a foreign film, *Terang Boelan* captured the local ethos and culture of Indonesia at the end of the nineteenth century.

The same can be said about the classic Malaysian film, *Laila Majnun* (Lovestruck Laila, 1933) directed by B. S. Rajhans. It is a love story premised on the Persian-Arabic tale, and its production was informed by Indian techniques and styles. While it is unanimously regarded as an important film, there are different views about it. For instance, Hassan Muthalib opined that the film was "only a film in the Malay language" made by foreign filmmakers from India. He asserts that Malay cinema, in fact, only started with P. Ramlee's *Semarah Padi* (Red rice, 1956). As opposed to the obvious Indian influences and features of *Laila Majnun*, Ramlee's film, he argues, highlights Malay culture, norms, and customs in a way that had never been seen before.[14] Regardless of the competing views regarding the significances of *Laila Majnun* and *Semarah Padi* in Malaysian film history, it is sufficient to note that both films represent a step toward the development of what eventually will be called Malaysian cinema. Without a doubt, prior to the prominence of Ramlee and other Malay filmmakers, Indian directors, such as B.S. Rajhans, facilitated the development of Malay/Malaysian cinema by delivering the early films using Malay language, actors, and setting.

Early films in Southeast Asia were intricately embedded in the distinct political, social, and economic milieu of the region. As Hassan Muthalib posits about Malaysian cinema, "The performances were not only to entertain; they usually imparted something of relevance to life as well as depicting the culture of the particular community in which they were presented. They were, in fact, reflecting man, his world, his world and his condition."[15] The same can also be said about the rest of the region.

At the end of the nineteenth century, cinema was one of the last legacies of Europe to Southeast Asia. However, despite the foreign origin of motion pictures, the social and cultural ethos of colonial Southeast Asia permeated the cinematic frame whether it was through the use of local languages or the employment of Southeast Asian cultural artefacts like musical instruments or traditional dance and costumes. Eventually, films were transformed and employed by Southeast Asians and became national cinemas. More importantly, the shared narratives of colonialism and images of nationalist fervor so evident in these national cinemas further served as fertile ground for creating and crafting the then embryonic Southeast Asian regional identity.

The Japanese Interlude

The Second World War had a profound impact on Southeast Asia. On the one hand, the Japanese conquest put most of the region under one colonial rule for the first time in history. On the other hand, Japanese films and filmmakers left an indelible mark among Southeast Asians. The Japanese took over the film companies and sequestered their cameras and equipment, using them to produce propaganda films—documentaries, feature films, and short news clips. The distress of the war was also manifested in the number of films produced.

In the Philippines, the Japanese confiscated various film companies owned by Americans and used them to make propaganda materials. In Malaya and Singapore, local and foreign personnel working for film companies were forced to work for a Japanese film company, Eiga Haikya Sha (Japan Film Distribution), which took control of the movie houses, film companies, as well as the distribution of films in Malaya and Singapore. The company also reviewed and censored films before allowing them to be publicly screened. In Singapore, Cathay Cinema became the most famous venue for Japanese-approved screenings. Old Indian films and Japanese propaganda were permitted while war films were prohibited. *Singapore Sokogeki*, *Marat Na Tora* (March to Singapore), *Shina No Yoru* (A Night in China), and *Tokyo Symphony* were some of the very few films allowed to be screened.[16]

Under the Japanese interregnum, anti-Western sentiments escalated, and nationalist ideas suffused in movies created by local and Japanese directors across the region. One example was Japanese filmmaker Abe Yutaka and Filipino filmmaker Gerardo de Leon's *Dawn of Freedom* (1944). With financial support from the Japanese Ministry of Army, the movie's plot revolves around the battle that launched Japanese capture of the Philippines (which was then still under American tutelage) in 1941. It depicted the Americans as the enemies of Asians and appealed to the nationalists in the Philippines to resist the West. This strong political allusion resonated with the Japanese pronouncement of "Asia for the Asians"—the core principle of the Greater East Asia Coprosperity Sphere. The Japanese promoted local culture and banned American films from being screened in the region.

The Japanese occupation had also left an impact on the style and technique of filmmakers in the region. For example, the acclaimed Japanese director Akira Kurosawa influenced Southeast Asian filmmakers. The Malaysian actor-director P. Ramlee's film *Kancan Tirana* (Kanchan Tirana, 1969) was based on Akira Kurosawa's *Sanshiro Sugata* (Judo saga, 1943). In the Japanese version, the main character decides to learn martial arts, which he eventually masters after a series of strenuous challenges and lessons from his instructor. In P. Ramlee's version, on the other hand, Kanchan (played by the Malaysian actor Jins Shamsuddin), a local boy who was bullied by a man named Sang Nila also decides to learn how to fight and get back at his opponent. Obviously inspired by Japanese martial arts films, P. Ramlee appropriated the plot into the Malaysian context. The characters speak Malay and are dressed in traditional Malay costumes, and the setting captures a typical Malay village with wooden houses.

At the end of Japanese occupation, the whole political landscape of Southeast Asia changed. The perceptions of the locals toward their former colonial masters also changed. The nationalist groups in Indonesia and Malaya acquired strength. The Filipinos looked forward to independence, which the Americans pledged to grant to the Philippines. Southeast Asian films also took a key turning point during this period. When the Second World War ended, Southeast Asian nationalists were ready to emerge and Southeast Asian national cinemas followed suit.

National Cinemas, Nation-Building, and Decolonization

The immediate years following the conclusion of the Second World War saw the rehabilitation and revival of cinemas in the region—the blossoming of the golden era of national cinemas. However, it is important to note that national cinemas in Southeast Asia did not emerge in isolation. They were transnationally connected. Traveling across borders to collaborate with one another, the producers shared their ideas, techniques of filmmaking, and political ideals. Hollywood productions also influenced their craft. All of these ideas and influences would find their way into the films that they created. Facilitating the transnational exchange and productions were the ethnic Chinese who funded a number of the films. Through these transnational exchanges, collaborations, and financial support, the postwar Southeast Asian film industry became notably vibrant and popular with the local population. The locals would embrace the films as valuable entertainment products and as significant parts of their social and cultural lives.

One of the foremost examples of these transnational cinematic productions in Southeast Asia is a work that resulted from the collaboration between Lamberto Avellana, a pioneering Filipino director, and P. Ramlee, who is known as a great, if not the greatest, actor, composer, director, and singer in Malaysian film history. *Sergeant Hassan* (Sergeant Hassan, 1958) is one of the most memorable films of postwar Malaysia, and by extension, of Southeast Asia. The film is set at the height of the Japanese invasion of Malaya and explores the story of a simple orphan turned soldier during the war. Hassan's parents die when he is young. His father's friend subsequently adopts him. Embittered by the attention that is lavished on Hassan, the latter's foster brother, Aziz, bullies him. As grownups, Aziz continues to hate Hassan because Salmah, a woman he likes, fancies Hassan instead of him. With the outbreak of war, the Royal Malay Regiment calls for volunteers. Aziz joins but Hassan is forced to stay at home to manage the land owned by his foster father. As a result, he is labeled a coward by the townsfolk. Hassan decides to leave and joins the regiment and is soon promoted to sergeant. Hassan proves to be a good and brave fighter and even saves Aziz when he is captured by the Japanese.

The entire film captures the dilemma of ordinary citizens at the height of the Japanese Occupation. It puts the narratives of resistance at the forefront of its filmic message. It argues for the awakening of Malay/Malaysian nationalist fervor. At a significant juncture in the film, the main character, Hassan, bravely proclaims: "Memang bangsa kita masih muda dan masih lemah. Aku tak peduli ito semua. Harapanku hanyalah kita sama bangsa bersatu-padulah hendaknya" (Even though we are still a young and new nation, I do not care. I hope we can all rise together).

Clearly, the film recognizes the state of the Malayan nation—its vulnerabilities at the stage of decolonization and its efforts to come to terms not merely with the Japanese Occupation but more importantly with the British hegemony. *Sergeant Hassan* envisioned the growth of a young yet sturdy nation. Moreover, despite the strong presence of the Malay—as a race and a group, as epitomized by the hero himself, P. Ramlee—it also incorporated other ethnic groups through key characters, such as the Chinese character who assists Hassan during the skirmishes. That this film was produced through collaboration and cooperation between Filipino and Malay filmmakers not only indicates the transnational relationship between the two countries' budding film industries, it also reflects their shared history and experience under the Japanese Occupation. In this respect, the film represents a shared vision—a common imagination within Southeast Asia forged through their experience under the Japanese rule. As in the film, the war disrupted lives of ordinary citizens in the region. While some Filipinos and Malays fought fiercely against the Japanese, as in the film, some also worked with the Japanese and facilitated their occupation.

Films such as *Sergeant Hassan* created opportunities for Southeast Asians to imagine not just the nation but also the cooperative region. By the 1950s, more transnational co-productions had transpired. Filipino directors traveled to Malaya and collaborated with local filmmakers. Their joint works resulted in transnational and hybrid narratives and styles that resonated with Filipinos, Malayans, and even Indonesians. Familiar with Malay culture and language, Filipinos cooperated easily and fruitfully with the Malayans. They also helped their counterparts to develop new shooting and lighting techniques—skills that the Filipinos acquired from the Americans.[17] The end result was films that connected with and inspired the peoples of the region.

Needless to say, pioneering Southeast Asian filmmakers were notably important in the development of their countries' national cinemas. Among them were Lamberto Avellana (Philippines), P. Ramlee (Malaysia), and Usmar Ismail (Indonesia), who took an active part in the construction of images—of the national self (and eventually the Southeast Asian self, albeit abstrusely) and the others (former colonizers, the United States and China, and the Soviet Union as others). Above all, through their cinematic productions, they interpreted the social and political milieu in their own countries as well as how they related to other countries in the region. The cinematic productions furnished their audiences with ideas and mental images to comprehend the region and regional developments as well.

In Indonesia, for instance, following the formal announcement of independence on December 27, 1949, new issues and questions surfaced. How should they promote economic development and social change? What kind of political system should be implemented? How should they project themselves to the world? Where do they go after independence? As these predicaments circulated in the realm of politics, Indonesian filmmakers and producers also scrambled to present possibilities in the marketplace of ideas. That very same year, under the leadership of Usmar Ismail, a group of Indonesians established the first film company in the country that was exclusively owned by Indonesians. They called the company Perfini. Also in the same year, Djamalludin Malik opened another Indonesian-owned company, Persari. These two pioneers are recognized as important figures in the history of Indonesian films. They employed films to stimulate the imagination and political consciousness of the Indonesians. In 1950, they produced more than twenty films in the country, though only one survived—Usmar Ismail's *Darah dan Doa* (Blood and prayer, 1950).[18]

Usmar Ismail's *Darah dan Doa* is generally considered the first truly indigenous film that was created in Indonesia by an Indonesian. Unlike films that contained narratives of vehement heroism and extreme nationalism, the film is about human fallibility, hunger to survive, and conflicted ideologies. Reinterpreting the history of Indonesia, the film details the journey of Captain Sudarto and his men, the Siliwangi Division, together with numerous civilians, including women and children, from Yogjakarta to West Java. The group has to constantly defend themselves against Dutch attacks. More importantly, the story accentuates how individual actions and whims impact the nature of the war. In essence, the film enabled Indonesians to reflect on their past—their roles and actions during the revolution, the memory of bloodshed, and the results of their struggles to survive as an independent nation-state. Viewed from this perspective, *Darah dan Doa* reflects Indonesia's postcolonial nation-building.

The case of the Philippines resembles that of Indonesia in many ways. After the Second World War, the country's film industry emerged from a three-year slump. Leading Filipino filmmakers, such as Manuel Conde and Gerardo de Leon, came out of it with a renewed and profound sense of creative imagination. Not long after the end of the war, the Philippine film industry entered one of its most productive and vibrant phases. Globally acclaimed Filipino classics were produced by the foremost founders and key shapers of Philippine national cinema.[19]

Upon the granting of independence in 1946, the general feeling among Filipinos was one of euphoria—of fervent nationalism as a newly independent state. This atmosphere was captured in films that depicted narratives of revolutionaries, war heroes, and guerrillas. At this point, it is imperative to underline a crucial similarity between Indonesian and Philippine cinemas. Whereas Ismail's *Darah dan Doa* epitomized the first masterful historical reimagining of the revolutionary struggle by an Indonesian, *Victory Joe* (Victory Joe, 1946) is the Philippines' early attempt to capture both the country's anxieties about the aftermath of the revolution and its changing relationship with its former colonizers. The latter film is a story about a young Filipina, Rosie, caught between her feelings for an American GI, Bob, and her deep affection for her Filipino lover, Eduardo, a guerrilla who was believed to have died fighting the Japanese during the occupation. Bob meets Rosie and falls in love with her. They spend romantic times together; he courts her; she teaches him some Filipino phrases and lectures him on the Filipino way of courtship.

Eventually, Rosie grows fond of Bob but could not forget Eduardo, with whom she was happy before the outbreak of the war. The story becomes even more complex when Eduardo turns out to be alive. One day, he returns to the village hoping to reunite with Rosie. A conflict between Bob and Eduardo ensues as Bob challenges Eduardo to a duel. But Bob realizes that regardless of what he does, Rosie was and has always been in love with Eduardo. In a conversation with Eduardo, Bob says, "She loves you, you fool. She always loved you. The more I tried to make her love me, the more she loved you." The film ends when Bob finally goes back to the United States, leaving Rosie and Eduardo to, presumably, live happily ever after.

The film explores a critical juncture in the history of the Philippines when it finally acquired its official status as a free and independent nation. It interrogates the complex relationship between the Philippines and the United States as much as it celebrates the departure of the Americans from the Philippine soil. In the film, Rosie is captivated by Bob in the same way that the Philippines was captivated by the glamour and allure of the United States. In the film, Rosie's heart remains loyal and profoundly committed to Eduardo and all she ever wants is to be with him—and even Bob understands this. The film instils a sense of nationalism and an ideological reference of reuniting the Philippines with the Filipinos. Despite the long relationship between the Americans and the Filipinos, 1946 marked the Filipinos' triumph over colonialism, a celebration of genuine nationalism and love for the country. The film reflects an attempt by Filipinos to make sense of the new international status of the Philippines and to redefine the country's relationship with the Americans. Simply put, *Victory Joe* celebrates the postcolonial hope of the Philippines to reconstruct itself as an independent and free nation.

The 1950s and 1960s also marked the golden age of Malayan/Malaysian. This period witnessed a surge in local film production and the rise to national prominence of key Malayan/Malaysian filmmakers and actors.[20] Concurrent with the political turbulence in the former British territories, the postwar film industry expanded in Malaysia. The Shaw Brothers reestablished the Malay Film Productions and structured it along the lines of the big studios in Hollywood. The company hired new actors, directors, and technicians from Malaysia and abroad. Prominent filmmakers from the Philippines, India, and even China, including B. S. Rahjans, B. N. Rao, Rolf Bayer, Ramon Estella, and Lamberto Avellana were recruited. These directors were tasked to conceptualize their own films. They even had to write the scripts. Indian films served as one of the major influences, after being adapted to the domestic taste and culture. Like in Indian films, Malaysian films incorporated music and dance into their narrative structure. Malay spectators welcomed these features because they saw the similarities between new films and *bangsawan*—the most popular entertainment before the introduction of film.

As independence from the British approached, films being produced continued to treat themes that presaged the emergent nation, despite the internal limitations and idiosyncrasies of its society. In *Semarah Padi*, for instance, P. Ramlee presents a model of governance of the emerging independent Malaya. The entire film is shot through with references to the foundation or origin of a community. It opens with a solemn invocation about *Semerah Padi*—a community of devoted Muslims in the Malay Archipelago. Combining a dramatic narrative and an intense romance, the film portrays an ideal village setting. That ideal setting is a Malay-Muslim community headed by a strong-willed chief whose power is immense and whose words are the law.

The film's narrative revolves around the themes of a triangular love story, crime, adultery, and punishment as seen through the lens of Islamic laws and values. Dara, daughter of the village head, is harboring feelings for Aduka, an assistant to Dara's father, and he loves her too. However, Dara's father decides that she should marry Taruna instead. The latter is also one of the village head's assistants. Being a dutiful child, Dara suppresses her own feelings and agrees to marry Taruna, who also genuinely likes her. At the time of their engagement, the peace and tranquility of the village are disrupted when a wounded villager named Kecewa is taken to the village head. He is beaten by his adulterous wife, Galak, and a man named Jejaka. Kecewa dies, thus prompting Dara's father to instruct Aduka to arrest the two culprits. Taruna then insists on accompanying Aduka because it is his responsibility as an assistant to the village head.

A fight ensues and ends up with the arrest of Galak and Jejaka. Adhering to the laws of the village, the chief orders death by impalement. The story then turns to another plot when Borek, Jejaka's brother, begins to assault the village—murdering locals and burning their houses to avenge Jejaka. Amid this chaos, Taruna is sent to aid the sultan's men against pirate attacks. While Aduka remains in the village to protect the people from Borek, the latter abducts Dara, who is eventually saved by Aduka. Swept by their feelings toward each other, Aduka and Dara engage in physical intimacy. Penitent for what they did, Dara weeps furiously and Aduka begs Taruna to punish him. In the end, Dara's father orders that each get one hundred lashes for their sins. Dara and Aduka then get married.

Despite the uncharacteristically tragic and even brutal conclusion, the meaning of the film especially within the cultural and temporal context of nation-building remains clear. It advances the idea of a nation based on historical and religious preconditions. The whole narrative explores the twofold process of securing peace and stability and defining the identity of the village. The community becomes the space for constructing the national identity. Islamic laws serve as the framework for maintaining order for Malaya/Malaysia's multiracial societies. At this point, one may argue that the film, in fact, is a rejection of a unified nation as it appears to enforce the Islamic rule by essentializing Malay cultural and Islamic tradition. Although this view has many valid concerns to consider, I look at it from a different angle. Certainly, the film interrogates the role of Islam and Malay people in the formation of the new nation, but it also attempts to incorporate non-Malays.

In one of the advertisements, for instance, the film is presented as "A picture of infinite appeal to all cinemagoers of all nationalities!" The film attempts to publicize itself as an experience that suits everyone regardless of their racial backgrounds. As such, in the process of watching the film, the audience is exposed to the foundational tenets of a stable and peaceful village but also prompted to accede to the saliency of Islam and Malay authority in the process of nation-building and its inherently chaotic nature. The film is a decisive portrayal of various levels of chaos and anarchy during the period, and therefore, the reflexive desire to endure as a robust and well-ordered society.

First, there is chaos within the village itself which reflects the internal divisions and conflicts in the emerging Malayan/Malaysian nation. The headman and Islam are presented as the pillars of the village. Individual desires and interests, as represented by Dara and Aduka's feelings toward each other, must be tapered, if not totally eliminated, for the overall well-being of the village, that is to say, the nation. This is the same message conveyed when Taruna forgives the two and when the village chief chooses to uphold the law and punish them. In this respect, in every character's individual story the prominence of the village/nation is evident. Although individual sacrifices over nation may not be the theme that resonates well with today's sentiment and mood, such a theme undoubtedly had a strong appeal during the period of nation-building after colonization

Second, the immediate external threat represented by Jejaka and Borek appears to be an indication, as mentioned, of the menace that lurks near the village itself. These perceived threats are the local communist groups and perhaps even the non-Malays who posed a danger to the formation of a new and independent nation. This does not mean that the film tries to exclude non-Malays. As I explained earlier, the publicity for the film was decidedly inclusive. The only prerequisite is the adherence to the overarching laws of the nation and, in the process, the curtailment of individual interests. A case in point is that even though Aduka and Dara were from the village, they gave in to their own desires and were punished as a result. This then indicates that the general well-being of the village, and also the nation, rests upon the dissolution of individual agency and the prominence of the ideological principle that keeps the whole nation intact and stable—again, messages that would have been suitable during the time of nation-building.

The third realm of chaos is signified by the pirate raids that imperil the sultan's domain. It can be seen as an allusion to the anarchy of the international political arena during the postwar period. The necessity of sending Taruna to aid the sultan hints at the obligation of the village, and certainly the nation, to safeguard peace and protect it from outside dangers (whether they be communists or colonizers). The main message, hence, centers on the defense of the nation, securing its survival amid different levels of threats. This tendency to construct the nation vis-à-vis the perception of threats is in a way a symptom of the eruption of widespread consciousness in Malaya to claim control over their fate and harness traditional power structures in nation-building.

From the emergence of embryonic nationalistic fervor up to the launch and implementation of the experiment of nation-building, it is evident from the foregoing discussion how films were crucial in two broad ways. On the one hand, they mirrored the complexities and nuances of the political, social, economic, and cultural milieus of the countries examined in this study. On the other hand, films carry with them a certain level of embedded message, that is, an ideological element that cuts across the plot and is conveyed from the most direct to the subtlest way. As a consequence of the colonial history of Southeast Asia, a vehement nationalist ideology emerged, lingered, and pervaded both the political and the filmic realities of the region.

Future of Films in Asia

Films are more than just the story or the business or the propaganda. While recognizing that films are essentially popular products and target to please or to draw in the audience, it is also imperative to assert that films do tell a story (or stories) about the time they were made. Cinema across Southeast Asia throughout the history underwent a significant shift from being a colonial product to an indigenized cultural product as Southeast Asians utilized films to conjure the earliest imaginations of their budding nations, the anxieties and equivocality in their decolonization, and their uncertainties about their future in navigating the international system.

National cinemas contain the prevailing beliefs of Southeast Asian leaders and have clear implications for foreign policy formulation. According to Sean Carter and Klaus Dodds, "International politics operates within and through a whole series of spatial imaginaries and formations."[21] This chapter furthers this argument by regarding cinema as a space for Southeast Asian imaginaries. However, this process of "imagining" continues up until today. The task of Southeast Asian nation-building remains an unfinished task, and cinema plays the same role as before.

Today, Southeast Asian cinema has begun to make its mark on the international stage in several ways. First, we have seen the emergence of many driven and talented Southeast Asians who are passionate about filmmaking and are not afraid of experimenting and exploring new styles and formats. Lav Diaz (Philippines), Brillante Mendoza (Philippines), Wee Meng Chee (also known as Namewee; Malaysia), Garin Nugroho (Indonesia), Riri Riza (Indonesia), and Tan Pin Pin (Singapore) are but among the many Southeast Asians who are now internationally acclaimed.[22]

Second, we have also seen the increasing number of Southeast Asian cinemas being screened at prestigious international film festivals, such as the Cannes Film Festival, Berlin International Film Festival, Venice International Film Festival, and Locarno International Film Festival. Lav Diaz's film *Season of the Devil* was screened at the 68th Berlin International Film Festival and was named Best Film in the Gems Section at the *Festival Internacional de Cine de Cartagena de Indias* (Cartagena Film Festival). At the 2018 Venice International Film Festival, several Southeast Asian filmmakers received critical acclaim, including Thailand's Phuttiphing Aroonpheng for the film *Manta Ray* and Indonesia's Aditya Ahmad for the short *A Gift*.

Finally, more and more Southeast Asian filmmakers are incorporating perennial social concerns and political issues into their projects. We are witnessing the continuous utilization of cinema as a space for political and social interrogation and intervention. The controversial war on drugs waged by the Philippine government has permeated the cinematic scape as seen in the works of Filipino filmmakers, such as Erik Matti (*BuyBust*, 2018) and Carlo J. Caparas (*Kamandag ng Droga*, Drug's poison, 2017). In Singapore, Siew Hua Yeo's *A Land Imagined* (2018) tackles the rarely examined narratives of immigrant workers, their struggles, living conditions, and efforts to dream and imagine in Singapore.

The stories of nationalism and decolonization in Southeast Asia are inevitably complex and dynamic given the heterogeneity of cultures and divergences in the historical and political narratives of Southeast Asian states. However, these stories find their nexus, a convergence of sorts, in the national cinemas that were produced by the Southeast Asians themselves. The development of national cinemas in the region served as a crucial platform for the emergence of multiple images and interrogations of the nascent national constructions by Southeast Asian states. Moreover, national cinemas following the Second World War reflected the ideological maelstrom during that period. National cinemas put forward a cultural narrative about anticolonialism, independence, and nation-building. These films reflect the creativity, resilience, and strength of Southeast Asians, and they continue to do so today.

Notes

1   *Enamorada* (A woman in love, 1946) was screened as a part of the "100 Years of Mexican Cinema," a film festival organized by the Embassy of Mexico in Singapore in May 2015.
2   By traditional history, I mean political and military history profoundly influenced by historians, such as the empiricist Leopold von Ranke, *History of the Latin and Teutonic Peoples from 1494 to 1514*, Translated by G. R. Dennis (London: George Bell and Sons, 1909), Robin George Collingwood, *The Idea of History* (New York: Oxford University Press, 1993), and Edward H. Carr, *What Is History?* (Cambridge: University of Cambridge, 1961).
3   I follow the pioneering works by cultural studies scholars and cultural historians, particularly those who employed cinema in their historical analysis: Theodore Hughes, *Literature and Film in Cold War South Korea: Freedom's Frontier* (New York: Columbia University Press, 2012); Kristin Hoganson, *Fighting for American Manhood: How Gender Politics Provoked the Spanish-American and Philippine-American Wars* (New Haven, CT: Yale University Press, 1998); Reinhold Wagleitner, *Coca-colonization and the Cold War: The Cultural Mission of the United States in Austria after the Second World War* (Chapel Hill: University of North Carolina Press, 1994); Robert Park, *Race and Culture* (New York: Free Press, 1964); Paul Kramer, *The Blood of the Government: Race, Empire, the United States and the Philippines* (Chapel Hill: University of North Carolina Press, 2006); and Tony Day and Maya H. T. Liem, eds. *Cultures at War: The Cold War and Cultural Expression in Southeast Asia* (Ithaca, NY: Cornell University Press, 2010). See, in particular, the essays by Francisco Benitez, Rachel Harrison, and Barbara Hatley.
4   In the book, *Past Imperfect: History According to the Movies*, film is presented as full of historical errors and flaws and therefore cannot be counted as a strong

source of history. See Mark Carnes, ed. *Past Imperfect: History According to the Movies* (New York: Henry Holt, 1995). In another work, Robert Toplin maintains that because films are produced for a particular purpose (to appeal to the audience and earn a profit) different than that of written history, then it must be regarded as different from other primary sources. See Robert Toplin, *History by Hollywood: The Use and Abuse of the American Past* (Urbana: University of Illinois Press, 1996).

5 See Jacob Burckhardt, *The Civilization of the Renaissance in Italy* (London: Penguin Classics, 1990). The work was originally published in 1860.

6 The end of the Second World War sparked an era of radical changes across Southeast Asia. Cold warriors, anticolonialists, nationalists, and imperialists operated to advance their interests across the region. Newly independent states strove to establish stable political and economic institutions, capable of enabling them to survive and stave off foreign interventions into their domestic affairs. Southeast Asian leaders furthermore articulated ideas championing regional unity, seeking to band together to protect their collective interests.

7 Malacca is located at the southern part of the Malay peninsula, about 148 kilometers from Kuala Lumpur, Malaysia.

8 See Nicholas Tarling, *Southeast Asia and the Great Powers* (London: Routledge, 2010).

9 Russell Fifield, *The Diplomacy of Southeast Asia* (New York: Harper and Brothers, 1958), 16.

10 Nick Deocampo, *Lost Films of Asia* (Philippines: Anvil, 2006), 3.

11 Throughout the chapter, I use "Malaya" to refer to the colonies and states in the Malay Peninsula under the British rule. After independence in 1963, the term "Malaysia" has been introduced to refer to the union of Malaya, North Borneo, Sarawak, and Singapore. In 1965, Singapore became a separate nation-state.

12 Jose Lacaba, *The Films of ASEAN* (Pasig, Philippines: ASEAN Committee on Culture and Information, 2000), 51.

13 *Keroncong* music is a traditional musical genre common to both the Malay Peninsula and Indonesia (though it originates from the latter). The ensemble commonly comprises flutes, a local ukulele (called *cuk* and *cak*), a guitar, a bass and a vocalist.

14 Hassan Muthalib, *Malaysian Cinema in a Bottle: A Century (and a Bit More) of Wayang* (Petaling Jaya, Malaysia: Merpati Jingga, 2013), 32.

15 Ibid., 11.

16 Ibid. See also William van der Heide, *Malaysian Cinema, Asian Film: Border Crossings and National Culture* (Amsterdam: Amsterdam University Press, 2002), 130–132.

17 Heide, *Malaysian Cinema*, 136.

18 Ismail's and Malik's works brought the political challenges and opportunities confronting Indonesia to the forefront of the people's imaginations. The Indonesian films reflected and constructed the nation-state's strategic culture and served as a means to shape Indonesia's national identity. As Karl Heider strongly asserts, "Not only do Indonesian films use the Indonesian language almost exclusively but, further . . . Indonesian films depict generalized behavior patterns. . . . And in doing so, these films have become an important medium for the shaping of an emergent national Indonesian culture." See Karl Heider, *Indonesian Cinema: National Culture on Screen* (Honolulu: University of Hawaii Press, 1991), 10.

19 Among Philippine classical movies are Lamberto Avellana's *Anal Dalita* (Child of sorrow, 1956); Manuel Silos's *Biyaya ng Lupa* (Blessings of the land, 1959); Gerardo

de Leon's *Huwag Mo Akong Limutin* (Forget me not, 1962); and Lino Brocka's *Tinimbang Ngunit Kulang* (Weighed but found wanting, 1974). See Bibsy Carballo, *Filipino Directors Up Close: The Golden Ages of Philippine Cinema, 1950–2010* (Manila: Anvil, 2010).

20 As mentioned, Malaya's early cinema shared its history with Singapore. They remained closely linked even after the Japanese Occupation. In 1957, Great Britain granted Malaya independence. In 1963, the Federation of Malaya merged with Singapore, North Borneo, and Sarawak to form Malaysia. Singapore left the federation in 1965 and became an independent state.

21 Sean Carter and Klaus Dodds, *International Politics and Film* (London: Wall-flower, 2014), 108.

22 Some notable films include Riri Riza's *Gie* (Gie, 2005); Namewee's *Nasi Lemak 2.0* (Fatty Rice 2.0, 2011); and Tan Pin Pin's *To Singapore, With Love* (2013), *Invisible City* (2007), *Building Dreams* (2002), and *Rogers Park* (2001).

Bibliography

Acharya, Amitav. *The Making of Southeast Asia: International Relations of a Region*. Singapore: ISEAS, 2003.

———. *The Quest for Identity: International Relations of Southeast Asia*. Oxford: Oxford University Press, 2000.

Aquilia, Pieter. "Westernizing Southeast Asian Cinema: Co-productions for Transnational Markets." *Journal of Media and Cultural Studies* 20, no. 4 (2006): 433–445.

Arifin, Sharuf Zinjuaber. *Sejarah Filem Melayu* [The history of Malay motion pictures]. Kuala Lumpur: Penerbitan Sri Sharifah, 1980.

Barnard, Timothy. "Decolonization and the Nation in Malay Film, 1955–1965." *Southeast Asia Research* 17, no. 1 (2009): 65–86.

———. "Film Melayu: Nationalism, Modernity, and Film in a Pre–World War Two Malay Magazine." *Journal of Southeast Asian Studies* 41, no. 1 (2010): 47–70.

Burckhardt, Jacob. *The Civilization of the Renaissance in Italy*. London: Penguin Classics, 1990.

Capino, Jose. *Dream Factories of a Former Colony: American Fantasies, Philippine Cinema*. Minneapolis: University of Minnesota Press, 2010.

Carballo, Bibsy. *Filipino Directors Up Close: The Golden Ages of Philippine Cinema. 1950–2010*. Manila: Anvil, 2010.

Carnes, Mark, ed. *Past Imperfect: History According to the Movies*. New York: Henry Holt, 1995.

Carr, Edward H. *What Is History?* Cambridge: University of Cambridge, 1961.

Carter, Sean, and Klaus Dodds. *International Politics and Film* (London: Wallflower, 2014).

Cheah, Boon Keng. *Malaysia: The Making of a Nation*. Singapore: ISEAS, 2002.

Chen, Kuan-Hsing. *Asia as Method: Toward Deimperialization*. Durham, NC: Duke University Press, 2010.

Collingwood, Robin George. *The Idea of History*. New York: Oxford University Press, 1993.

Day, Tony, and Maya H. T. Liem, eds. *Cultures at War: The Cold War and Cultural Expression in Southeast Asia*. Ithaca, NY: Cornell University Press, 2010.

Deocampo, Nick. *Cine: Spanish Influences on Early Cinema in the Philippines*. Manila: National Commission for the Culture and Arts, 2003.

———. *Film: American Influences on Philippine Cinema*. Manila: Anvil, 2011.

———. *Lost Films of Asia*. Manila: Anvil, 2006.

Fifield, Russell. *The Diplomacy of Southeast Asia*. New York: Harper and Brothers, 1958.

Hanan, David. *Films in Southeast Asia Views from the Region: Essays on Film in Ten Southeast Asia-Pacific Countries*. Hanoi: SEAPAVAA, Vietnam Film Institute, and National Screen and Sound Archive of Australia, 2001.

Heide, William van der. *Malaysian Cinema, Asian Film: Border Crossings and National Culture*. Amsterdam: Amsterdam University Press, 2002.

Heider, Karl. *Indonesian Cinema: National Culture on Screen*. Honolulu: University of Hawaii Press, 1991.

Hoganson, Kristin. *Fighting for American Manhood: How Gender Politics Provoked the Spanish-American and Philippine-American Wars*. New Haven, CT: Yale University Press, 1998.

Hughes, Theodore. *Literature and Film in Cold War South Korea: Freedom's Frontier*. New York: Columbia University Press, 2012.

Kramer, Paul. *The Blood of the Government: Race, Empire, the United States and the Philippines*. Chapel Hill: University of North Carolina Press, 2006.

Kurniasari, Triwik. "Reviving Usmar Ismail's Legacy." *Jakarta Post*. June 24, 2016. http://www.thejakartapost.com/news/2012/06/24/reviving-usmar-ismails-legacy.html.

Lacaba, Jose. *The Films of ASEAN*. Pasig, Philippines: ASEAN Committee on Culture and Information, 2000.

Muthalib, Hussan. *Malaysian Cinema in a Bottle: A Century (and a Bit More) of Wayang*. Petaling Jaya, Malaysia: Merpati Jingga, 2013.

Park, Robert. *Race and Culture*. New York: Free Press, 1964.

Said, Salim. *Shadows on the Silver Screen: A Social History of Indonesian Film*. Jakarta: Lontar Foundation, 1991.

Tarling, Nicholas. *Southeast Asia and the Great Powers*. London: Routledge, 2010.

Toohey, Aileen. "Badjao: Cinematic Representations of Difference in the Philippines." *Journal of Southeast Asian Studies* 36, no. 2 (2005): 281–312.

Toplin, Robert. *History by Hollywood: The Use and Abuse of the American Past*. Urbana: University of Illinois Press, 1996.

Vasudev, Aruna, Latika Padgaonkar, and Rashmi Doraiswamy, eds. *Being and Becoming: The Cinema of Asia*. New Delhi: Macmillan, 2002.

von Ranke, Leopold. *History of the Latin and Teutonic Peoples from 1494 to 1514*, Translated by G. R. Dennis. London: George Bell and Sons, 1909.

Wagleitner, Reinhold. *Coca-colonization and the Cold War: The Cultural Mission of the United States in Austria after the Second World War*. Chapel Hill: University of North Carolina Press, 1994.

Wang, Gungwu, ed. *Nation-Building: Five Southeast Asian Histories*. Singapore: ISEAS, 2005.

11

Afghan Media and Culture in Transition

■■■■■■■■■■■■■■■■■■■■■■■■■

ALIREZA DEHGHAN

This chapter reviews the spread and consumption of television channels and Facebook, an online social media and social networking website, in today's Afghanistan. In addition, the chapter interprets the quantitative spread and consumption of television and Facebook in Afghanistan culturally, using some relevant theoretical concepts and explanations as well as the historical, political, and cultural realities of Afghanistan. The basic data and general informative sources referred to in this chapter are relatively and inevitably inconsistent. This, to some degree, is an understandable shortcoming, given Afghanistan's political situation, where about 60 percent of the country is currently not under the control of an internationally recognized government.[1] Formal and trustworthy databank centers, such as Asian Development Bank and International Data Base lack some basic data for Afghanistan, although the same data may be readily available for many neighboring countries. Such data are not regularly collected in Afghanistan under its unstable political circumstances.[2]

Although my focus is on the consumption of nongovernmental television channels and Facebook in Afghanistan, it is important to understand the more general Afghan media context since media do not operate in a vacuum. Rather, media are affected by broader political and social specificities of the nation within which they are produced and consumed. Physical insecurity and political instability, for instance, have overshadowed Afghanistan for decades. As an example, on November 22, 2018, *Daily Outlook Afghanistan*, an Afghan English language newspaper, published a news story entitled "Bloodshed Amidst Peace Talks": "An attack was carried out in Kabul in which more than 50 people were killed and tens of others were wounded. The attack came after a new international peace talk meeting."[3] Such an incident has been a common occurrence in Afghanistan since the collapse of the Taliban in 2001. In such a political and military environment, Afghanistan can be described as a country of explosions. Political instability brings about cultural struggles and hinders formation of a unified national identity. Thomas Barfield,[4] for instance, discusses how governing Afghan people was relatively easier when power was concentrated in a small, dynastic elite. He argues that the American invasion after the September 11 attacks in late 2001 toppled the Taliban quickly, but that intervention did not lead to the birth of a viable state easily. Under such unstable political governing, cultural and political freedom is hardly achievable in Afghanistan.[5]

Poverty is another critical issue in Afghanistan. In an estimated population of 35 million, nearly 40 percent of the entire population lives below the national poverty line. A large portion of the urban population is living in slums, and the majority of the population has no access to electricity.[6] Issues related to an unequal distribution of wealth are the characteristics of the nation frequently reported in the current Afghanistan print media.[7] The gap between the rich and the poor seems to be increasing. The rich, namely a small group of landlords, tribal heads, and religious leaders who own properties worth millions of dollars, are greatly privileged and lucky, residing in larger urban centers.[8] In sharp contrast, millions of the poor are forced to live their lives in the remotest areas, struggling for food, clothes, shelter, education, and security. There are approximately 3 million Afghan refugees who work under difficult conditions in Pakistan and Iran.

The third major problem easily seen in Afghan society is gender discrimination. For several reasons, including tribal and religious values and traditions, Afghanistan can be described as an extremely male-dominated society. Hence, natural and social rights of women are frequently violated in different forms and situations. In 2015, for instance, 8.8 percent of women between the ages of 20 and 24 married before they were 15, while 34.8 percent married before they were 18.[9] This is an important indicator regarding women's social situation in Afghanistan. The mentioned rate is much higher than that of neighboring countries, such as Azerbaijan, Georgia, Kazakhstan, Pakistan, Tajikistan and Uzbekistan.[10] Many instances are reported in Afghanistan where women are physically tortured, beaten, or even burned.[11]

Gender discrimination goes beyond the private sphere and enters the public realm and work places. One study related to journalists in Herat City, the western part of Afghanistan, indicates that female respondents have less access to information compared to male journalists, as news sources are often not available for female media workers. According to the data obtained from an online survey, among a total of 388 Afghan journalists (298 male and 90 female), 78 percent of female respondents and 31 percent of male respondents said, in terms of gender, the work conditions seemed unbalanced and unfair. Female journalists often feel discriminated at work as they are paid less than their male colleagues. Interestingly, however, female journalists feel more secure in their job than male journalists. This may be due to the fact that most women in Afghan media are working inside media offices and are accordingly less vulnerable to unexpected threats (physical as well as emotional) that they might face in the outside, public spaces.[12]

Media Explosion in Afghanistan

Amid such a volatile political and social context and especially for the past 15 years, there has been a significant increase in media access and usage in Afghanistan. Since the collapse of the Taliban in 2001 in particular, the media scene in Afghanistan has exploded: "Under the Taliban, only one government radio station was allowed to operate, and there were no independent media. Ten years later, the Afghan media scene is a lively place, with more than 175 FM radio stations, 75 TV channels, four news agencies, and hundreds of publications, including at least seven daily newspapers. Internet cafes can be found in major cities, and 61 percent of Afghans have mobile phones, which some use to listen to radio."[13] Evidently, there has been a rapid growth of both the old and new media in Afghanistan in spite of the society being characterized by internal military struggles, poor resources, underdevelopment, and vulnerable democracy backed by a foreign military presence.

The so-called media explosion continued, although its speed reduced. In another media survey conducted in 2014 and released in 2015, some changes were noted.[14] According to this report, the pace of the growth of new media outlets in Afghanistan slowed down, but there were about three TV channels created each year compared to around nine channels in 2010. In addition, in 2014, the types of TV programs remained the same as those of 2010, which included news packages, drama series, entertainment programs, and political debates. The only difference was the start of sports programs in 2014. Internal producers were eager to take part, but were faced with financial, social, and political difficulties.

Why is commercial television the dominant model of broadcasting in a country where the economy is not flourishing? The dominance of commercial television in Afghanistan is the result of the nation's political transformation during two recent decades. Since the collapse of the Taliban, Afghanistan has been in close association with international interventions to change its political governance system. These interventions are described as a promotion of cultural policies, encouraging and strengthening independent, plural, and free media. Indeed the policy of media commercialization, supported by an international coalition in general and the United States in particular, is part of generalizing democracy and human rights in Afghanistan. This policy demands abolition of government monopoly regarding media ownership and accelerates participations of all political, social, or cultural groups as well as ordinary people active in social development and growth.

A report released by Altai Consulting Media Group, a nongovernmental media research team operating in many countries, including Afghanistan, for instance, indicates that Afghan media channels can be divided into six groups, including private generalist channels, language specialists, religious channels, party-backed channels, regional channels, and a governmental channel (RTA).[15] These are mostly privately owned channels funded by foreign support and investment.[16] As for the viewer demographics, television viewers are mostly those residents living in urban centers, while rural residents listen mostly to radios. On the other hand, there are more female viewers than male viewers.[17] As already mentioned, not all parts of the country have access to electricity. This, coupled with the high rate of low-income households in many parts of the country, is one of the factors that prevent further growth of television viewing in Afghanistan.

Despite the relatively high degree of satisfaction among ordinary television viewers who have access to commercial television, the popularity and growth of television channels in Afghanistan are not received positively by national associations and independent social activists who are especially concerned about negative cultural impacts of television commercials.[18] Most commercials in Afghanistan are interlinked with entertainment programs. A heavy concentration on entertainment productions has resulted in the weakening of other more important and socially impactful areas, such as education and development.

Theoretical Orientation

What theoretical concepts and explanations can we use to understand the current expansion of both the old and new media in Afghanistan and its cultural consequences? There, of course, are several useful theoretical frameworks in media and cultural studies available for researchers and scholars. However, many of these theories, such as agenda-setting theory,[19] knowledge gap theory,[20] or cultural cultivation theory,[21] are mostly concerned with Anglo American and European societies. Consequently, they fail to account for the specific political, cultural, and social realities of Afghanistan and how they inform media production and consumption in the country. Benedict Anderson's idea on the origin and spread of nationalism highlights this challenge quite accurately. Mass media in the history of nationalism often contributed significantly to the notion of a symbolic nation. Benedict Anderson in his *Imagined Communities* (1983), for instance, describes the creation of national communities. According to Anderson, "Nation is an imagined political community. It is imagined because members of even the smallest nation will never know most of their fellow members, meet them, or even hear of them."[22] Therefore, for Anderson, the rise of print technology was essential to create the deep horizontal solidarity as it quickly spread ideologies and influenced perceptions of people at a larger scale. This solidarity, despite its socially constructed nature, is also genuine and deep-seated, and explains why nationalism can drive people to fight, die, and kill for their country and its people, who are mostly anonymous to them.

Anderson's idea on the relationship between media and nationalism could lead people to conclude that sudden spread of media can strengthen national identity. Anderson's explanation has been a relevant conceptual tool, although arguably, especially when considering established nation-states with a thriving print media industry. This, however, is not the case when we refer to the Afghan society. The nation's low literacy rate (estimated at 38 percent) renders print media less popular in Afghanistan. Access to print media is also challenged by the insufficient infrastructure and insecurity. As a result, print media, most notably newspapers, have less to do with the formation of national identity and solidarity in Afghanistan. Moreover, as mentioned previously, one of the major problems that Afghan society is facing is the tribal and religious conflicts that prevent the formation of national solidarity and social cohesion. With such a high degree of diversity in the nation, reaching the national unity and solidarity seems a lot more complicated.

The same can be said about radio listening. Currently, radio can reach rural Afghans a lot better than print media, television, or the internet. Radio has long been considered the significant and popular medium in Afghanistan with Salam Watandar Radio Service, a national radio service providing leading news, information, and entertainment, being the main provider of the nation's radio programs.[23] Radio programs in Afghanistan consist of the news, entertainment, and education (including religious teachings). Most stations broadcast in a mix of Dari and Pashto languages,[24] depending on the population of each language group in each region. While this style of multilingual broadcasting environment may be regarded as an example of media pluralism, this may also discourage the spirit of nationalism and a unified Afghan nation. It is hence clear that in spite of Anderson's otherwise eloquent theorization of the relationship between media and nationalism, in the case of Afghanistan, the role of media (print media and radio in particular) has been less significant in the formation of national identity and social cohesion.

Nevertheless, there are other Western-originated theories that are relevant and applicable to Afghanistan and its media culture. Chris Rojeck, for instance, explains that the development of search engines such as Google has greatly changed the production, dissemination, and consumption of news stories, movies, and other forms of communicative activities.[25] These changes, of course, do not take the same form and meaning in every social setting. However, some patterns of these changes can be said to be universal. One may notice that mobile commerce and web-dating or personal/intimacy affairs are more common in Anglo American and European societies, although in Afghanistan, these are hardly the main internet-related activities. Rather, news making and distribution, chatting/communicating, and the disclosure of public officials' political and economic corruptions are the pervasive forms of internet activities. On the other hand, "personals" seems to be the common type of online activity in both the Northern Hemisphere and Afghanistan. By personals, Rojeck means file-sharing as well as free downloading of film and music facilitated by companies like Napster, Kazaa, and Morpheus.[26] In the case of Afghanistan, the same type of online activity is quite common among urban settlers.

What is also relevant to Afghanistan is John Thompson's argument that mass media cannot disseminate information without touching other dimensions of social life. Using mass media includes creating new methods for users to relate socially and altering the existing methods for communicating. In using communication media, people initiate new forms of interactions that differ from face-to-face interactions. One very important aspect of the new methods of communicating and interacting is that social interactions can be detached from a physical place and location. Interaction does not require persons to be in the same place at the same time. However, the traditional mass media or new social media do not necessarily destroy traditional beliefs, ideologies, and practices. Accordingly, in sharp contrast to some of the classical communication scholars, such as Daniel Lerner, who adopts a modernization approach, Thompson claims that media both uproot and revitalize traditions. This is the point I plan to return to later in the chapter.[27]

Another useful theoretical concept is the mediatization theory. "Mediatization" refers to the changes in communication media and their social and political environments. According to Jesper Strömbäck, mediatization can be described as a four-phase process.[28] In the first phase, the mass media become the most important channel of communication and diffusion of information between people, including political institutions and actors. In the second phase, media begin to operate based on the media logic rather than merely following political institutions' and actors' wishes. Both the autonomy of media, that is, the selection and appropriation of messages, and the professionalism and commercialism increase in this phase.

In the third phase, the power of media increases even more significantly. In this phase, the power of media logic, such as formats, grammar, and rhythm, is pervasive to the point that social and political institutions and actors have to adapt to the logic. In the fourth phase, the political institutions and actors employ the technical characteristics of media and media formats. If one examines the development of both the old and new media in Afghanistan based on these four phases of mediatization, it seems that Afghanistan has already entered the first phase and is experiencing the second phase, especially given the ever-growing access to the internet and the spread of social media, most notably, Facebook. In the following pages, I first outline the consumption of commercial television in Afghanistan and its cultural consequences. I will then explain access to the internet in general and the influence of Facebook in particular.

Access, Consumption, and Cultural Influence of Commercial Television Channels in Afghanistan

The most viewed channels in Afghanistan include Tolo TV, Ariyana Television Network (ATN), and Kurshid TV. Tolo TV belongs to the Moby Capital Group, which is a very powerful media organization in Afghanistan owned by Saad Mohseni and his brothers. It is headquartered in Kabul, with many branches in other parts of Afghanistan. ATN is a part of the Bayat Foundation established in 2005 by Esanolah Bayat, an American-Afghan, after the collapse of the Taliban. Bayat foundation also operates Afghan Wireless Communication Company. Khurshid TV, on the other hand, started in 2011. A close look at some of the most important programs broadcast by these three commercial television channels during prime time (from 6:00 P.M. to 9:00 P.M.) indicates that soap operas, music shows, competition shows (game and quiz shows, for instance), lifestyle programs (such as cooking and fashion shows), and news packages are the dominant genres in the current privately owned Afghanistan television channels (as of May 2017).

Tolo TV prime time programs include two music programs, five television drama series (three Turkish, one Indian, and one Pakistani series) concentrated on family conflicts, love and friendship, seduction, hate, treason, thriller, and comedy. It also broadcasts two news packages at 6:00 P.M. and 8:00 P.M., two entertainment talk shows, and one competition show. ATN prime time programs, on the other hand, include three music programs, two news packages, one in the Pashto language at 6:00 P.M. and the other in Dari at 8:00 P.M. Three television drama series (two Indian and one Turkish), again focused on conflicts, violence, and treason, two lifestyle programs about food and cooking, and two talk shows about Persian language/literature and crime control are also included. Lastly, Khurshid prime time programs include three music shows, four television drama series (three Turkish and one Indian) with similar themes, two news programs, one in Dari at 6:00 P.M. and the other in Pashto at 10:00 P.M., and five lifestyle programs (cooking, gaming, fashion, education, and politics).

These prime time television programs broadcast by major television channels lead us to generalize some notable orientations of television consumption in Afghanistan and how these programs may influence the society at large.[29] For instance, Tolo TV on April 21, 2017, in its internal section of 6:00 P.M. news released five news items: (1) ten Taliban fighters attacked Camp Shaheen, the headquarters of the Afghan National Army near Mazar Sharif. The attack was the deadliest against the Afghan army since the collapse of the Taliban; (2) an investigation on the attack was called for; (3) some experts criticized military leadership in regard to the Taliban attack; (4) foreign investigations indicate the increasing casualties of the security forces in various events all over the country; and (5) Parliament members reacted to the Taliban attack and criticized the performance of the political administration. Here, one can note that the prime time news program is filled with hostility, fear, and bloodshed.

Similarly, Khurshid TV provided a news package on the same day with the following concentrations: (1) the death toll regarding the Taliban attack announced by the formal sources cannot be trusted. The government doesn't state the real figure; (2) members of the Parliament criticized the performance of government security forces; (3) the North Atlantic Treaty Organization (NATO) is still committed to supporting security forces in Afghanistan; (4) Kazakhstan minister of foreign affairs said he was worried about Afghanistan's worsening security in the Shanghai meeting; and (5) political chaos and conflicts between the Afghan Cabinet and the Parliament are worsening.[30]

In other words, news of war incidents, war casualties, Taliban attacks, peace talks and meetings without hopeful results, and the government's inadequacy in general security all over the country seems unending. This, in fact, has been the pattern since the collapse of the Taliban in 2001. It is not just the news that is heavily concentrated on violence and conflicts. Afghan television series and commercials also display conflicts, tensions, and verbal and physical violence. In the following discussion, I refer to some scenes from a popular television series aired in 2017 to provide relevant evidence in this regard. This particular series is still running in Afghanistan and has been hugely popular.

Tolo TV has been airing a drama series called *Bahar*. In episode 203 of this show, aired in July 2017, one of its main characters sends a postal parcel to another character. Inside the parcel is a letter of will and a revolver. The letter of will encourages hostility and revenge. In another episode (episode 301), the audience is faced with another violent action. A woman sets a seaside house on fire with residents inside. In the next scene, a heavy truck hits a car from the back, and the car falls into a valley. In a subsequent scene, Bahar (the main character) is lying on a hospital bed. Someone, disguised as a nurse, sprays acid on her face. In the next three scenes, those trapped in the seaside house on fire cry helplessly, the car fallen into the valley is burning, and Bahar is screaming, her face badly burned.

The prevalence of violence in Afghan commercial television shows should not be surprising. In fact, this seems to be the pattern globally. After all, scholars have noted that "fear is a universal emotion and easy to exploit."[31] More specifically in the case of Afghanistan, however, television channels seem to capitalize on violence and fear even more due to the fact that there are many themes that cannot be displayed in the country as a result of the religious and cultural beliefs and values. Sexuality and explicit romance, for instance, are common popular themes in many other parts of the world and their television shows. These themes, however, are largely tabooed in Afghanistan. Hence, commercial television channels in Afghanistan turn to violence to attract and entertain viewers.

Commodification of culture is another facet of television consumption in Afghanistan. Commercial television channels in Afghanistan, of course, cannot be aired without the financial support of commercial companies. For instance, a news package named *News at Six*, produced by Tolo TV, is financially supported by the International Bank of Afghanistan and an energy drink company Carabao. At the beginning of the news hour and at the end of it, the audience notices a caption that reads, "This program brought to you by International Bank of Afghanistan and Carabao Energy Drink."[32] In some music programs, on the other hand, numerous commercials will be displayed after each song. Finally, the television series *Bahar* is financed by a home appliance company, whose commercials appear frequently during the intervals of the show.

Television commercials, of course, are common in many other parts of the world. The notable point about them in Afghanistan, however, is that these commercials have started appearing quite suddenly and unexpectedly in Afghanistan, which is still a very traditional society with a large economic gap between a small number of the rich and the extremely poor who constitute the majority of the population. The Afghan commercial television channels, by aggressively displaying commercial goods that most Afghans are unable to afford, can cause a sense of hopelessness and deprivation among most viewers. One can therefore argue that the explosive growth of commercial television channels and their commercials are deepening the problem of poverty and the gap between the rich and the poor in Afghanistan.

Another important issue to consider is how the consumption of television channels is influencing people's political perceptions and attitudes in Afghanistan. Is there any meaningful relationship between the television consumption and the public evaluation of the government's performance? While in 2013 about 58 percent of the Afghan people said that the country was going in the right direction, in 2016 the figure reduced to 29 percent, signaling a sharp increase of pessimism among people in a period of just three years.[33] This is rather disappointing given the nation's move toward democracy and the expansion of more diverse media. Furthermore, in 2016, more than half of the Afghan people (53 percent) said that they felt fear while voting in national or provincial elections. Also, according to the 2017 survey, 69.8 percent of Afghans reported feeling fear for their personal safety on a daily basis.[34] Asian foundation Survey has also explored whether television viewership affects public perceptions in three areas: support for women's rights, confidence in government, and perceptions of insecurity.

Respondents who spend more time watching television are more likely to support women's rights, while these same respondents are less likely to express confidence in various levels of the Afghan government.[35] Television viewership also affects the perception of insecurity. Respondents who watch more television are more likely to say that the Islamic State of Iraq and the Levant (also known as the Islamic State of Iraq and Syria, ISIS) is a threat to their area than those who do not watch television as often. They also tend to report a higher level of insecurity and fear for their personal safety.[36] While this kind of relationship between media and the audience has already been indicated in numerous research studies,[37] the case of Afghanistan is worth considering more deeply given its particular sociopolitical context as well as the relatively delayed growth of commercial television channels.

Access to and Consumption of the Internet and Facebook

Internet growth in Afghanistan has especially accelerated since 2001. A recent study, for instance, indicates that currently 4.5 million Afghans use the internet, and 2.1 million Afghans use Facebook. The majority of these internet users spend about 5 hours per day on the internet on average.[38] There are several factors to consider when thinking of internet use in Afghanistan. First of all, internet services in Afghanistan are fairly inexpensive compared to some neighboring countries, such as Uzbekistan. Likewise, social media are more easily accessible in Afghanistan with less government control and censorship. Secondly, the new constitutional law in Afghanistan strongly asserts freedom of expression, thereby creating an environment where new platforms for communication and expression are welcome. Therefore, private businesses providing internet services are eagerly competing for more customers and more commercial gains. Lastly, we have to consider the sociopolitical instability of the country. Despite the emergence of a semidemocratic government, because of the weakness of the overall security of the nation, there is an intense need for people in Afghanistan to get daily news updates and be informed about what is happening in the country. As a result, more people in Afghanistan are turning to media generally and the new media, such as Facebook, in particular.[39]

According to a recent study based on a sample of 400 Facebook users in Balkh, the northern part of Afghanistan, 70 percent of the Facebook users answered that they use Facebook in order to get daily news updates.[40] These same users also log into Facebook four times more frequently than those who use Facebook to communicate with their friends and families. According to the same study, Facebook is the first social media choice for news updates in Afghanistan followed by Google Plus, Viber, and Twitter.[41] An example that captures the power of Facebook in Afghanistan is the popular Facebook page called *Kabul Taxi*. The page posts stories narrated by a fictitious taxi driver whose passengers are high-ranked government officials. The imaginary dialogues between the driver and his passengers reveal stories that are critical of public officials in Afghanistan, drawing attention to the flaws and inadequacies of their work. Indeed, Helena Malikyar, an Afghan political analyst writing for Aljazeera online, wrote an article about it on November 17, 2015:

> Today Afghan humor has found online social media as a more suitable vehicle for reaching a larger and younger audience. *Kabul Taxi* is a Facebook page that often uses fictitious dialog between the rather caustic taxi driver and his VIP passengers to highlight the government's flawed policies, corruption and inefficiencies. The site captured international attention in August, when its criticism sparked the fury of Mohammad Hanif Atmar, the country's national security adviser. Under the headings "Atmar's Choir Boys," *Kabul Taxi* described the National Security Council's advisers as inexperienced children of influential men who were receiving absurdly high salaries and privileges. The NSC reportedly detained a journalist suspected of being behind the anonymous post and blocked the page for more than a month.[42]

Facebook in Afghanistan leads to two somewhat contradicting consequences. On the one hand, it is transforming the Afghan society into a more stable and reliable democracy by offering a platform for free and open expression and communication. On the other hand, Facebook perpetuates public officials' greed for visibility. After all, Facebook in its essence is a platform for self-promotion. What is important to note, however, is that public officials favor visibility only if they can be in charge of it. These public figures used to control their own desired degree and form of visibility and publicity within the realm of more traditional media, such as radio, television, or print media. This, however, is no longer the case with the emergence of new media such as Facebook.[43] Within these new media platforms, where users actively participate not only to consume but also to produce and disseminate information, public figures no longer have a firm control over their visibility. This certainly is an unwanted outcome for those who hold military, political, or economic power. As a result, Facebook with its capacity to disclose and disseminate news potentially increases government accountability and the general public's interest and sensitivity toward it.

Putting it all together, the sudden explosion of various media in Afghanistan in general and commercial television channels and Facebook in particular indicates that the society is participating in the global media trend, although the mediatization in Afghanistan must be considered within its specific sociopolitical and historical context. The increasing consumption of the Turkish and Indian television series in Afghanistan also signals how Afghanistan is participating in the inter-Asian media flow and embracing the Pan-Asian identity. Political implications and consequences of Facebook are especially worth noting in the context of Afghanistan. As noted, Facebook has become the first source of political news and information for many youth in Afghanistan, especially those who are educated and reside in the urban centers of the country. For these users, Facebook has provided an alternative space where they can more openly discuss what used to be sensitive issues, women's rights, sexual life, sexual crimes, political and economic corruption, and tribal/religious discrimination, for instance. These issues are still considered to be profane in non-media spheres and in more traditional medial platforms. Commercial television channels and Facebook, as noted in this chapter, however, are indeed changing this social landscape.

Notes

1 Simon Tisdal published an article, "The US and Afghanistan: Can't Win the War, Can't Stop It, Can't Leave." The title clearly indicates how the situation in Afghanistan is critical and unstable. In the article, Tisdal further highlights how this political instability poses challenges to researchers in their attempt to gather information about the country and conduct research. For the full article, see Simon Tisdal, "The US and Afghanistan: Can't Win the War, Can't Stop It, Can't Leave," *Guardian*, May 1, 2018, https://www.theguardian.com/world/2018/may/01/the-us-and-afghanistan-cant-win-the-war-cant-stop-it-cant-leave.

2 For instance, according to the webpage of Asian Development Bank (ADB), 39.1 percent of the population in Afghanistan lives below the national poverty line. This figure, however, is for 2013. Data for the next three years, 2014 to 2016, are not available. By contrast, relevant data are more up to date for neighboring countries such as Kazakhstan, Azerbaijan, and Tajikistan. For further information, visit the webpage: https://www.adb.org/countries/afghanistan/poverty.

3 "Bloodshed amidst Peace Talks," *Daily Outlook Afghanistan*, last modified November 22, 2018, http://www.outlookafghanistan.net/editorialdetail.php?post_id=22280.

4 Thomas Barfield, *Afghanistan: A Cultural and Political History* (Princeton, NJ: Princeton University Press, 2010).

5 It seems even the coalition of the United States and Afghanistan central government is now unable to bring political stability to the Afghan society. See Barfield for more information.

6 To see more indicators discussing poverty in Afghanistan, visit https://www.adb.org/countries/afghanistan/poverty.

7 Such issues of poverty are often highlighted in *Daily Outlook Afghanistan*, the country's pioneering English language publication available both in print and online. For more information, see http://outlookafghanistan.net.

8 Dilawar Sherzai, "Class Differences and Afghan Society," *Daily Outlook Afghanistan*, last modified April 18, 2013, http://outlookafghanistan.net/topics.php?post_id=7139.

9 "Key Indicators for Asia and the Pacific 2017," Asia Development Bank, last modified September 2017, https://www.adb.org/publications/key-indicators-asia-and-pacific-2017.

10 Ibid.

11 Alissa Rubin, "Flawed Justice after a Mob Killed an Afghan Woman," *New York Times*, December 26, 2015, https://www.nytimes.com/2015/12/27/world/asia/flawed-justice-after-a-mob-killed-an-afghan-woman.html.

12 Bashir Ahmad Behravan, "An Evaluation of Media System in Afghanistan" (master's thesis, Faculty of Social Sciences, University of Tehran, 2016).

13 Peter Cary, *An Expulsion of News: The State of Media in Afghanistan* (Washington, DC: Center for International Media Assistance, 2012), 4.

14 "Local Radio in Afghanistan: A Sustainability Assessment," Altai Consulting for Internews, accessed February 21, 2018, https://internews.org/resource/local-radio-afghanistan-sustainability-assessment.

15 Ibid.

16 Cary, *An Expulsion*.

17 Nancy Hopkins, *Afghanistan in 2012: A Survey of Afghan People* (San Francisco: The Asia Foundation, 2012), https://asiafoundation.org/resources/pdfs/Surveybook2012web1.pdf.

18 Najiburrahman Hadid, "The Private Television and the Challenge of Participating in Provision of Public Goods in Afghanistan" (PhD diss., Faculty of Social Sciences, University of Tehran, 2017).

19 Agenda-setting is the capacity of media to raise the importance of an issue in the public's mind. See Werner J. Severin and James W. Tankard, *Communication Theories: Origins, Methods, and Uses in the Mass Media* (New York: Longman, 2001).

20 Knowledge gap theory is the idea that there is a relationship between the socioeconomic status of people and the ways in which this status impacts how they get information from media. See Severin and Tankard, *Communication Theories*.

21 Cultivation theory is the idea that long-term exposures to television, regardless of its specific programs, cultivate people's perceptions, attitudes, and values. See Severin and Tankard, *Communication Theories*.

22 Benedict Anderson, *Imagined Communities: Reflections on the Origin and Spread of Nationalism* (London: VERSO, 1991).

23 "Local Radio in Afghanistan."

24 Dari and Pashto are the two official languages in Afghanistan, basically using Arabic letters. It is estimated that about 50 percent of the Afghan population speaks Dari and 35 percent Pashto. In addition, about 11 percent of the population speaks the Uzbek language. There are other languages spoken in Afghanistan, although not as common as Dari and Pashto.

25 Chris Rojeck, *Cultural Studies* (Cambridge: Polity Press, 2007), 18.
26 Ibid.
27 Daniel Lerner argues that as media develop, they weaken the traditional forms of authority, such as religious and tribal institutions and actors. See Daniel Lerner, *The Passing of Traditional Society: Modernizing the Middle East* (London: Macmillan, 1958) and John Thompson, *The Media and Modernity: A Social Theory of the Media* (Stanford, CA: Stanford University Press, 1995).
28 Jesper Strömbäck, "Four Phases of Mediatization," *International Journal of Press/Politics* 13, no. 3 (2008): 228–246.
29 Hadid argues that the news packages provided by Tolo TV and Khurshid TV are saturated with the narration of violence. See Hadid, "The Private Television."
30 Ibid.
31 See, for instance, George Gerbner and Larry Gross, "Living with Television: The Violence Profile," *Journal of Communication* 26, no. 2 (1976): 175.
32 Hadid, "The Private Television."
33 "A Survey of the Afghan People: Afghanistan in 2016," Asia Foundation, last modified December 7, 2016, https://asiafoundation.org/publication/afghanistan-2016-survey-afghan-people/.
34 Ibid.
35 Ibid.
36 Ibid.
37 For a comprehensive review, see Robin L. Nabi and John L. Sullivan, "Does Television Viewing Relate to Engagement in Protective Action against Crime? A Cultivation Analysis from a Theory of Reasoned Action Perspective," *Communication Research* 28, no. 6 (2001): 802–825.
38 Sekandar Maihanyar, "A Study of Facebook as a News Source" (master's thesis, Faculty of Social Sciences, University of Tehran, 2016).
39 Melvin L. De Fleur and Sandra Ball-Rokeach, *Theories of Mass Communication* (New York: Longman, 1975).
40 Research evidence related to the exact extent and consequences of using social media in Afghanistan is hardly available. For a recent study, however, see Sekandar Maihanyar, "A Study of Facebook."
41 Another reason that explains the popularity of Facebook in Afghanistan is that Facebook is more apt to reach out to larger public or large groups of people, whereas other social media are used mostly for bilateral, closed-group communications. For further information, see Sayed Asef Hossaini, "How Social Media Is Changing Afghan Society," The Green Political Foundation, February 14, 2018, https://www.boell.de/en/person/sayed-asef-hossaini?dimension1=ds_digitalasia.
42 Helena Malikyar, "*Kabul Taxi:* You Talkin' to Me?," Aljazeera, November 17, 2015, https://www.aljazeera.com/indepth/opinion/2015/11/kabul-taxi-satire-afghanistan-151112070657966.html.
43 John Thompson, "New Visibility," *Theory, Culture, and Society* 22, no. 6 (2005): 31–51.

Bibliography

Anderson, Benedict. *Imagined Communities: Reflections on the Origin and Spread of Nationalism*. London: VERSO, 1991.

Barfield, Thomas. *Afghanistan: A Cultural and Political History*. Princeton, NJ: Princeton University Press, 2010.

Behravan, Bashir Ahmad. "An Evaluation of Media System in Afghanistan." Master's thesis, Faculty of Social Sciences, University of Tehran, 2016.

"Bloodshed amidst Peace Talks." *Daily Outlook Afghanistan*. Last modified November 22, 2018. http://www.outlookafghanistan.net/editorialdetail.php?post_id =22280.

Cary, Peter. *An Expulsion of News: The State of Media in Afghanistan*. Washington, DC: Center for International Media Assistance, 2012.

De Fleur, Melvin L., and Sandra Ball-Rokeach. *Theories of Mass Communication*. New York: Longman, 1975.

Gerbner, George, and Larry Gross. "Living with Television: The Violence Profile." *Journal of Communication* 26, no. 2 (1976): 172–199.

Hadid, Najiburrahman. "The Private Television and the Challenge of Participating in Provision of Public Goods in Afghanistan." PhD diss., Faculty of Social Sciences, The University of Tehran, 2017.

Hopkins, Nancy. *Afghanistan in 2012: A Survey of Afghan People*. San Francisco: The Asia Foundation, 2012. https://asiafoundation.org/resources/pdfs /Surveybook2012web1.pdf.

Hossaini, Sayed Asef. "How Social Media Is Changing Afghan Society." The Green Political Foundation. February 14, 2018. https://www.boell.de/en/person/sayed -asef-hossaini?dimension1=ds_digitalasia.

"Key Indicators for Asia and the Pacific 2017." Asia Development Bank. Last modified September, 2017. https://www.adb.org/publications/key-indicators-asia-and -pacific-2017.

Lerner, Daniel. *The Passing of Traditional Society: Modernizing the Middle East*. London: Macmillan, 1958.

"Local Radio in Afghanistan: A Sustainability Assessment." Altai Consulting for Internews. Accessed February 21, 2018. https://internews.org/resource/local-radio -afghanistan-sustainability-assessment.

Maihanyar, Sekandar. "A Study of Facebook as a News Source." Master's thesis, Faculty of Social Sciences, University of Tehran, 2016.

Malikyar, Helena. *"Kabul Taxi:* You Talkin' to Me?" Aljazeera. November 17, 2015. https://www.aljazeera.com/indepth/opinion/2015/11/kabul-taxi-satire-afghanistan -151112070657966.html.

Nabi, Robin L., and John L. Sullivan. "Does Television Viewing Relate to Engagement in Protective Action against Crime? A Cultivation Analysis from a Theory of Reasoned Action Perspective." *Communication Research* 28, no. 6 (2001): 802–825.

"Poverty in Afghanistan." Asian Development Bank (ADB). Accessed March 16, 2019. https://www.adb.org/countries/afghanistan/poverty.

Rojeck, Chris. *Cultural Studies*. Cambridge: Polity Press, 2007.

Rubin, Alissa. "Flawed Justice after a Mob Killed an Afghan Woman." *New York Times*. December 26, 2015. https://www.nytimes.com/2015/12/27/world/asia /flawed-justice-after-a-mob-killed-an-afghan-woman.html.

Severin, Werner J., and James W. Tankard, *Communication Theories: Origins, Methods, and Uses in the Mass Media*. New York: Longman, 2001.

Sherzai, Dilawar. "Class Differences and Afghan Society." *Daily Outlook Afghanistan*. Last modified April 18, 2013. http://outlookafghanistan.net/topics.php?post_id =7139.

Strömbäck, Jesper. "Four Phases of Mediatization." *International Journal of Press/Politics* 13, no. 3 (2008): 228–246.

"A Survey of the Afghan People: Afghanistan in 2016." The Asia Foundation. Last modified December 7, 2016. https://asiafoundation.org/publication/afghanistan-2016-survey-afghan-people/.

Thompson, John. *The Media and Modernity: A Social Theory of the Media*. Stanford, CA: Stanford University Press, 1995.

———. "New Visibility." *Theory, Culture, and Society* 22, no. 6 (2005): 31–51.

Tisdal, Simon. "The US and Afghanistan: Can't Win the War, Can't Stop It, Can't Leave." *Guardian*. May 1, 2018. https://www.theguardian.com/world/2018/may/01/the-us-and-afghanistan-cant-win-the-war-cant-stop-it-cant-leave.

12

A Semiotic Analysis
of Symbolic Actions of
Iranian Instagram Users

HAMID ABDOLLAHYAN AND
HOORNAZ KESHAVARZIAN

Before we offer our argument and analysis, it is necessary to note that the culture and practices of Instagram use discussed in this chapter, of course, are not specific to Iran only, and Iranians' use of Instagram is in line with its global use. However, discussing Instagram in the context of Iran is important, as Iran is the country that is often viewed in a specifically prejudiced way by the West. Attributing an unreal schema, such as "axis of evil" as defined by the United States, to Iran is one example. Regardless of how Western media have disseminated ignorant and unfair pictures of Iran, Iran is a fast-changing, modern society with a large population of digital users. Understanding Iran's Instagram use hence sheds new light on Iran and helps us to understand better the country, its culture, and its people. One example is how Iranian society, which is best known for its long history, is beautifully incorporating its traditional social networking quality into modern social media networking practices. This has contributed to Iranian society becoming even more network-based than before.

It should also be noted that in this chapter, we treat Western theories as being universal, just as the development of Marxist capitalism has brought most of the social elements in the world under capitalist regulations. Today's world economy substantiates this point—otherwise Iran and its people would not have suffered from the economic sanctions imposed upon them. Accordingly, Iran can be productively discussed in a global context, while many of the Western theories discussed in this chapter offer useful insights into an Iranian context. What we aim to do, especially in our later analysis of some selective Instagram images posted by Iranian Instagram users and the controversial Instagram page called "Rich Kids of Teheran," however, is to better understand how Iran with its cultural, social, historical, and religious specificities intersects with and further refines these Western theories, leading to more nuanced discussions of them.

Having said that, we can now begin our chapter with a reference to Gary Cronkhite, who argues, "The defining commitment of the communication discipline is to study human symbolic action in the various contexts of its performance."[1] This definition gave us an idea to work on Instagram—the image-based application and social networking site—with special attention to Iranian Instagram users and how their use of Instagram can be socially and culturally understood. To use Pierre Bourdieu's term, Instagram transforms into a zone to exhibit users' "capitals."[2] That is to say, Instagram provides users opportunities to ostentatiously display their wealth—economic, social, cultural, and so forth. This chapter hence offers a study of Instagram and its symbolic action of display. It also explores how the technological specifications of Instagram inform in particular ways what content can be displayed and consumed by its users. By looking at the use of Instagram in Iran specifically, we would also like to consider more deeply the relationship between medium and context. In other words, we will question whether the Iranian sociocultural and temporal context influences the ways in which Instagram as a medium produces and helps consume certain messages.

Out of the entire population of 82 million people, 56.7 million Iranians use the internet, leading to a 69 percent internet penetration rate.[3] Most of these internet users in Iran are also active social media users (about 40 million people), and Instagram, a photo and video-sharing application launched in 2010, is the second most popular social media platform in Iran.[4] With 24 million users, which amount to 29 percent of the entire population of the country, Iran is the seventh biggest market for Instagram. The popularity of Instagram in Iran is partially attributable to the fact that unlike Facebook and Twitter, Instagram is not blocked by authorities. Therefore, having an access to Instagram in Iran is less complicated than having an access to, for instance, its parent company, Facebook. More significantly, however, what makes Instagram popular is its technological capacity that enables its users to fashion their self-presentations in the ways that they desire. With its photo-filtering application and hashtags, which allow users to easily find any particular images and contents, Instagram has opened up a new window for people to display their highly fashioned and aestheticized moments as quite natural activities. Thanks to Instagram, we now observe photos that can never be found in old family albums. Photos of a plate of food, just done nails, newly purchased shoes, or selfies are all available, often publicly, over the existing Instagram practices. In this chapter, the term "display" is used as opposed to terms such as "show" or "representation." We believe that display conceptually relies on the quality of representation, expression, disclosure, or pretension. Moreover, the notion of display does a better job at emphasizing the significance of the spectator through which any message, image, or performance can be finally realized. Our main concern in this chapter is whether and how Instagram provides a context for expression and display for Iranian users.

Conceptual Framework: Field of Display

In order to examine practices of Iranian Instagram users, we consider Instagram as a field of display or a display field. We also turn to theories by Pierre Bourdieu, Erving Goffman, Marshall McLuhan, and Guy Debord and further specify these theories in our analysis of Instagram images by locating them in the Iranian situation. Display field simply means a context. Many Iranians are using Instagram as their context to exhibit their symbolic and social capitals and to communicate with and impress their audience. The word "impress" brings us closer to Thorstein Veblen's term "conspicuous consumption,"[5] which is a clear manifestation of capital before the eyes of others. Likewise, Instagram helps exercise and demonstrate conspicuous consumption because many account owners publicly display their consumption as a way to gain prestige and to impress their audience. Similarly, Guy Debord in *The Society of the Spectacle* (1970) generalizes the notion that social relationship between people has become image-mediated.[6] What becomes important, then, is the role of a medium, which reminds us of Marshall McLuhan's well-known quote, "The medium is the message."[7] McLuhan in *Understanding the Media* (1964) has noted that the medium brings out "psychic and social consequences."[8] By this, McLuhan means that "the personal and social consequences of any medium—that is, of any extension of ourselves—result from the new scale that is introduced into our affairs by each extension of ourselves, or by new technology."[9] Hence each medium reconstructs human association based on its own specific patterns. More importantly, these patterns manipulate in particular ways behaviors of actors/users. In McLuhan's own words, "the message of any medium or technology is the change of scale or pace or pattern that it introduces into human affairs."[10]

Along the same line, Instagram as a virtual field of display provides a context for many Iranians to manifest and display their capitals. Moreover, the interactive nature of Instagram further encourages expressions of capitals. More specifically, the model for field of display features the following qualities: capital display, presence of viewers, orientation of image, and trend acknowledgment. As for the capital display, according to Pierre Bourdieu,[11] capital, unequally distributed assets that secure distinction, comes in economic, social, cultural, and symbolic forms. With Instagram, the exhibition of these capitals is the prerequisite for interaction to be performed, and only the photographable moments are worthy of display. Lavish lifestyle, business and academic achievements, social relationships, leisure and entertainment, clothing and appearance, eating habits, and accessibility to certain facilities can all be considered as indices of capitals, provided that they are impressive or extravagant. Instagrammers often practice an ostentatious display of wealth and share luxurious moments of their lives to gain distinction and social prestige. A tour of Europe, for instance, can perfectly exhibit the economic capital of a typical Iranian Instagram user.

Presence of viewers, on the other hand, refers to the fact that the display of capital on Instagram is performed before the eyes of the physically absent viewers. Images need to be worthy in the eyes of these viewers. On Instagram, the audience's admiration is shown by likes. What is interesting to consider, however, is that although Instagram users seek distinctions while practicing and displaying conspicuous consumptions in many different ways, they tend not to step out of the Instagram community and what the community as a whole generally practices. This is not to be alienated from their audience. This echoes Erving Goffman's idea about how a performer stages himself or herself always in relation to a particular audience: "A performer often engenders in his audience the belief that he is related to them in a more ideal way than is always the case."[12] This relationship between performer and audience applies to a mediated online context like Instagram where one's activities are witnessed and approved by the online audience.

Orientation of image means that capital display on Instagram occurs in the realm of image where the content is visual rather than verbal. Pierre Bourdieu perceives photography as an object of sociological study.[13] To him a photographic act is "the ontological choice of an object which is perceived as worthy of being photographed, which is captured, stored, communicated, shown, and admired."[14] The technological specifications of photography make possible creation of visually appealing content. Likewise, users of Instagram choose to communicate via photographic acts, while adhering to the specifics of the given medium and its technologies that may make the acts and displays more admirable and desirable. Lastly, trend acknowledgment implies that new users of any platform and any field of display always take their cues from early adopters. Similarly, Instagram users imitate existing modes of visual narration and self-expression. Such imitations are greeted by likes, helping users feel safe and assured that they are following the existing online protocol. By online protocol, we mean practices that align with the existing Instagram trends. Accordingly, in order for users to survive as well-liked participants on social media, they need to respect online-visual norms and display the right content. Users also adjust themselves to the features of Instagram and try to meet expectations of the audience. More specifically, Instagram users present their selected, rightly fashioned selves by using means of photography. More to this phenomenon, we can also argue that "a performer tends to conceal or underplay those activities, facts, and motives which are incompatible with an idealized version of himself and his products."[15]

Investigation into Iranian Instagram users and how they perform and practice their symbolic actions helps us put the theoretical model of field of display into practice. We can, for instance, consider many wedding photos easily found on Instagram accounts all over the world. Wedding ceremonies require time and money, but people seem to move toward conspicuous display so that the time and money spent on ceremonies will be rewarded by the audience's admiration. Therefore, the to-be-couples would like to have their moments captured by professionals. Pierre Bourdieu in the same regard has mentioned that "the wedding photograph was accepted quickly and generally only because it met the social conditions of its existence: just as waste is a part of festive behavior, the purchase of the group photograph, a conspicuous consumption which no one can escape without loss of face, is felt to be obligatory, as an homage to the married couple."[16] Bourdieu's emphasis on "loss of face" in the case of wedding photography acknowledges the presence of a judgmental audience and one's desire to be liked.

Similarly, couples in Iran are willing to sacrifice spending money and time on other aspects of their wedding so that they can spend more resources on photography. More than anything, many couples want their big day to be depicted gracefully. This is where Instagram functions perfectly as a field of display and of conspicuous consumption. Numerous Instagram pages regarding wedding photography and videography are followed by Iranian users, while the would-be couples prefer to have their memory visually captured on Instagram. Some of the videos are specifically produced to fit the Instagram page. In other words, since the running time of a video clip cannot exceed one minute on Instagram, wedding video clips are customized based on the features of this specific platform. Couples display both their economic capital and their symbolic capital, that is, love, before the eyes of their online audience.

Methodologically speaking, our main idea comes from Roland Barthes who argues, "All these imitative arts [drawings, paintings, cinema, and theater] comprise two messages: a denoted message, which is the analog on itself, and a connoted message, which is the manner in which the society to a certain extent communicates what it thinks of it."[17] Having mentioned that, it is clear that some semiotic approaches need to be employed so that we would be able to collect data from pictures and analyze them based on their sign structures and characteristics that determine how meanings are conveyed. Therefore, in the following section of the chapter, we will consider images on Instagram as our units of analysis and observation.

Semiotic Analysis of Images

Roland Barthes in *Image, Music, Text* (1977) offers two main techniques that we in this chapter followed in our reading of the Instagram images.[18] These techniques include, first, the main connotation procedures for photographic images in which the trick effects, pose, objects, photogenia, aestheticism, and syntax are of our analytical interests. Barthes also refers to different levels of meaning that could be classified into three levels. The first level is the information or communication level. This level indicates that if a meaning has to be extracted, then we need to look into communicative actions where information takes shape and is reflected in social constructs. Images are part of such social constructs. This level of meaning deals with the obvious, as Barthes would put it. The second level, on the other hand, can be understood as a symbolic level, that is, referential or diegetic symbolism. Taken in its entirety, "this second level is that of signification. Its mode of analysis would be a semiotics more highly developed than the first, a second or neo-semiotics, open no longer to the science of the message but to the sciences of the symbol (psychoanalysis, economy, dramaturgy)."[19] The last, third level is related to significance or semiotics of the text. Barthes argues that the third type of meaning takes its form from theoretical individuality. This third level deals with punctum, which may be very small and lightning-like, but has the potential to expand. The third level of meaning, according to Barthes, "is a signifier without a signified,"[20] or is obtuse. This means that individual and society get involved in the production of meaning. According to these techniques and models, Instagram functions as a context in which practices of (visualized) meaning-making take place. Images along with hashtags, emojis, and captions, therefore, are units of observation and analysis for us. In our analysis of Instagram, we studied captions, including hashtags and emojis, based on Barthes's anchoring procedure and types of signs (semiotics). We looked into all three levels of meaning and their elements carried by captions in order to figure out how Iranian Instagram users use images in order to convey meanings to their audience.

In our study, we decided to use an Instagram account owned by one of our researchers, Hoornaz Keshavarzian, through which we accessed other Iranian Instagram users. This was to avoid occasions where Instagram accounts under our investigation change from public to private unexpectedly and beyond our control. At the time of conducting this research in 2016, Keshavarzian had 185 followers in her account. We considered three criteria for sampling: (1) Instagram users with more than 70 images, (2) Instagram users who were the users for at least 80 weeks, that is, more than one and a half years, and (3) Instagram users who had more than 100 followers. Using the combination of these three criteria and considering gender distribution, six users with 511 images were eventually selected to constitute the sample size of this study. Users' images were then regarded as the units of analysis and observation.

To understand meaningful actions of Iranian Instagram users, we selected 511 images shared by the sample users and classified them into three major categories: group, display component, and capital. In the first "group" category, images were classified into eight groups in accordance with their content: selfie, travel, friends, leisure, occasion, fashion, food, and pets. Display component as the second category refers to elements in images. We analyzed these elements by looking into the content or form (including the location) of the images posted by Iranian Instagram users. Importantly, too, we regarded only those elements that were clearly visible in the images as the elements of display component. The third component is capital. Pierre Bourdieu categorizes capital into three different and major types: economic, social, and cultural. There is also a fourth type of capital that is extracted from cultural capital, which Bourdieu calls symbolic capital. Bourdieu keeps it as a special type in his argument. To him, symbolic capital can be drawn from cultural capital, but it is mainly individual and can die when its bearer dies.[21] The following results represent the most favorite groups of image based on their frequency:

1 Travel: 50 percent (256 images)
2 Friends: 32 percent (166 images)
3 Selfie: 21 percent (109 images)
4 Leisure: 14 percent (70 images)
5 Food: 10 percent (53 images)
6 Occasion: 8 percent (39 images)
7 Fashion: 8 percent (35 images)
8 Pets: 2 percent (10 images)

The most frequently reflected capitals include the following:

1 Economic capital: 65 percent (334 images)
2 Social capital: 32 percent (166 images)
3 Symbolic capital: 31 percent (157 images)
4 Cultural capital: 3 percent (16 images)

Additionally, the most frequent display element was location, with 276 images in total. Three indices with the highest total frequency were travel, location, and economic capital. Statistically, 29 percent of the images encompassed more than one capital.

Image Analysis

We would now like to analyze some selective Instagram images in order to elaborate on the aforementioned results. What all these images that we have examined have in common is that they contain within themselves a combination of content category, capital, and display component: travel (content category), economic capital (capital), and location (display component). The following images also remind us of what Pierre Bourdieu said about photography and holiday: "Photography is what one does on holiday, and also what makes a holiday."[22]

The statement from Bourdieu, "The true honeymoon is the honeymoon in Paris,"[23] may be the most accurate description for the first image (fig. 12.1). This

FIG. 12.1 Image of a honeymoon moment in Eiffel Tower. (Courtesy of the account owner.)

image, posted by an Iranian female Instagram user and taken during her honeymoon from the terrace of the Eiffel tower, shows Paris in all its glamour. The image is visually appealing thanks to the high angle camera shot and the filtering feature being applied to the photo. The account owner of this Instagram page is attached to this spectacular object, the Eiffel tower, and the owner's decision to post this specific image indicates, borrowing Bourdieu's words again, "an exceptional moment in [her] life and a place that is exceptional by virtue of its high symbolic yield."[24] As far as the economic capital is concerned, images of holidays in Europe imply a possession of high economic status, especially for Iranians who have to go through the costly process of applying for a Schengen visa. Apart from the economic capital, a minor cultural capital is displayed through the brief caption, "This is Paris," written in French. This, of course, is in tune with the location of the image itself, but also reveals the account owner's knowledge of the French language. One may conclude that this cultural capital, too, is used symbolically, indicating the distinction and prestige of the account owner.

The next image from the same user displays continuation of her romantic honeymoon in Paris (fig. 12.2). For this image, an English caption was chosen to express the cultural capital. According to Bourdieu, cultural capital can exist in the form of "institutionalized state," which is seen in "educational qualifications."[25] Therefore, speaking "the most prestigious language on earth,"[26] that is, English, manifests distinction. For Iranian people in Iran, who are barely exposed to English, speaking English fluently and accurately is regarded as a great achievement. This English caption, then, is a way for the account holder to show her distinction and prestige as a fluent English speaker in Iran. Additionally, by capturing "locks of love," the image also displays one of the strongest versions of social capital that any couple may seek to possess—love and romance. Moreover, display of this particular social capital enables the Instagram user and her husband to associate themselves with other happy couples. By doing so, they complete their own social circle. Of course, it is needless to mention that by identifying herself with Notre-Dame and the Seine, the account owner succeeds to display her economic capital, which bears a clear symbolic message to her audience.

If you were an FC Barcelona fan and the opportunity of watching AC Milan versus FC Barcelona in San Siro stadium came along, this would definitely be an unforgettable experience. It is almost impossible for an active Instagram user not to share this moment. The next image (fig. 12.3), still coming from the same Instagram user, is doubly special due to the fact that Iranian women are not allowed in Iranian stadiums due to the local and traditional restrictions in Iran. In order to discuss the importance of this photo, we need to consider the limitations that women face in Iran. Some restrictions are imposed by Islamic rules. However, there are other rules that restrict women based on some unwritten

FIG. 12.2 Image of love padlocks attached to a fence of the Pont des Arts bridge over the Seine River in Paris. (Courtesy of the account owner.)

rules. Women, for instance, should not express themselves in a way that could result in attracting attention. In other words, flamboyant behaviors or clothes are not tolerated. Women are forbidden from entering sports stadiums because they are not allowed to witness men's sports. Apart from this, some public areas are segregated based on gender. These include public transport like buses and subways, libraries, schools, and certain ceremonies (weddings and funerals). Thus Instagram offers some female Instagram users in Iran degrees of flexibility through which self-expression may be practiced regardless of the offline obstacles. Once again, in this Instagram image, the account owner has acknowledged her own presence in this specific location by applying the location feature to her post. On the other hand, she has utilized the tagging feature to indicate that she was accompanied by two others—their names are tagged on the photo. These friends ("the brothers"), who are tagged and therefore become part of the display, help the account owner to state her social capital. As

FIG. 12.3 Image of spending time at San Siro stadium. (Courtesy of the account owner.)

mentioned in English in the caption, she was "surprised" by her brothers, and this emotional expression in turn highlights the quality of her social capital.

Data Interpretation Based on Marshall McLuhan's Approach

According to Marshall McLuhan, it is the technology (that is, the medium) that configures and reconstructs human work. As he puts it, "Characteristic of all media [is] that the content of any medium is always another medium."[27] The best place to start the argument is to refer to the aestheticism, as it is the most frequent connotative signification procedure on Instagram. This is also the only procedure related to the framework and features of Instagram, and users achieve this procedure by applying color filters to their images. All examined images in our study indeed underwent this specific aesthetic creation procedure.

Another element to note is the location feature, which is the most frequent display element in the Instagram images that we studied. In all images, locations, from where the images were taken, are clearly indicated through the location tagging feature of the Instagram. In other words, generally speaking, images on Instagram are not necessarily fancy by themselves. Rather, it is the location of display including names of European countries, nice neighborhoods of the cities, and places of entertainment that contributes to the symbolic qualities and sentiment of the images. Location is a technical and content-less facility. This can confirm the claim that Instagram's technical features create its content. In our study, we were able to conclude that a typical Iranian Instagram user induces a desired display interpretation by using this location feature of Instagram. Statistically, images using this feature account for 54 percent of the entire images that we selected and examined (511 photos). All locations are signifiers of various types of capital. Travel, the most frequent content, owes its frequency to its association with location. To put it another way, the content of travel has been created because travel is often identified with its destination, that is, location.

It is especially true among Iranian Instagram users that the image-oriented nature and technical features of Instagram give more space to certain types of capital and sweep other capitals aside. What can tangibly be displayed in an image finds an opportunity to come to the surface, whereas what does not fit in the image and other visual channels is marginalized and finds no opportunity to be expressed. Cultural capital with the lowest frequency is an example of the marginalized capital in the field of display. This is because this type of capital is less obviously representable, although it finds its way within a symbolic capital that is apparent, omnipresent, and conspicuous in all images. Photos of a university, library, books, and other cultural products, for instance, can function symbolically as cultural capital.

However, scientific knowledge, intellectual assets, and academic titles cannot naturally be displayed, and the content of images and visual expressions do not directly represent cultural capital. It may thus be concluded that the cultural capital of Iranian Instagram users can be better represented in publications, and such image-oriented spaces, Instagram included, are not suitable for displaying such achievements. Contrary to this capital, economic and social capitals have found an opportunity to be shown in the display field of Instagram. The expressions of economic and social capitals can be realized at two levels. They can be defined upon the audience's approval and measured based on the likes and comments. Thus it is again the technical features of Instagram that determine the content and lay the ground for visual representations.

To put it differently, absolute manifestations of expensive travels, luxury houses, brand new cars, and luxury goods are all tangible and observable. Therefore, economic capital has not only accounted for the highest frequency but has also found a suitable environment to shine on Instagram. Social capital can also be defined based on one's association with a certain group. This capital, being the capital with the second highest frequency, is also highly displayable on Instagram. One can consider photos with friends in this regard.

The Instagram page "Rich Kids of Tehran" is the gist of this argument in which the economic capital is displayed in its boldest. This page captures compellingly how Instagram caters for such practices. The photos on this page testify to the conspicuous consumption of Iranian users on Instagram and also breach the sociopolitical protocol. For instance, users on this page are seen drinking alcoholic drinks and being dressed in bikinis, practices which are not allowed in public domains in Iran. The performance of leisure shown in these photos does not necessarily represent an Iranian culture, as Muslims are forbidden from drinking alcoholic drinks. The sports centers, or more specifically all swimming pools in Iran are all gender-separated. Yet women on this page are shown drinking alcohol and swimming with men in private swimming pools. This means that the production of content is driven by the visual medium rather than the actual cultural context that users inhabit.

A specifically and personally culturalized fashion is exhibited in many images posted on "Rich Kids of Tehran," signifying a symbolic capital. This capital must be examined against the historical context of Iran. Muslim women have to wear hijab in public, and the Iranian dress code is a uniform called manteaux along with the veil. Similarly, the dress code for men forbids men from wearing shorts or a vest top in public. A large number of photos found on this particular Instagram page show how these dress codes are violated by both women and men. The economic capital, on the other hand, is most strongly reflected on this page. Users exhibit themselves wearing the latest fashion, Nike shoes and Louis Vuitton bags, for instance. Especially in the case of women, their hijab barely covers their hair. Thus users of this particular Instagram page have deliberately chosen to reflect their favored capitals, making stark contrast with the social, cultural, and historical contexts of Iran.

Conclusion

The initial research question in our study can be reframed in plain language as follows: What do Iranian Instagram users do? Nevertheless, if we have to phrase this question according to our formal research approach, it is more fitting to ask: What does Instagram do to its Iranian users? The concluding answer reads like this: The person who forms the message adjusts the content to the specific communication medium of Instagram, and the medium ultimately forms the message.

Display is the ultimate point of action on Instagram. Instagram is a place for visual representation of assets and ownership, to display subjects and objects with their actual and symbolic values. Before the creation of this image-oriented network, such visual representations were not as prevalent and common. Instagram's technical features have made possible numerous opportunities for visual representation, while also allowing people to make their images more appealing by using color filters, adding captions and locations, and tagging people.

Instagram may be the very first social network site that has provoked its users within the framework of boastful displays of their moments. We use the term "provoke" to emphasize the fact that this digital space has the energy to lead its users to take certain actions—that is, action to display and represent a wide range of capitals. Every technology has its own spirit that provokes its users to be converged with technology. Investigations of Instagram and Iranian users' convergence with it show how we indeed turn ourselves into images.

Notes

1 Thomas Lindolf and Bryan Taylor, *Qualitative Communication Research Method* (Thousand Oaks, CA: Sage Publications, 2002), 6.
2 Pierre Bourdieu explains that "capital, which, in its objectified or embodied forms, takes time to accumulate and which, as a potential capacity to produce profits and to reproduce itself in identical or expanded form, contains a tendency to persist in its being, is a force inscribed in the objectivity of things so that everything is not equally possible or impossible." For more details, see Pierre Bourdieu, "The Forms of Capital," in *Handbook of Theory and Research for the Sociology of Education*, ed. John G. Richardson (Westport, CT: Greenwood Publishing Group, 1986), 46.
3 "Latest Data on Iran: Surge in Social Media Use," *Financial Tribune*, last modified February 06, 2018, https://financialtribune.com/articles/sci-tech/81536/latest-data-on-iran-surge-in-social-media-use.
4 According to the same article from *Financial Tribune*, Telegram is the most popular social media platform in Iran.
5 Thorstein Veblen, *The Theory of the Leisure Class: An Economic Study in the Evolution of Institutions* (London: Macmillan, 1899).
6 Guy Debord, *The Society of the Spectacle* (Kalamazoo: Black & Red, 1970).
7 Marshall McLuhan. *Understanding Media: The Extensions of Man* (Toronto: McGraw-Hill, 1964).
8 Ibid., 4.
9 Ibid., 7.
10 Ibid., 8.
11 Pierre Bourdieu, *Distinction: A Social Critique of the Judgment of Taste* (Cambridge, MA: Harvard University Press, 1984).
12 Erving Goffman, *The Presentation of Self in Everyday Life* (Edinburgh: University of Edinburgh, Social Sciences Research Centre, 1956), 40.
13 Pierre Bourdieu, Luc Boltanski, Robert Castel, Jean-Claude Chamboredon, and Dominique Schnapper, *Photography: A Middle-Brow Art* (Cambridge, MA: Polity Press, 1990).
14 Ibid., 6.

15 Goffman, *The Presentation of Self*, 40.
16 Bourdieu et al., *Photography*, 20.
17 Roland Barthes, *Image Music Text* (London: Fontana Press, 1977), 20.
18 Ibid.
19 Ibid., 52.
20 Ibid., 68.
21 Bourdieu et al., *Photography*, 36.
22 Ibid.
23 Ibid.
24 Ibid.
25 Bourdieu, "The Forms," 47.
26 Robert McColl Millar, *Trask's Historical Linguistics* (New York: Routledge, 2015), 18.
27 While Instagram may fail to capture such cultural capital by using its strictly visual means, captions can readily verbalize and hence highlight this kind of capital to the audience.

Bibliography

Barthes, Roland. *Image Music Text*. London: Fontana Press, 1977, 20.
Bourdieu, Pierre. *Distinction: A Social Critique of the Judgment of Taste*. Cambridge, MA: Harvard University Press, 1984.
———. "The Forms of Capital." In *Handbook of Theory and Research for the Sociology of Education*, edited by John G. Richardson, 46–58. Westport, CT: Greenwood Publishing Group, 1986.
Bourdieu, Pierre, Luc Boltanski, Robert Castel, Jean-Claude Chamboredon, and Dominique Schnapper. *Photography: A Middle-Brow Art*. Cambridge, MA: Polity Press, 1990.
Debord, Guy. *The Society of the Spectacle*. Kalamazoo: Black & Red, 1970.
Goffman, Erving. *The Presentation of Self in Everyday Life*. Edinburgh: University of Edinburgh, Social Sciences Research Centre, 1956.
"Latest Data on Iran: Surge in Social Media Use," *Financial Tribune*. Last modified February 6, 2018. https://financialtribune.com/articles/sci-tech/81536/latest-data-on-iran-surge-in-social-media-use.
Lindolf, Thomas, and Bryan Taylor. *Qualitative Communication Research Method*. Thousand Oaks, CA: Sage Publications, 2002.
McLuhan, Marshall. *Understanding Media: The Extensions of Man*. Toronto: McGraw-Hill, 1964.
Millar, Robert McColl. *Trask's Historical Linguistics*. New York: Routledge, 2015.
Veblen, Thorstein. *The Theory of the Leisure Class: An Economic Study in the Evolution of Institutions*. London: Macmillan, 1899.

Acknowledgments

First of all, I would like to thank Frederick Luis Aldama for encouraging me to work on this project. Thanks to him, I have now found a new scholarly interest in media studies and narrative intersection. I would also like to mention Maya Dodd, who initially planned to work on this book project with me but could not do so due to personal reasons. Nevertheless, Maya spent numerous hours with me talking about the book and offered invaluable emotional support. I deeply thank Priyanka Aidasani, Shriya Kuchibhotla, Aman Sakhrani, and Seema Aidasani for volunteering to work on the cover image of the book. I could not have been happier with the outcome of their collaborative work. Writing and editing of the book were possible thanks to my home institution, Bellevue College. The sabbatical leave from the college enabled me to focus on the book and deliver it on time. My gratitude also goes to the professional team at Rutgers University Press, including the executive editor Nicole Solano. Nicole was attentive, prompt, efficient, and gracious from the very beginning stage of the project till the end of it. My most sincere thanks, of course, goes to all of the fourteen contributors to this book. Without their hard work, insights, expertise, patience, and commitment to the project, this book would not have been possible.

Finally, I thank my family in South Korea (and Sarath for being always patient and consistent with me even when I am not) and all my teachers, including David Herman and Jim Phelan. They inspire and humble me on a daily basis.

Notes on Contributors

HAMID ABDOLLAHYAN received his PhD in Sociology in 1996 at Carleton University, Ottawa, Canada, and joined University of Tehran, Iran, in 1997. He is now a professor of communication at the Department of Communication, University of Tehran. His research interests include new media and cultural differences, media and public sphere, cultural studies and generational gap, consumer culture and automobile industry, research methods in communications studies, comparative dimensions of sociology, communication and history, social networking, and human–computer interaction. His publications include *Conceptualization of Reality in Historical Sociology: Narrating Absentee-Landlordism in Iran* (2004) and *Comparative Perspectives in Sociology, Anthropology, and Communication* (2008). He has also published a number of articles in journals such as *Critical Middle Eastern Studies, Asian Journal of Social Sciences, Journal of Media and Religion, Space and Culture, Iranian Social Science Letter, Communication and Culture*, and *Global Media Journal*.

REA AMIT is a visiting assistant professor of Asian studies at Knox College, Illinois, United States. He received his MA from Tokyo University of the Arts in Aesthetics, and his PhD from Yale University in Film and Media Studies and East Asian Languages and Literatures. He has published on Asian media, aesthetics, and theory in journals such as *Philosophy East and West, Positions: Asia Critique, Participations: International Journal of Audience Research, New Ideas in East Asian Studies*, as well as a chapter on miscommunication in J- and K- horror films in an edited volume on horror cinema. He is currently writing a book on televisuality in postwar Japanese cinema.

SHUBHDA ARORA is a media sociologist currently working as an assistant professor of communication at Indian Institute of Management, Lucknow. She completed her doctoral degree in Communication for Social Change from Mudra Institute of Communication, Ahmedabad, India. Most of her research and publication is in the area of environmental and disaster communication as well as in audience studies. She has been associated as a guest researcher with the Central European University in Budapest, Freie University in Berlin, and the University of Chile, Santiago.

ASANTHA U. ATTANAYAKE is a senior lecturer attached to the University of Colombo, Sri Lanka. She received her PhD from Jawaharlal Nehru University, New Delhi, India, and was a Fulbright Advanced Teaching and Research Scholar at Pennsylvania State University, United States. She also won a scholarship to attend Harvard Kennedy School Executive Education (HKSEE) course at Harvard University. She has written extensively on the need for context-specific teaching methodologies and has designed a number of curricula for undergraduates in many universities across Sri Lanka. Her thesis, *Undergraduate ELT in Sri Lanka: Policy, Practice and Perspectives for South Asia*, was published in 2017. Her second book, *Post-colonial Curriculum Practices in South Asia: Building Confidence to Speak English*, came out in 2019. Currently she is co-authoring two other books, *Technology in the ESL Classroom* and *An Action Research Handbook for English Language Teaching in South Asia*, with her husband, Colonel Adam L. Barborich.

ALIREZA DEHGHAN graduated from University of Tarbiat Moderess, Iran with an MA in Social Sciences and from New South Wales University, Australia, with a PhD in Social Sciences. Upon completing his studies, Dehghan joined the Department of Communication Studies at the University of Tehran, Iran, and currently teaches mass communication theories and print media studies for undergraduate and graduate students as well as culture and communication theories for PhD candidate students. He has published numerous research articles in academic journals in the areas of social sciences and communication and media studies. His areas of research interests include mass media, culture and communication, media and public sphere, and mediatisation theory.

MAYA DODD received her PhD from Stanford University in Modern Thought and Literature. Subsequently, she received postdoctoral fellowships at Princeton University and Jawaharlal Nehru University, India. She also taught in the Department of Anthropology at Princeton University and in English departments at Stanford and the University of Florida. She has chaired the Centre for South Asia and Department of Humanities and Languages at FLAME University, Pune, India, where she teaches literary and cultural studies. Her research interests include digital humanities, South Asian studies, and cultural studies, and her teaching is focused on the digital classroom and archiving practices.

DARLENE MACHELL DE LEON ESPENA is an assistant professor of humanities at Singapore Management University (SMU), Singapore. She earned her PhD in Southeast Asian History (2017) and her MSc in Asian Studies (2012) from Nanyang Technological University, Singapore. Her research interests include cinema, culture and politics in Cold War/postcolonial Southeast Asia, and political and cultural discourses on Singapore education and economy. Before joining SMU, she was a research fellow at Singapore's National Institute of Education (NTU). She also held teaching positions at De La Salle University and the Ateneo de Manila University, Philippines.

JOHN GAGNON is an assistant professor of rhetoric and composition and former director of the Writing Center at the University of Hawaii at Manoa, United States. He is a cultural rhetorician interested in the rhetorical framing of human rights issues, and has published in *Reflections, Poroi, Present Tense, Interdisciplinary Humanities*, and the *Journal of War Crimes, Genocide, and Crimes against Humanity*. He earned his PhD at Michigan State University, JD and MS degrees at Tulane University, and his BA at Andrews University.

SABIHA HUQ is a professor of English at Khulna University, Bangladesh. She is an alumnus of University of Dhaka (BA Hons and MA in English Literature) and University of Oslo (MPhil and PhD in Ibsen Studies). She has had a career in teaching for more than eighteen years in the fields of cultural studies, performance studies, translation studies, and English literatures. Her research interests also include modern drama and Henrik Ibsen, postcolonial literature, and women's writing and migration literature. She was the coordinator of a collaborative international project on "Locating Post-Partition Amnesia in Memory and Literature: An Indo-Bangladesh Perspective" on behalf of English Discipline, Khulna University. Her publications include both critical and creative writings in international journals, books, newspapers, and magazines.

JUHI JOTWANI is a student pursuing undergraduate studies in FLAME University, Pune, India. She is majoring in Literary and Culture Studies and taking courses in sociology. Her research interests are gender, caste, and media studies.

HOORNAZ KESHAVARZIAN ranked the first in Iran in the MA entrance examination in the field of social communications in 2012 and received her master's degree from University of Tehran, Iran, in 2015. She is particularly interested in online self-expression and identity display. Her current focus is on youth online engagement on social media.

DOROTHY WAI SIM LAU is an assistant professor at the Academy of Film, Hong Kong Baptist University, Hong Kong. Her research interests include stardom, fandom, Asian cinema, digital culture, and screen culture. Her publications have appeared in journals such as *Positions: Asia Critique, Continuum, Journal of Chinese Cinemas, Journal of Asian Cinema*, and a number of edited volumes. She is the author of *Chinese Stardom in Participatory Cyberculture* (2018). She is currently writing her next book monograph tentatively titled *Reorienting Chinese Stars in Global Polyphonic Network: Voice, Ethnicity, Power* (under contract).

HYESU PARK received her PhD in English from the Ohio State University in 2014 and is currently an associate professor of English at Bellevue College, United States. In 2015 and 2016, she was a visiting professor at FLMAE University, Pune, India. Her research interests include American and Asian literatures, graphic narrative, media studies, South Korean literature and popular culture, emotion research, and cognitive and rhetorical narratology. Her articles have appeared in *Image and Narrative, Studies in Twentieth and Twenty-First Century Literature*, and *American Book Review*. Currently, she is working on a book monograph tentatively titled *Media Trends in South Korea: Mukbang TV, Webcomics, and Literature* (under contract).

W. MICHELLE WANG is assistant professor of English at Nanyang Technological University, Singapore, where she teaches seminars in postmodern and contemporary literature, war in literature and film, and the graduate seminar in the history of literary theory. Her research areas are in twentieth and twenty-first century fiction, East Asian televisual narratives, and aesthetic and narrative theories. She is co-editor of *Narrating Death: The Limit of Literature* (Jernigan, Wadiak, and Wang 2019) and the forthcoming *Companion to Death and Literature* (Jernigan, Murphy, and Wang). Her articles have been published in the journals *Narrative, Review of Contemporary Fiction*, and *Journal of Narrative Theory*, while her book monograph entitled *Eternalized Fragments: Aesthetic Lucidity in 20th and 21st Century World Fiction* is forthcoming.

HIROKI YAMAMOTO was born in Chiba, Japan, in 1986. He graduated in Social Science at Hitotsubashi University in 2010 and received his MA in Fine Art from the Chelsea College of Arts, University of the Arts London (UAL) in 2013. From 2013 to 2018, Yamamoto worked as a research fellow at UAL's Research Centre for Transnational Art, Identity and Nation (TrAIN), where he completed his PhD in 2018. He was previously a research fellow at Asia Culture Center (ACC) in Gwangju, South Korea. He was a postdoctoral fellow at School of Design, The Hong Kong Polytechnic University, Hong Kong, and is currently teaching at Tokyo University of the Arts.

Index

Printed and bound by CPI Group (UK) Ltd, Croydon, CR0 4YY

16/04/2025

14658333-0004